RIVER BOOTS

A Fish Warden's Tales
of Pennsylvania Fish and Game Law Enforcement

Robert Lynn Steiner

Fish on!
Bob Steiner

DEDICATION

To my wife, Linda. She was there,
through it all, loving me.

And Sneed.

RIVER BOOTS

A Fish Warden's Tales
of Pennsylvania Fish and Game Law Enforcement

Copyright © 2022 Robert Lynn Steiner

ISBN: 9798501017191

All rights reserved. No part of this publication may be reproduced, stored in a retrieval system or transmitted in any form or by any means, electronic, mechanical, photocopying, recording, or otherwise without the prior permission of the author, who can be contacted at P.O. Box 207, Cooperstown, PA 16317. Additional copies are available from Amazon Books online.

TABLE OF CONTENTS

Introduction 7
Foreword...7
Disclaimer 9
Explanations 10
How It All Started...10
About Collecting Money in the Field 11
About Trout Stocking and Management..12

CHAPTER 1: Thrills on Wheels..15
CHAPTER 2: Trout Tales..28
CHAPTER 3: Guys and Gals in Green (Fish) 49
CHAPTER 4: Checkmate 58
CHAPTER 5: Trouting Culprits...76
CHAPTER 6: Warmwater Culprits 96
CHAPTER 7: Things That Go Bump in the Night 104
CHAPTER 8: Don't Drink the Water 112
CHAPTER 9: Thou Shalt Not Litter 121
CHAPTER 10: Publicity Stunts...128
CHAPTER 11: They Walk on Water 133
CHAPTER 12: Afloat in a Boat 140
CHAPTER 13: In Front of the Bench..150
CHAPTER 14: Snakes and Turtles and Frogs, Ah-ha.................160
CHAPTER 15: Game Calls 166
CHAPTER 16: Out of My League..180
CHAPTER 17: Tricks of the Trade 182
CHAPTER 18: Bad Habits 186
CHAPTER 19: The Clients..193
CHAPTER 20: Barrels of Fun 202
CHAPTER 21: Fun with Wildlife 209
CHAPTER 22: The Rest of the Job..221
CHAPTER 23: Rescues and Recoveries 234
CHAPTER 24: Sex in the Long Grass (Rated R)..........................240

About the Author 253

INTRODUCTION

Outdoor humor writer Patrick McManus introduced his readership, of which I was one, to his fish and game warden character, Sneed. Sneed was respected by the outdoor fraternity for doing the job their license money paid him to do fairly and without favoritism. Mostly Sneed had a presence that was always with you when you were engaged in hunting, fishing and similar outdoor pursuits, whether he was there or not. He showed up when least expected and didn't when expected...until you let your guard down. It was Sneed that I strived most to emulate when carrying out my sworn duties.

FOREWORD

There is no job like it in the world. You make friends and enemies out of the same people, all in one day, and it has nothing to do with what you say or do. It all has to do with what they are doing when you arrive.

Without the violators, this is just another 9-to-5 job. Many of them are good people that have gotten themselves into bad or compromising situations. Some of them are hardened outlaws that represent generations of disrespect for the resources we are sworn to protect. All of them make the job interesting.

They all have an excuse or reason why they were doing what they were caught at. You listen to them all. You warn some and arrest some. Most of them put a smile on your face when you are back in the car and leaving. Other cases you don't smile about until years after they are over. But sooner or later they all make you smile.

The Pennsylvania Fish and Boat Commission Waterways Conservation Officer job lets you work with some of the most environmentally dedicated people in the world. The other Waterways Conservation Officers, the Pennsylvania Game Commission Game Wardens, the deputies from both commissions, the fish truck drivers, persons from every department in both agencies and all the good people that in some way touch your career, be they professionals or sportsmen, are what make it all worthwhile.

Over 27-plus years, two raising fish and 25 in law enforcement, I came to realize that there is one common thread running through this occupation. The people you deal with all have an interest in the outdoors and somewhere in their makeup, because they are an outdoorsman, there is a sense of humor. I hope to make that dedication and humor shine through each and every one of these tales.

The accounts that follow are a collection of recollections, from a 27-year career with the Pennsylvania Fish and Boat Commission that spanned parts of three decades, by a guy that can't remember what he had for breakfast today. I am sure that some of these tales are not exactly true, although none of them are purposely fictionalized. They are told as I remember them.

Names have been changed in some cases on purpose to protect other officers from ridicule and in some cases to ensure it. The players "in black" in many cases have also had their names changed because I may not be legally accurate in the telling of the tale and because I have no real animosity toward anyone that I prosecuted in my career. Once they pay the fine or do the time, I feel they are rightfully done paying, but without their many contrived escapes from prosecution, there would be no reason to write these accounts.

If anything in these accounts is contrary to the policies of my old employer or the laws of this state or any government, the act either took place before the policy or law was enacted or the tale is an outright lie. I know I would have never done anything wrong or anything that would have jeopardized my employment with as fine an employer as the Pennsylvania Fish and later Fish and Boat Commission.

I had the opportunity during my career to work with many fine and some not-so-fine officers. These officers represented a vast period in conservation law enforcement. I worked with at least one officer from each Game Commission and Fish and Boat Commission class. Some of the old officers I worked with had personally worked alongside the dozen or so wardens originally appointed when the agencies began to take their mandated "protection" duties seriously.

I was part of the "third" generation. I worked a year or two with a few fellows, at the end of their careers, who had worked a year or two with the originals. Though occasionally these jobs only amounted to a day at a fair booth or attending a meeting, it makes me proud to be one of the ties that bind the original Fish Wardens with new, spit-polished Conservation Officers.

I always loved history and folklore. When things got slow on a joint patrol, at a show or on break, I'd extract as much of the "good old days" as I could. I used this information to become what I felt was the perfect Fish Warden. Not necessarily the one the Fish Commission was looking for, but the one that the perfect fisherman would want to encounter. After all, that's who I worked for.

Having worked with wardens that were politically appointed, wardens that were tested extensively and a few that never did neither, just showed up on the roster, I have seen all kinds. The new system of Civil Service testing and hiring is certainly the most fair and most consistent at providing quality raw material for the officer mold. All were great in their own way. Some were like gems in the rough; some were finely polished jewels. All gave me a reason to laugh and enjoy my job.

I have had over 30 deputy wardens serve under my control. Many of them are successful in their "real life" occupations and looked to this as a diversion. Four went on to become full-time wardens. Some had no success at life or as deputies. Some, when they got a badge, it so swelled their head that their hat wouldn't fit. But, for the most part, they were a dedicated bunch of persons that had nothing more than the best interests of fishing and boating safety and the resource at heart. They gave freely of their time and money, so that the persons of the state that use our waterways and water-related sports could better enjoy their time in these most-beautiful areas of the state.

Game deputies were no different. They worked hard to make Pennsylvania's outdoors a better place to play in on your day off. From time to time, these two groups have caused my sides to hurt from laughter as we rode a boat, dealt with fishermen or sat in a darkened car in the middle of nowhere waiting for a poacher's shot to be fired.

Deputies, overall, I believe were responsible for most of the good laughs. Perhaps it was because they weren't caught up in the day-to-day trappings of the fish and game warden jobs. Without these guys and gals, many of these wonderfully funny experiences would have been nothing but lonely days and lonely nights.

There are many others that contributed a part to a story or laugh in these pages. They represented many agencies at all levels of government and clubs too numerous to mention. They were just as integral a part of my day-to-day life in green as were the rest.

Not to be forgotten are the families that supported a spouse that spent long hours "somewhere" alone or with "somebody," trying to catch bad guys. Not knowing when dad or mom was coming home was always a worry and an inconvenience, yet these families for the most part persevered. They, too, gave of their lives so that the Commonwealth's wild resources would be protected.

I've sorted out these tales from the hundreds of others that flowed through my brain during the more than 20-year construction of this book. It is a monument to a way of life. I'm sure some persons will feel slighted; it was not meant to be. There are many other tales that could and would have been included, had I had more energy, time and money.

Most of all, I guess I am happy to be writing this as a tribute to the many beautiful waterways of this state on which I have been able to serve. When times got rough and I was confronting what seemed to be insurmountable odds, be it polluters, poachers or other violators, I needed only to pull the car alongside the road and shut off the motor. I would walk to a little stream and listen to its plea to keep it clean or listen to the winds in a streamside white pine and know that as long as there is one drop of clean water or one breath of fresh air, it is still all worth fighting for.

DISCLAIMER

Nobody is perfect. Once you turn 70, you remember what you want, the way you want, and just hope that everyone else that remembers the event either remembers it the same way or is at least decent enough not to call you on the error in front of the world. I am over 70 and this is the way I remember it, possibly embellished in the telling, but essentially true. Some of these tales may not be mine. They may be the tales of the great old-time storytellers in green that I worked with all those years. But, because I am over 70 and have told them myself so many times, I now believe the tales are mine. If anything the officers in these tales or I did was illegal, unlawful or unconstitutional, I must have remembered incorrectly.

EXPLANATIONS

You should know that I covered primarily southern Luzerne County and Venango County in my career, but at first roved around the 31 northwest, southwest and north-central counties. In addition to these assignments, I filled in at one time or another in Forest, Carbon and Warren counties. I also was never bashful about pulling a badge case from my pocket when I witnessed a violation anywhere in the state. To simplify and clarify, you also need to know that at first there were Fish Wardens. I just missed being one of them by a few years. I was hired as a Waterways Patrolman and then the title changed again to Waterways Conservation Officer (WCO). The Fish Commission also became the Fish and Boat Commission (PFBC) during that time. I try to use "Officer So-and-so" in the beginning of each tale when referring to a Fish Commission officer, then resorted to first names or nicknames to keep these tales from becoming police reports. Throughout these pages you will meet some wonderful characters. Many are Deputy Waterways Conservation Officers. I will refer to them as deputy and their first name. For those reasons, you the reader need to know there was more than one deputy Jim, Don, Gene, Stan, Earl, etc. Names are not important, but the stories are. Enjoy them.

Our counterparts in the Game Commission (PGC) were Game Protectors, then Wildlife Conservation Officers (WCO) and now are Game Wardens. The Department of Environmental Resources (DER) used to include pollution, state parks and forestry. Now the Dept. of Conservation and Natural Resources (DCNR) umbrellas over parks and forestry and the Dept. of Environmental Protection (DEP) is the water pollution agency.

Fish, Game and DCNR officers have authority to cite persons violating the other agencies' laws and regulations, but they seldom are assigned to primarily patrol for the other agencies. I understand that nowadays they all have authority under all laws of the state.

Additionally we worked closely with the Soil Conservation Service (SCS), the Natural Resource Conservation Service (NRCS), the Army Corps of Engineers (ACE), the Environmental Protection Agency (EPA) and the Fish and Wildlife Service (USFWS).

HOW IT ALL STARTED

At a sportsmen's club meeting, after a talk by the game warden, my dad pointed at him and said, "There's what you want to be, boy. They don't have to work too hard." I was sold. I read about forest rangers, fish and game wardens and all kind of outdoor things and jobs.

Unlike today, when children are not required to begin looking for a job until they are 30, in sixth grade we had to write a letter to an employer to determine the hiring requirements for some position. I wrote to the Somerset office of the Pennsylvania Fish Commission and asked about being a "warden." Somehow I had located their address.

I got a reply from John Buck, supervisor of that contingent. If I remember right, he told me that I had to be 23 years old, a military vet, and 5'8" or taller and under 6'6". I needed to weigh 165 to 250 pounds and have perfect eyesight and hearing. I took him seriously. I played football a few years, ran track a few years and wrestled for five. I joined the U.S. Coast Guard and was in boot camp 13 days after high school graduation.

While still in the service, I talked to the personnel manager for the Fish Commission and found out that I wouldn't be old enough to be a warden when I completed my four-year enlistment. She suggested I take the test for a job in the fish hatchery system, since the minimum age was lower. I did and quickly got a call wanting to hire me before my enlistment had ended. I couldn't make it happen. I listened to offers of enlistment bonuses, a jump to pay grade E-6 or a shot at Officer Candidate School. Then I got out. I returned to my parents' home with my wife of two years and lazed around for awhile.

Seven months after my discharge from the Coast Guard, I was hired by the Fish Commission. I went to work as a Fish Culturist at the Walnut Creek Fish Culture Station, in Erie County. We were supposed to be raising salmon, but a lot of the time we didn't have any fish; they were all at other facilities. Eventually I got to attend Fish Culture School and really wowed them with my academic performance.

After that, I was put in charge of a dry-diet feeding program for Esocids (muskellunge and northern pike) at Union City hatchery in the summer and would return to Walnut Creek for the fall, winter and spring. Hatchery work was enjoyable, and I especially enjoyed gathering wild brood fish, salmon and northern pike, for spawning.

I was just starting to get into my new niche in life, when the boss walked into the lunch room one day and suggested I take the Waterways Patrolman test. "Those wardens treat us all like dummies," he said. "Why don't you take that test and show them what we are really capable of." We often had wardens loafing in the lunchroom between their undercover shifts on salmon detail. We didn't like them.

Well, I took the test and against all odds finished in the running, interviewed well despite a ponytail I wore at the time, and off I went to fish warden school. The pay raise was substantial, so I was happy to have readjusted my career. As I sit back and write this, I can't help but wonder what I would have accomplished in the line of fish culture and research, had I stayed in the fisheries end of things. I also can't help but wonder if the boss would have encouraged me to take the test had we gotten along better.

ABOUT COLLECTING MONEY IN THE FIELD

All officers understand that they need to write citations and settle cases. Compliance with the law is not voluntary. That is what law enforcement is about. In many of my early years, salaried officers such as myself carried a field receipt book. We explained a violator's rights to a magisterial trial and subsequently a jury trial, if he or she felt they were not guilty. If they choose to admit their guilt, we could collect the fine on the spot and give them a receipt. They paid only the fine, no additional court costs. Later in my career that Field Acknowledgement of Guilt was still in effect with a time frame for mail-in payment. But a violator requesting a citation had to post the fine and court costs with a magistrate to obtain a trial. Non-residents were governed by a pay-or-stay situation, where they had to either plead guilty or post fine and costs before they could leave the state. We carried envelopes so they could post their fine and costs by mail and not have to stay in Pennsylvania overnight or the weekend, waiting on a magistrate. Deputies did none of the paperwork until quite late in my career. They only observed and gathered information. Throughout history, for some reason known only to our state legislature, all boating cases always had to receive a citation and thus pay the additional court costs. Now I understand the Field Acknowledgement of Guilt for Fish and Game cases has finally, deservingly, gone by the wayside. Citations only are issued and include court costs, whether you plead guilty or not guilty.

ABOUT TROUT STOCKING AND MANAGEMENT

Pennsylvania trout fishermen have the best of both worlds. They have a profusion of streams that make wild brook, brown and rainbow trout. These trout are wary and the apple of many dedicated trout anglers' eye. These are the fish that set my trout fishing urge to thumping. These are the resource fish.

We trout fishermen also have a multitude of recreational trout. They come to a nearby stream in a big, white Fish and Boat Commission hatchery truck. The "great white fleet" stocks millions of these scrappy fish annually. They are not as hardy or pretty as the resource fish, but they are fun to catch. For many anglers, due to where they live and fish, they are the only trout they will ever love.

The fish wardens assist with stocking trout. This was always a labor of love with me. When asked by an eager fisherman why I didn't just put them under the bridges, I responded, "I am on the side of the trout. Somebody has to cheer for them."

I liked getting trout into the chill waters of our Commonwealth, with an eye toward actually giving them a chance, however remote, to become a holdover for the next year. To this end I used helicopters, rubber rafts, 4WDs, ATVs, float boxes and people-labor to get fish into stretches of approved trout streams that could possibly give the trout a chance and, if not, at least provide a worthwhile experience to the fisherman that finally catches them.

If you live in suburbia or urban America and get an opportunity to sit on a grassy bank along a clear stream and fish for trout, it may be a quality angling experience for you. For another, it may be a small lake in a park that does it for him or her. Sitting at a picnic table, drinking a can of soda-pop and watching a bobber may be as good as it gets. It is and always has been important that some fish be stocked where these types of fishermen may enjoy the thrill of a catch.

However, it is just as important that some trout be placed into streams where catching them is a little more demanding. This can be farther from the road or just tougher to get to. Perhaps it is rough because of the quick fall of the stream. It may be all of these factors. Possibly this place is better because the scenery is nicer. These folks, too, deserve to thrill to the tug of a trout.

If you fish for trout but are not familiar with trout-stocking programs, you may have studied maps for remote areas and decided to fish a few. Planned your vacation and dreamed away a winter with expectations of what you were going to catch in your secret, hard-to-get-to spot.

When summer came and you finally got to this "find" of yours, you enjoyed the experience, but caught no fish. You were disillusioned. You failed to consider what it takes to get a fish into such places. Time restraints, overtime costs, sources of volunteer help and a host of other external factors dictate trout stocking methods and capabilities.

I have had both a suburban and a rural district. I found that the closer a place is to a major population center, the better the chance that a remote area will get stocked. It is an oxymoron of a sort, but I think the psychology of it goes something like this. Although the same percentage needs a wilderness experience, where there are more people, this percentage will be a larger group. Also there are fewer local wildernesses. Therefore more persons are focused on the same wilderness, and the area is easier to get support for and easier to get help when stocking trout there.

In rural areas, there are fewer persons and more wildernesses. The experience is not as heavily sought since it is easier to find and there are more such places. Stocking help is scarce. Anything outside the general "run a bucket and dump them" type of stocking is therefore a result of volunteer help.

With production and transportation costs always on the rise, it only makes sense that the Fish and Boat Commission stays afloat while stocking millions of trout by conserving time, energy and money at every possible opportunity. To leave a truck idling and a driver sitting on overtime, while a float box is pulled, is just not good economics. Whenever possible, I used whatever it took in the way of volunteer labor and effort to spread the fish out and get them into those back-in areas. Some resulted in near tragedies, some in belly chuckles, and almost all in a memory worth telling often.

Stocked trout are managed as a recreation. There is no real aspiration that they will ever repopulate a watershed and bring forth generations of wild trout. Some of them certainly do survive and spawn, but not many and not enough to support the recreational fishery that exists. Fishermen spend millions of tourist dollars each year pursuing stocked fish. They are a product that, when properly used, provides a terrific recreational opportunity for hundreds of thousands of anglers and keeps many rural economies afloat.

It is a shame that many of the officers that are responsible for the stocking of these fine fish come to despise them and the "circus" atmosphere that often accompanies them. This attitude is the result of long hours, in all kinds of adverse weather, doing hard labor. Buckets full of fish weigh nearly 40 pounds each and are often carried a hundred yards. At 35 fish to the bucket, this adds up to miles of carrying each year, which eventually take their toll. When you add to the labor the encounters with "hog fishermen" that each officer is sure to have, it can spoil an otherwise good attitude about stocked trout.

Through a lifelong love of fishing for trout, I have avoided falling prey to the attitude problem. However, I have had to overcome some experiences with "hog fishermen" and other despicable types that tend to be part of the ugly side of trout stocking.

Commonwealth of Pennsylvania

PENNSYLVANIA FISH COMMISSION

TO ALL TO WHOM THESE PRESENTS SHALL COME, GREETINGS:

KNOW YE, That reposing especial trust and confidence in the prudence, integrity and ability of

Robert L. Steiner

AND under the authority of the Constitution and Laws of the said Commonwealth, in such case made and provided, we have appointed and do by these presents commission him

WATERWAYS CONSERVATION OFFICER

For the Commonwealth of Pennsylvania

HE IS, THEREFORE, to have and to hold the said office, together with all the rights, powers and privileges thereunto belonging, or by law in anywise appertaining so long as he shall behave himself well.

This appointment to compute from *February 28, 1972*

Given under my hand and the Seal of the Pennsylvania Fish Commission at the City of Harrisburg, this *28th* day of *January* in the year of our Lord one thousand nine hundred and *eighty-five* and of the Commonwealth the two hundred and *ninth*.

President of the Commission

Executive Director

CHAPTER 1:
Thrills on Wheels

If you want a man to go to the moon you need to give him a rocket ship. If you want a man to build a house, you need to give him the right tools. If you want a man to do fish and game, timbering and gas and oil drilling operation patrols on rural roads through the spring thaw and the snows and ice of winter, you give him an AMC Matador to drive.

CASE OF THE PIPELINE JEEP

It was a brilliant sunny Sunday afternoon. Native brook trout had led me to patrol a remote stretch of Wright's Creek, up in the PGC game lands. After deciding nothing was going on there, I noticed some fresh Jeep tracks on the old railroad grade that ran through the area. Since trout season was still a week away, I decided to follow the Jeep tracks and see how they got in and out, as long as the path stayed "good." "Good" for the Matador was also "good" for a Jeep. The white Matador had been through terrifically tough terrain and never left me sitting ... for too long.

I was following along with a deputy, just enjoying the sunshine and talking, when I looked in the rearview mirror. Bearing down on me was a new model 4WD Jeep truck. Now, I was on the only hard path on the gas line at this time. The access road had been built up in this area. Obviously, the Jeep driver either didn't recognize the state vehicle or didn't think I could catch him.

He pulled behind me to within 50 yards and then veered around me into a marshy-looking area. Despite the fine reputation of the vehicle he was driving, he was down for good in mud up to his door handles.

My deputy and I greeted the occupants as they crawled out the Jeep's windows. We took the necessary information to prosecute the violation of the Game Law and then gave the guys a ride to the nearest phone. They were left making arrangements with the Game Commission, a wrecker service to extract their vehicle and a friend for a ride.

I turned over the information to Game Protector Nolf the next morning and the citations were issued. The gas company got wind through the magistrate's office that a vehicle had been buried on their gas line and the culprits apprehended. This was a problem they had been dealing with for some time with no luck. They sued for damages and were awarded around $10,000 from the two Jeep drivers.

It was a fitting end to a situation that had been tough to control. After the newspaper articles, it was years until we again saw any vehicle tracks in that section of game lands.

LIFT YOUR FEET

The Matador was the wrong car to issue me as a first new vehicle in a district that contained both interstate highways and miles of game lands roads.

I avoided the highways as often as I could, while putting as many miles as possible on the game lands access roads along streams.

Nothing much was going on this early fall day. The tourists were all home for school and the locals hadn't gotten into their hunting season mode yet. Deputies Earl, Stan, Don and I were out for a routine patrol in the Matador, when suddenly it veered off the pavement and went careening into the woods on a barely perceptible logging trail, near Penn Lake. Soon we were on the road to high adventure.

We were following Jeep tracks and trying to figure how and where they came from. We were hopelessly lost in the vast Pocono wilderness above F. E. Walter Reservoir. I kept jockeying from logging road to logging road, following the Jeep trails. Then we came to a low rock barrier with a severe mud puddle on the near side. Once across, we would be on a game lands road that I recognized and for which I had a gate key. I gunned it. The Matador leaped into the air and bounced over the row of basketball-sized rocks.

We were up on the road and no low-oil warning light came on. In the rearview mirror, all I could see was Earl's knees. A rock had forced the floor in the backseat to bulge upwards, pushing his knees up into view. He got out and got a rock and proceeded to flatten the hump.

Earl had almost finished the bodywork, when he realized the rock he was using to pound the floor back into place had been covered with little "piss" ants and now the car was swarming with them. About a half hour later, we had eradicated them using manual snubbing as our primary method and were on our way.

We took the Jeep tracks to a gas line and then followed them down over a severe hill onto an access road to a water company gate, which we were able to circumvent by going over a smallish log. As usual, the Matador had proven its mettle.

THE GAS LINE CHALLENGE

Bob Nolf was the sharpest game warden I ever worked with. He thought of all the angles, all the time. He seemed to live in the heads of some of the violators that he caught, and he always was working to find a better hiding place, a different view of a given valley or hillside.

It was a frosty morning in mid-November. A dusting of snow covered everything as Bob and I patrolled in my white Matador, along Big Wapwallopen Creek. We had taken the white car at Bob's urging, since it would allow us to get a little closer, undetected, with the white groundcover, than the Game Commission green car would.

The morning had been uneventful, so I pulled over in a sunny spot along the creek and poured a coffee from the Thermos. You didn't dare spend much time in coffee shops those days, and you couldn't afford counter coffee on our wages, anyway. As we sat drinking the coffee, Bob looked across the road to a steep gas line that had a 4WD trail going up it. In those days there were no ATVs, so it was a Jeep track.

"I wonder where that goes," he said.

"When I finish this coffee, we'll find out," I replied.

"You can't go up there with this. We'll need a Jeep," he said, beginning to show fear in his eyes.

"Betcha I can," I offered.

"A quarter you don't get to the top," he replied.

That was all that it took.

I rolled down the window and dumped the coffee. I got a straight line on the track and headed up. Bob clutched the dashboard with both hands. The Matador screamed. Rocks flew from the tires and pounded the undercarriage, as the car climbed and fishtailed ever nearer to the top. At times it wanted to go sideways and roll to the bottom, but judicious use of the gas and brake pedal kept it ever climbing. Then a drainage ditch bounced the tires free of their traction, and we sat spinning, only gaining inches.

Bob's face now matched the color of the car. Slowly he turned toward me. Never taking his eyes off the icy mountain dead ahead, he spoke. "I'll give you a buck if you quit and go back down."

At the bottom he handed me a dollar from his wallet, without saying anything, and just kept shaking his head. He obviously had forgotten that I was still just a kid.

Note: Along with its many other features, the Matador was white with a black interior. This allowed the glare from the hood to ruin your eyes, while the interior heated up and melted you in the summer. One day, with the windows down, moving on the highway, I placed a thermometer under the seat. When I stopped, I immediately checked. It was 117 degrees under the seat out of the sun. I could lose five pounds on a routine patrol. That's probably why they issued it to me.

THE LITTLE ENGINE THAT COULD

We were on a roll. Deputy Bob accompanied me that early fall Sunday afternoon and we had gotten several good cases. We were towing the boat, a 14-foot "Tin Lizzy" with a small outboard on it, when he spotted a Jeep running a power line right-of-way on the game lands. I set the Matador on pursuit and we began up the very steep power line, boat in tow, in hopes of putting an end to the heinous crime in progress.

The adrenalin of sport often overrules judgment in mankind. This had just happened to me. As I neared the top of the mountain, the old Matador labored and the wheels spun. Soon smoke flew and I gave up. The Jeep disappeared into the sunset.

I decided to back down; unlike me. As I began to do so, the trailer jackknifed. This left me but one option. I had Bob uncouple the trailer while I turned the car around on the steep hillside without rolling it, and then he would try to re-couple the trailer.

The boat was light. With a little rubber burning, I turned the car around. As I looked in the rearview mirror for the boat's location, I was left halfway between a giggle and a serious worry. My aged deputy, short, rotund and bald, a stogie hanging from his mouth, went running by the car with the trailer tongue in his hand.

Once he got it turned, he couldn't get the trailer stopped to hook up. Rather than ram the car with the tongue, he narrowly missed the collision. However momentum got the best of him and, along with the inevitable, gravity, he now made quite a sight. He looked like the "Little Engine That Could," stuck in reverse.

Boat, trailer and deputy made it to the bottom of the hundred-yard hill, with only a few small nicks in the engine prop where it had touched the dirt, while the tongue bounced skyward several times, lifting Bob from the ground.

THE LOW CLOTHESLINE CAPER

There were some big sections of woods up behind Mountain Top, and I always felt it was my obligation to get to know it all or at least where all the logging roads would take you. It seemed that jacklighters would disappear into thin air in this area. I figured they had to be pulling into the woods on these remote tram roads and vanishing when we came looking for the source of the shots.

The way to beat them was to know how they disappeared. Game Deputy Del was my sidekick for many of these exploratory trips. Some of the things that we found while running these missions were good to have found. Others were not.

Unfortunately, the Matador was what I had to run these tram roads with. I figured that the brass knew what the job was like. Most of them having been field officers at one time, they would expect you to get the job done with the equipment they gave you.

Del and I had been weaving around for hours, making our way west, when I happened to look down over the hillside onto a branch of the logging track we were on. I could see a house rooftop.

Rather than get the car committed and not be able to get it out, I took a quick hike and realized I had discovered a real bonanza.

"Are you sure we can get out down there?" Del asked.

"Trust me," I replied.

Del just rolled his eyes and fastened his safety belt. I turned onto the angle tram road and soon was careening down the steep side of the mountain. As I got to the edge of the woods, the road out was but 50 yards in front of us.

"Now how you going to get us over there?" Del queried.

"Just get out and get a stick and hold up that clothesline so my antenna clears it. I wish they wouldn't mount them on the top of these cars," I responded.

"You're going right through their yard?" he asked, incredulous.

"We can't back up that hill," I said.

Reluctantly, Del got out and held up the clothesline and I drove under it, between the swing set and the flower garden, onto the driveway and out to the road.

A woman came running out of the house and flew into Del.

"She was pretty mad," Del said, as he jumped into the car.

"Did you tell her that we were lost?" I asked.

"She knows me from church. I wasn't going to lie to her," he responded.

"So what did you say?" I asked.

"I told her the next time a bear eats her rabbits, not to call me if that's the way she was going to be."

"Did it work?" I asked, looking at him sheepishly.

"Must have. She said we could use it anytime, as long as the yard was dry and we didn't leave ruts."

We did use it a time or two later, when we felt that poachers were watching the roads into the area and using CB radios to tip each other off about our approach.

BEFUDDLED BY A MUD PUDDLE

Deputy Game Protector Del and I were just ending up a routine patrol of the Crystal Lake area of Luzerne County. It was some big country and we were in the northeast end of the tract, looking for a way to get out on a hard road, without having to go back the way we had come. We were near an access road around one of the lakes and knew there was a gate ahead. Del thought that he had a key for that gate.

As I eased the Matador through one stretch of woods, a long, bottomless puddle came into view. "I ain't goin' back," I said.

"Let me out. I'll walk. See you over there," he said, pointing.

He cleared out of the way and I fired up the engine. I knew the best thing to do with the Matador was to get all the horses running at full throttle, and then let the water, mud and saplings try to stop it. I had learned the technique driving a 1966 Chevy Malibu Super Sport on the sand roads of the vast Wharton Tract in southern New Jersey. In big, deep puddles, momentum was your only ally.

I dropped it into gear and pushed the pedal to the floor. The horses whined and the tires grabbed, the mud was flying 20 feet in all directions as I fishtailed, trying to only hit trees that weren't big enough to dent fenders. I came charging out the other side, with the engine hissing in its new layer of wet mud. Del just shook his head, laughing.

Just before we got to the gate, there was a little creek and a ford that I had run earlier with Nolf, the Game Protector. Today, however, the beavers had backed up the downstream culvert and we were looking at a formidable lake. There was no crossing it, not even with the Matador. It was over a hundred yards wide and looked to be six or seven feet deep where I would have to hit it.

Downstream was another crossing, but it had washed out badly and was too short and steep for the length of the car. We would get stuck between the banks for sure. It was getting dark as we resigned ourselves to failure and turned the Matador around for the long ride home on logging roads.

It was dim when we got back to The Puddle. It was getting quite cold and Del elected to stay in the car, but he held on for dear life. I looked the puddle over and fired up the Matador. The return trip through started well. Water flew, we fishtailed and were just getting to that point of puddle crossing where you begin to breathe again, when I felt the driver's side front tire get sucked to the left, miring us hopelessly.

We crawled out the windows into 18 inches of cold water and slogged to the shoreline, 30 yards away. Just before dark set in, we saw a Jeep quite a ways ahead of us.

"He must be a caretaker or at least have a key to one of the gates," Del stated.

"I'll catch him," I said, sprinting off with a flashlight, trying to get his attention. He never slowed down.

"He either doesn't have mirrors, doesn't ever look in them, or didn't want anything to do with game wardens," I offered upon return.

The six-mile march in wet boots was not fun. Around ten at night we arrived in a little housing development near Mountain Top.

"I know some people that used to live here," Del said. "I'll bet they will let us use their phone."

After knocking repeatedly, an older man answered the door in a robe. Once we explained our dilemma, we were welcomed in to make our call.

"Who we going to call?" Del asked.

"Nolfie?" I suggested, quizzically.

"All he has is a sedan, just like the one that's stuck," Del reminded me.

Dr. Pat, my fishing and hunting buddy, was just getting into bed when his phone rang. He made the mistake of answering it.

"Pat? This is Stein. Whatcha doin'?"

"I got my pajamas on. I'm heading for bed," he replied.

"I could use some help. Need a 4WD and a lot of cable and chain," I explained

"I knew I shouldn't have answered," he muttered. "Where're you at?"

"We're in Mountain Top at that little development. We'll be standing under the streetlight at the entrance," I responded, and we hung up.

Pat arrived and picked us up. His wife, Shirley, was with him. Around midnight we got back to the car. With a little fancy maneuvering, we were able to get Pat's Blazer in front of the Matador. We stretched every inch of tow chain and cable he had brought, and I slogged toward the Matador, on feet that felt frozen, with the end. We were about two feet short.

Pat remembered his tire chains, stashed by the spare. Using them to extend our tow chain, I got hooked on the frame below water level, sacrificing yet one more extremity to the rigors of cold, muddy water. Pat, an expert with a dentist drill, also proved his capabilities as a tow truck driver that night. He got the Matador pulled out, and we worked our way back through the woods onto the hardtop road around 2 a.m.

Del was a little grouchy, but that is expected of men who haven't eaten for 14 hours and have exercised hard. He swore he would never ride with me again. He didn't mean it; the very next weekend we patrolled together again. Pat even began answering his phone again in a year or so.

HOW TO AIR CONDITION A WINDSHIELD

Game Protector Bob Nolf had wanted to go into this remote mountain section. The morning was frigid as I eased the old Jeep back a tram road. I had been given an old, decommissioned Jeep when the Matador died an untimely death. The Jeep's driver's seat was held upright by two tires wedged between it and the backseat. The massive body of the officer that drove it before had destroyed the seat back. It was the perfect car for me.

There was a tree stub jutting from alongside the trail at windshield height. Bob offered to get out and move it.

"They make Jeeps for times like this," I responded.

I eased up tight against the stub, which was as big around as a man's fist, expecting it to slide out of the way. It was a little cold driving home with the hole in the windshield, but duct tape fixed it for the duration of the winter. In summer the breeze was nice.

Eventually, the Jeep was re-decommissioned. When I finished off a car, it was finished off.

I HEAR THAT TRAIN A-COMIN'

New is generally good. But when you have too many new things, you may not have enough experience with any one thing for the situation. So was the case on this late March day. I had a new Pennsylvania Fish Commission pickup truck, with a brand new radio. I was traveling with Tom, a new young game deputy on a railroad grade that was recently opened. The snow was reasonably well melted, so we figured we would go exploring.

At White Haven, we swung onto the abandoned railroad right-of-way alongside the still-active line and headed down along the Lehigh River. The scenery on this stretch of river is breathtaking and the whitewater is intriguing to watch as you travel along. We saw no one and negotiated the few remaining snowdrifts with little or no trouble. As evening came on, we were some 34 miles below our starting point and the truck was black from the fine railroad soot.

We got to the gate at Jim Thorpe and tried all the keys I had, but none worked. I tried the new radio, knowing that WCO "Fritz" Ohlsen would have a key. At any time, Fritz had keys for every lock in the world on several rings on his belt, but he did not answer, due to my inefficiency with the new radio. I did not want to drive the 34 dirty, rough miles back to White Haven, so I looked for an alternative means of escape from the rail grade.

I was at the end of a grocery store parking lot, so yanking the gate out was out of the question. Too many witnesses. As I looked around, I noticed some planks lying alongside the active line. I quickly understood them to be an unauthorized temporary crossing. I got out of the truck and maneuvered the planks to create a ramp of sorts that would let me bridge the rails, two wheels at a time. In fairness to Tom, I should say that he had voted for the long ride back.

I got the truck lined up and revved the engine to be sure I had proper lift and headed up the makeshift ramp. The front wheels cleared both sets of rails nicely, but the truck didn't have the power of the old Matador and landed the rear wheels between the rails. I backed against one side and gunned it but it wouldn't jump clear. I tried again and repositioned the boards. Still no luck. This process went on for about 10 minutes, with occasional breaks to try to radio Fritz, who still did not answer.

I contemplated walking over to the pay phone across the parking lot and calling Fritz at home, when I noticed the man walking his dog at the lower end of the parking lot, about a hundred yards away, downgrade. He seemed enthralled by the beautiful spring day, just walking and waving.

Waving? Yeah, waving with both hands and pointing down the track. Then I heard it and felt it in the rails. He could see a train coming. This act was soon going to have to end. I immediately thought of the boss's reaction when I called him Monday and explained about both the truck and its week-old radio system.

Tom was already out of the truck and running. The train was rounding the corner in sight, closing the gap rapidly. I would have one more chance. The boards were in place, and I revved it again in idle and slapped the truck into gear. It jumped up, spun on top of the rail, rocked, and the drive wheel caught and catapulted me onto the parking lot, throwing sparks when the rear bumper scraped the rail. It cleared the 20 yards to the edge of the parking lot, and I jammed the brakes and watched the train go by in the rearview mirror.

When the train passed, Tom crossed the tracks to the truck, looking much relieved. When he got in, I turned the truck around and headed back toward the tracks. "Goin' back that way, aren't we?" I quizzed. Tom was speechless, but the look in his eyes said he would rather not, and we didn't.

BOUNCING BLAZER

People that do not spend every day in a 4WD for a hundred miles underestimate the rugged utility of these vehicles. When I got to the Venango County district, my first new assigned car was a GMC Blazer.

Giving me a new 4WD vehicle is like putting perfume on a pig. It is wasted. I treat vehicles as an implement in which to cover ground you don't want to or can't walk. It doesn't matter who owns them, me or the company, they are for useful purposes, not for pampering and preening.

I was checking out a stretch of Sandy Creek for access. The stretch was to be stocked for the first time, and I was trying to determine if I could get a fish truck streamside. It is important to know your stocking points and access capabilities to evenly distribute the trout of spring in the most equitable and efficient manner.

Pittsburgh Joe, an interested sportsman, was accompanying me. He had a desire to see some of the county and was a good companion for the off-season. He was also a "mupp-ear." A "mupp-ear" is a term used by WCOs in the northcountry for sportsmen from south of I-80. The scenario that leads to the name goes like this.

"How's fishin'?" asks the warden.
"OK," replies the sportsman.
"Where you from?" continues the warden.
"I'm up here from Pittsburgh," replies the sportsman.
Thus, they are "mupp-ears" from Pittsburgh.

Joe and I traveled the cobble of the abandoned railroad bed and then, having seen and noted the access and truck-ability of the grade, I made my determination of where I would stock. I saw a smallish log, about five or six inches in diameter, that had been laid down across the gas line to discourage traffic.

Now, the gas line had been my exit on an earlier trip. It would eliminate several miles of rough cobble riding to get back on the pavement. I gassed the Jimmy and hit the log in full stride, bouncing over it and just juggling the contents of the Jimmy a little.

From there I ran the gas line out and swung onto a short piece of logging road that took me into a driveway. The driveway went around an old camp and came out behind the Polk Elementary School. It was only a short run along the woods edge until you dropped on their paved parking lot and were on your way.

When we got on the pavement the "mupp-ear" closed his gaping mouth and eased his grasp on the dashboard. He had been paralyzed with an anxiety attack. He was recovering well when I spotted the desk-sized boulders used to prohibit entry onto the next section of railroad right-of-way.

I stepped on the accelerator and sent him into a writhing, clutching, defensive posture. He was convinced by now that I was going to ram them. I stopped the Jimmy and grinned at him.

"Just kidding," I said.

His breathing became regular again about halfway through lunch.

BLAZERING UP AN ICY HILL

It was a warming day in late spring. The sun had made the melting ice very slick, as I took another state employee, who is also a close friend, with me on a tour of a recently opened railroad grade in my newly issued GMC Blazer.

Now, this person is one of the world's nicest guys, but a wimp. He does not like taking risks. Every time I would come to an old train trestle or icy spot, he would whine and carry on about the consequences of wrecking the state iron in a place like that. I had a hard time making him understand that places like that are what jobs like mine are all about.

When we came to the high trestle over the Allegheny River, I let on I was going out across it, just to check his heart. It seemed to be working all right, so I figured it was time to take him some place even better.

I knew that from where we were to the hard road would be either a long ride back up the bumpy railroad grade or up a logging road I had used once before. The logging road was precarious, icy and steep. Perfect for a day of adventure in the wilderness for my desk-jockey friend.

As I turned the Jimmy around, he was still trying to get his whining under control from the trestle. I quickly dodged off the railroad grade and onto the logging road. Before he could begin whining again, he was frozen with fear as I bounced and roared up the tram road. When it seemed that I was going to have to back down, I would ease the side of a wheel against the dirt embankment on his side and let the revolutions of the tire pull me like I was on a cog railroad.

Slow but sure, we worked to the top. A dry patch would catch and we would catapult forward, then an icy patch in the sun would slide us nearly sideways, but always we were gaining toward the top. He was speechless, clutching the dash and passenger-side handle over his door. He was looking down off the high side at a 300 to 400-foot hillside, with nothing but a dirt bank against the wheel to keep us from going over.

Naturally when I got to the top, I just did a U-turn and started as though I were going back down. His language was unbecoming a man in his influential position. I then turned around again and went about my patrol, with him resting peacefully beside me on the seat, eyes glazed.

EASY OVER BLAZER

I was stocking fish along the East Sandy Creek railroad grade one drizzling mid-May afternoon. I was driving, looking to pick out easy spots to carry the buckets (on this creek there are none) and talking to my copilot. Suddenly I hung the left front wheel off into the loose railroad ballast, where it dropped three feet. Before I could do anything, the Blazer was in dire risk of rolling over. Luckily, I had lots of stocking help along. Ten or twelve guys came up alongside and, with me shifting the 4WD into low range, held the Blazer upright until I could get it back on the flat again. Had I been alone, it may have ended differently and this story been a bit more interesting.

MILLER FARM ICE RIDE

When you approach the Miller Farm bridge from the Pleasantville side, you travel a mile on the relative flat. Then you begin a rapid descent as you leave the open hardwoods and start down through the hemlocks into the gorge, to Oil Creek. At the bottom of a long, downhill, straight stretch of road, you make a 90-degree turn to the right. Or at least you are supposed to.

My father and mother were visiting for the weekend. I had stocked fish on Friday, the day before they arrived. It was early March. The bike trail along Oil Creek had been mostly passable, having been cleared of snow by the state park crews and melted off during the few warm days we had just experienced.

Saturday morning dawned bright and clear, and I suggested to my dad that he ride along and see my new district. I could do a patrol and visit with him as we rode. Things were usually very slow this time of year. We checked along the lower reaches Oil Creek, drove through Petroleum Center and up over the hill through the park. I suggested we cross at the Miller Farm bridge and head to Titusville for lunch. This area had struck me as beautiful and I wanted to share it with Dad.

I made the turn by the Pleasantville Rod and Gun Club grounds and headed west, toward the creek. I was getting hungry, so I was clipping along about 20 miles an hour. The mud and dirt under my tires showed no sign of use, and I wasn't worrying about encountering another oncoming car.

I rounded the little bit of a bend at the end of the hardwoods and was catapulted onto a sheet of ice under the hemlocks. It had gotten just warm enough to make the top wet. We were in for a ride.

Now, my father wasn't one for cursing. He smoked a corncob pipe almost constantly, and at this moment it was tightly gripped between his broken teeth. He was frozen speechless in terror.

I am an old hand at ice driving, having done similarly stupid things many times before. However, at the moment I was totally engrossed in my effort to miss obstacles and slow down the sled. I tried neutral gear and the car built speed. I tried pumping and then locking the brakes, and we just kept surrendering faster and faster to the force of gravity. I even tried reverse.

It became obvious that the best plan was to brake just enough to help steer and let 'er fly. Fortunately, before you get to that 90-degree right-hand turn at the bottom, you have about 100 yards of relative flatness that is again in hardwoods. When I first noticed the glaze was off the ice and we were gripping, I was closing on the turn at what seemed like 70 miles an hour. I got the vehicle stopped without any damage; only the front wheels went into the ditch where I failed to make the turn.

For the first time since the top of the hill, I breathed and looked at Dad. He took his pipe from his mouth and studied it.

"Damn near bit the stem off, boy," was all he said.

HIGH BRIDGE OVER TROUBLING WATERS

I was always fascinated with train tracks. They went someplace and came back again. Someday I would find out where.

It was an icy, late January day when I stumbled onto the abandoned train track at the Mercer County town of Sandy Lake. It was a slow day, and I would just see where the old rail bed led. I am sure that riding an abandoned railroad grade over the cobble with a 4WD vehicle is as nerve-wracking as riding a train on the rails is soothing. This time there were no rails.

I bounced and jostled along and, nearly an hour later, after crossing three small trestles, found myself staring at a large railroad bridge over the Allegheny River, at Belmar. I could see that on the other side there were no ties or rails there, either, and the grade continued on. Several times I eased the front wheels onto the first set of ties, but eventually I gave myself the lecture about discretion being the better part of valor and turned and went on back to the road. But it bugged me.

As the spring passed, I eventually ran the line on the other side of the river almost into Clarion, but again I hesitated to go across the bridge. I knew it would be solid; all the other trestles were. We had taken fish trucks across them when stocking East Sandy and Sandy creeks, but I just couldn't find a reason to be on the trestle over the Allegheny River in the state vehicle.

Then one sunny July day, as I sat staring at the bridge, wishing I was on the other side so I could do a patrol of East Sandy and wishing I didn't have to drive the whole way into Franklin and around, I heard a dirt bike coming. He weaved around the state car at what seemed like a hundred miles an hour and never let off the gas as he hit the bridge. In a flash he was over it and I was following him, slowly.

The bridge had several ties, then an iron girder that sat several inches lower. The structural pattern was repeated over and over the whole way across. How that screaming bike went across there without dislodging the rider or turning the front wheel is beyond my comprehension, but he did.

When I got to the other side I got out and had a look. The bridge was extremely high and what I had done was stupid, but I thought that at least I had done it once and would never have to do it again. I discontinued my patrol, and then thought of the fun I would have with the fish truck drivers when we were stocking East Sandy and got to the end by the trestle. I would just lead right out on it and see if they followed.

Before the stocking truck came the next spring, I ran down the grade and checked the rail bed for ice and blockages. It was in great shape, except for one place. They had welded a gate shut on either end of the Allegheny River Bridge. I could no longer cross the river, one tie at a time.

CASE OF THE MISSING MIDNIGHT ROAD

It was a rainy Wednesday in the fall. Nolf, the Game Protector, and I were driving around on a brushy strip mine job, trying to figure out the exits the deer poachers were using. A white buck was being seen there and was sure to attract attention. This area near Eckley was nothing but a maze of strip mines.

We thought we had it all figured out. When we went home at dark, we had a plan. He and I would work in the strippings, while several carloads of deputies would seal off the perimeter if we had any action.

Saturday night came and we were once again met with fog and rain. As was the custom, once we got off the state highway, all lights went out. Driving around a strip mine without lights at midnight is bad enough. On a foggy night it's even worse.

We were slowly easing our way to our hideout, when something didn't look right. Nolfie stopped the vehicle.

"Something ain't right," he said.

"Looks fine to me," I replied.

By the rusted-out machinery on the edge, I knew this was the same access road we had been on several days before.

"Hate to get out to look, the lights will come on," he said.

"Looks fine to me," I replied.

Nolfie's door swung open and the dome light came on. He stepped out into the wet, black night. Not 10 feet in front of the car was a hundred-foot sheer wall, freshly dug since Wednesday.

For once I was glad I hadn't chided him into "going for it."

CHARIOT AFIRE

Joe Kopena, the Forest County fish warden, was my neighboring officer for years. When things got slow in the early spring or fall, we would do a joint patrol on the county line and enjoy a lunch together.

It was one of those wet, snowy, early spring days when Joe and I went to the Sky Jet Restaurant for a bowl of soup. We had ordered lunch and were sitting there awaiting its delivery, when a log truck driver came through the door. He walked back to us and said, "Joe, your Jeep's on fire out there."

"Just steam," Joe answered calmly. "Always does that."

The guy shook his head and went over to the counter.

Another log truck driver sauntered through the door, stepped the few steps down and came back to us, too.

"Joe, I think your Jeep's on fire," he offered.

"No, just steam. Does it all the time," Joe said. "They better get me a new one soon. That one has about had it."

Then long, tall Tom Greenley, then president of the Pa. Game Commission, came through the door and right to us, in a bit of a hurry.

"Joe, your Jeep's on fire," he opened.

"Just steam," Joe said again.

"No, it's fire!" Tom hollered. "I can see the flame melting your radio!"

Everybody was up and running. Soon a fire extinguisher was exhausted on the blaze and the Jeep hood battered open with logging bars. Flames shot ten feet in the air when the hood popped.

I went back to the restaurant booth. The fire department had been called and nothing could be done now except get hurt. Joe was doing some kind of primal fire dance around the Jeep and chanting in Polish. Best I just went and sat down.

The soup had been delivered to our table while this was all going on. It was homemade chicken noodle. I ate mine and watched the firefighters trying to spray the Jeep around the hopping, chanting form of Joe. His soup would be wasted since it was getting cold, so I ate it, too. Finally all was calm and Joe came back to sit a minute, eat and figure our next move.

"Who ate my soup?" he bellowed.

"I did, Joe. It was getting cold," I answered.

He cursed in Polish. Then we made some calls and got a tow for the Jeep and a ride for ourselves to my car. It wasn't until the next day that Joe realized I let him pay the lunch bill.

CHAPTER 2:
Trout Tales

Each year several million trout travel from the Fish Commission's hatchery system to the many cool, clear streams of the Commonwealth. They are paid for by sportsperson's licensing dollars. They arrive in large, white tank trucks that travel six, four and two-lane highways, paved country roads and dirt roads along mountain streams. They also occasionally get on gated roads to access prime waters, with the hope of providing a special "wilderness" experience for avid backcountry fisherman. Like all vehicles, they wreck, quit, don't fit and get stuck.

SEVEN YEARS AND NEVER BEEN STUCK
No tale of stocking truck mishaps would be complete without the story of Joe. Joe was a veteran of seven years of truck driving in the northwest region. I was a rookie officer freelancing in the northwest, with nothing to do but help other officers stock trout and take pictures. I can't remember the stream, but I know it was in McKean County and Wilbur Williams was the officer in charge. He had a particularly nasty logging road for an access and he began leading Joe, driving the stocking truck, down it. It was downhill, snow and ice covered and sloped to the right.

We stopped at one particularly bad place and got out to look it over. Joe joined us and Wilbur said, "What do you think?" Joe responded with, "No problem. I've been driving for seven years and never been stuck."

We got back in our vehicles and proceeded. Joe was a little too cautious driving and lost his momentum. The rear of the truck slid sideways on the ice, went off the road and hung precariously over the bank.

While we waited for a tow to arrive, I had nothing to do but take pictures, so I did. After getting them developed, I had a nice 8x10 glossy made up and mailed it to a mutual friend of mine and Joe's at the hatchery at Corry. He saw that it got put up on the crew bulletin board. It had a handwritten inscription that read, "I've been driving for seven years and never been stuck."

DON'T CROSS THOSE LINES
Lake Irena was a special place to my way of thinking. It provided a spot for folks to fish who didn't have any means to get anywhere else. They only had to jump on the bus headed to the mall and walk across the park to be on the shores of this fine, little, 20-acre gem. It certainly deserved to be stocked with trout, but I'm not sure it should have gotten the tens of thousands that it did.

Back then, we announced the day we were stocking. Because of the large number of fish put into the lake and the relative closeness of a large population center, Lake Irena was usually shoulder to shoulder. Often persons stood behind those angling, waiting for someone to limit out so they could have a place to fish. This was maximum utilization of product, space and personnel.

A problem developed when the hatchery went to the quick-release stocking truck. The fish came with instructions to dump them using the hose. We could no longer scatter the fish with buckets. We were going to save time and money by shooting them in. Everyone wanted to have the fish dumped near them, but nobody wanted to give up their spot for fear they would not get it back when the stocking was over.

After having a few stocking helpers superficially hooked in their garments or lesser-used body parts, I decided that I would have to take some initiative to solve this problem before it led to gunfire. The next in-season stocking, I arrived early and chose my stocking place before the crowd could arrive. Using the edge of my boot, I scratched out two lines in the mud at the edge of the pond and told the two fishermen on either side that I would be arresting anyone that I caught fishing between the lines.

To my surprise, when I got there with the truck, I had about 20 feet of open shoreline, from boot mark to boot mark. As I stocked, the guys nearest the line kept yelling at the people behind them to, "Quit pushing, you're going to shove me over the line and I'll get arrested." I knew I was onto something.

When I completed stocking, I usually took the truck driver across the road for a coffee and then returned to do a patrol, after completing the necessary paperwork in the restaurant.

"Can we fish there now?" someone asked.

"Not until I get back from the restaurant," I replied.

I figured when I got out of sight the no-fishing zone would be invaded. To my surprise, when I returned there wasn't a footprint in the mud. I got my rod and a lure out and made a few casts to be sure the trout had dispersed properly and, after catching a few, declared the zone open to fishing.

Until I left Luzerne County, this was the way we stocked Lake Irena when a quick release truck was used. It just amazes me that so many people think we wardens can and do actually make the laws.

THREE TRUCKS STUCK, LEHIGH

A big storm was predicted locally for the day we were to stock the Lehigh River. I called the hatchery at Carlisle the afternoon before and told them they had better hold the trucks. The hatchery superintendent lamented the confusion that rescheduling three trucks would cause. I relented and told him I would call again in the morning.

When I called, the snow was falling blizzard-like. Up in Luzerne County, we had a foot and were expected to get more. The hatchery super said the roads were dry down south and he wanted to send the trucks. I argued, but finally gave up and got the troops rallied. We would try to get the fish off as fast as possible and get the trucks headed south again.

It wasn't to be. When the trucks arrived, they had no chains and the tires were nothing to write home about. Two deputies took two of the trucks and I took the third. We headed for our respective routes to get the show on the road. I would start in the White Haven area and work downstream. I pulled into the first parking lot along the river and the driver began to back down when the bottom went out from under him. He was stuck but good.

A call to a towing service soon had us back on the road again, but with a $70 bill to greet the hatchery superintendent attached to the trip sheet. I certainly didn't plan it, but figured it would give the super a little more faith in my judgment from then on.

Eventually we emptied the tanks and returned to the meeting place. No other trucks were back. I had a coffee with the driver, then left him in the diner, eating an oversized hamburger, and went looking for the other trucks. On a dead-end road, I found the second one sitting off the side in a ditch. The tow was summoned for the second time that day. The bill now was up to $140. This would be a lesson well learned.

Back to the diner, again. Another coffee and still no third truck. As I was walking out, a passerby waved me down and asked if I was looking for a fish truck. I assured him I was. He then told me where to look for it, in the White Haven Poconos development, hopelessly mired.

Three tows was a record for me in one day. It probably still stands as a statewide record. The bill jumped once again, proportionately. Though the next time when I sounded the snow alert, it was heeded.

BE REASONABLE OR BE ARRESTED

Stocking the Lehigh was mostly remote, with a short piece right in the town of White Haven. We had to jockey around the narrow streets with the oversized fish trucks, but since we have very professional drivers, it was never a problem. Never, except once.

We were coming out of the parking lot above the bridge and I turned left. It was a wet, miserable day and Jack, the driver, didn't see me turn, so he started up the hill, under the railroad overpass. When he got under it, he realized that with the slope, he wasn't going to fit. He looked in his rearview mirror and went to back up, when a big, old Ford LTD came around the corner, got tight against him, and began honking the horn. He couldn't move.

The LTD driver was a greasy redneck, boisterous, adamant about Jack moving the fish truck, and probably drunk. Jack was short, heavy and looked like a prizefighter with a lot of tough years. Though he was getting older, he still had a lot of spunk.

When I realized Jack wasn't behind me, I turned the Matador around and went back looking for him, figuring he had either not seen me turn or gotten stuck. What I didn't expect was what greeted me. I rounded the bend and there was Jack reaching through the window of the LTD. He had the ruffian by the scruff of the shirt neck and about to make him look like a prizefighter, too.

I got out and using my best law enforcement rationale got Jack to let go. I then demanded information from the instigator so I could cite him for something. I wasn't sure of what; I was making it up as I went along. Once things got quieted down and cooled off, I got Jack back in the fish truck and told the troublemaker to get out of there while the getting was good. Which is exactly what he did. Trout stocking is never boring.

HAYES CREEK CROSSING

If you drove fish truck in the late '70s and early '80s, some runs were cushy and others struck fear into your heart. If you were going to Steiner's district, fear was usually the first response. I hated doing anything easy. The fish and the fishermen always deserved better than that. Drivers never knew what I had in store for them.

The Lehigh River was big and brawling and had some tricky accesses. It was a fine piece of fishing water. I was always looking for new accesses to spread the trout out and make the fishing more sporting. One day while patrolling, I was told of an old-time stocking point. It was simple. All you had to do was go down the gravel road bank, cross Fawn Run, then go along the steeply slanting gravel road for a hundred yards down into Hayes Creek, cross under the railroad tunnel on the right-hand side, drop the few inches onto the sandbar, and climb up the sandy shore to the logging road. This then took you right to the Lehigh's edge. I liked it!

I ran the route a time or two in a friend's 4WD and decided it was certainly doable. Risky, but doable. Three fish trucks would usually arrive for this stocking. Whichever truck driver got the short straw would be off with me, while the deputies did the easy, everyday accesses with the other two trucks.

Jack got the short straw this particular day. The rain was hard at times, but Jack had a long history with the outfit and I had no fear of his abilities. I made the upper stops as fast as possible, and then headed for the "Hayes Creek crossing." When I parked the Matador and jumped into my deputy's 4WD, Jack sensed trouble, like a fox sniffing a trap. But before he could quiz me and try to talk me out of it, we were rolling.

The ascent to Fawn Run was steep in and out and just long enough to keep from getting both of the fish truck's bumpers stuck at the same time. They did both scrape, though. I saw Jack hand-motioning me when I looked in the rearview mirror. I just smiled; he hadn't seen nuthin' yet.

We jumped out of Fawn Run. The dirt path slanted to the point that Jack had to keep momentum up or slide off. This was good, because as he rounded the turn, he was plunging into Hayes Creek without a chance to think about it. When we hit the creek with the 4WD, I noticed that the water was up a foot or two since yesterday. Water pushed up over the hood of the 4WD and onto the windshield. Got to love them old Scouts!

"Keep 'er rolling, Stan, Jack's on our tail,' I guffawed.

Stan's knuckles were white on the steering wheel. The Scout lunged off the concrete tunnel bottom and jumped into the swirling hole below. It choked, coughed and grabbed ground and pulled up the sandy bank like a first-time swimmer spewing inhaled water. Then down the logging road toward the Lehigh we went.

The stocking truck was on our heels like a hound on a rabbit. He had scraped his mirror on the underpass, hugging the side to avoid going into the deepest part of the creek. We arrived at the cleared camping area along the river. I jumped out of the Scout and climbed up on the truck and grabbed a dip net like nothing had happened. Jack came out, questioning my sanity in words you certainly cannot use in a book like this. As he was explaining to me in no uncertain terms the consequences of maneuvers like this, I was busy trying to convince him that he should be thanking me for putting a little adventure into his mundane life. We stocked this area a few times after that one, but it always was with a new driver and always when the Hayes was running low. It was never as much fun again.

HELICOPTER STOCKED WOODS

Helicopter stocking of the Lehigh River above the F. E. Walter Dam was extremely popular among real fishermen. It was a place with trout where you didn't have to put up with the truck followers, if you were willing to expend a little effort. Each year during one of the in-season scheduled stockings, I would try to make arrangements for such a stocking. Where we would load the chopper had a lot of variables figured in. I always left that up to the pilot. I would adapt the truck location to suit the flying conditions.

This particular fine May day we were operating from the upper parking lot, on the west side of the reservoir. The pilot would load water from the dam and fly up to us. We would load 300 trout in the bucket and then he would head for the upper reaches of the Lehigh. Only the pilot knew where the fish landed in the river. Fishermen would then hunt them, knowing that there were 1,500 or 2,000 fine trout for them to find and catch in the four or five-mile stretch.

As we finished the third load, we signaled for the pilot to lift off. He lifted and had begun his slow swing up over the point toward Bear Creek, when it happened. The bucket malfunctioned. Water and trout began to spray from the bucket in a steady stream. For 300 yards, he laid a path of damp trout on the ground.

The fish truck driver and I quickly passed out buckets with a little water in them and sent our volunteer sportsmen ground crew scampering for the fish. After a half hour, they returned with about 50 trout in various stages of stress from being out of the water. We assured the sportsmen that they had gotten all the fish "but a few," and we went on as though it never happened.

The next several runs went without a hitch. Fishermen reported good fishing all summer and trappers reported that the raccoons were a little heavier than usual in that area in the fall.

RAFT STOCKING

There is a stretch of the Lehigh River from Thornhurst to the upper end of the still water at Francis E. Walter Reservoir that is as remote as anywhere in the state of Pennsylvania. To get to it takes a walk of over an hour. It is rugged, brushy and full of bears, rattlers and blackflies. It's a perfect place to trout fish.

To get to it, you either walk through the Pocono pucker-brush or run your boat across the lake and walk upstream. I spotted the remote stretch on a map and just had to get fish into it.

Before the helicopter became available, I had made the acquaintance of the owners of a rubber-rafting company. They rented weekend whitewater thrills on the Lehigh to city people. I worked closely with them, convincing them that loaning rafts to our trout stocking operation would go a long way toward alleviating the animosity toward their operation held by fishermen who were plagued by inconsiderate city thrill-seekers on the weekends.

The raft owners bought into the idea. We lined up TV, radio and newspaper coverage and set up to float trout into this upper stretch of river. It was a big production. Several friends and deputies volunteered for the first run.

Eighteen inches of snow fell through the night, but my efforts to cancel the trucks fell on deaf ears at the hatchery. They had the trucks loaded and it wasn't snowing down in Carlisle. They were on their way. I got everything set up and my float teams donned wet suits and waited. Each raft was inflated to the maximum and loaded with cold river water. The trucks rolled in, the cameras rolled and clicked, we dumped hundreds of trout into each raft, and they shoved off down the "river of no return."

Hours passed and night came on. Eight hours later, six wet, nearly frozen adventurers finally stepped from the rafts at the dam. The wind on the still water had nearly defeated them, and I had been too damn dumb to figure out the problem and go to their rescue with a powerboat. But all had worked well.

The following year, the stage was set again and the stocking and TV crews were ready. This was taking on the color of an annual event on par with Punxsutawney Phil. Again it snowed, the wind blew, the fish got stocked, but this time a "rescue" boat was waiting for the rafters when they hit the still water. Once more the program was a success.

When year three rolled around, the deputies and their friends were getting a little smarter. They figured out that while I sat in the car, basking in warmth and glory, they were freezing off parts of their anatomy that only they normally saw. The bright lights of the cameras were warming me against the weather and inflating my hat size. I was becoming the star of the silver screen.

I am not sure whether it was my desire to get in on some of the action or their desire to watch me slowly freeze to death, as they had, that led them to a concerted effort to coerce me into being a rafter. They would don uniforms and bask in the lights and glory, and I would ride the frigid "river of no return." I reluctantly consented, fearing mutiny if I balked.

When the day arrived, the logistics had become routine. Everyone knew their part, had rehearsed their lines and was ready to roll. The trucks showed on time. Only one thing had changed. Instead of a foot of blustery snow, we had a 70-degree bluebird day. I wore the wet suit, but could have gone in shorts. I was more worried about sunburn than frostbite. The stocking went without a hitch. Instead of hunkering down into the raft out of the wind on departure, I made a grand exit for the cameras, not unlike the famous portrait of Washington crossing the Delaware.

After the stocking and all the fanfare, it was the crew's tradition to don dry clothes and retire to a local restaurant/pub and partake of good food and strong drink, originally to chase the chill from the participants' bones, and watch the TV newsreel of our adventures. Since at least two stations covered each year's activities, we found it necessary to watch both the 6 o'clock and 11 o'clock news. The time in between was spent throwing darts and reliving the day's adventures. Talk was of trout and seasons of yore.

I used the five hours effectively chiding the crew about what "wimps" they had been in years gone by, "yammering" about the harshness of the task. I had taken the challenge and had found all their concerns to be unfounded. It had proved neither cold nor windy nor arduous.

As I chided them, they were already trying to conceive a plan to get me in the raft again and a way to guarantee unsettled weather. As my luck has always been, I took their challenge. But before I could begin to worry about the next spring's ordeal, a gauntlet of frigidity, a white knight rode to my rescue. He rode in on a helicopter. When the offer came to use a helicopter with a fire-fighting water bucket to stock the remote regions of the river, I immediately accepted, escaping the inevitable forever. I assured all the participants of the necessity of spreading the wealth of goodwill and TV coverage around and never again had to think about snowstorms and rubber rafts.

THE BANK ROLL

Dads like to think that their kids like to help stock trout. Kids think they would like it, until you hand them a 40-pound bucket on a hundred-yard run. Then they don't. One in a hundred thinks it is fun after that. I believe I haven't been out with my one-hundredth kid yet, and I'm retired.

After age 16, kids see trout stocking as a way of attaining status; then they are good help.

"You ain't goin' to let an old fat man out-carry you, are you?" I'll ask after I make several good runs.

"Never happen!" comes the reply.

These teens are already thinking of the glory the next day, when they tell their buddies how they out-carried a grown-up fat fish warden all day. They will be a hero with their friends for a day or two. I'd carry just enough to make them think that I was putting the pressure on, and they would keep carrying. It's an old trick I learned from Mark Twain, and it still works today. They don't have Mark Twain video games, so aren't wise to it.

Earl was my deputy and his son, Russell, was just out of school at the end of his sophomore high school year. Earl thought Russell would like to stock fish with me. I thought he would, too. Russell wasn't sure, but we convinced him he would. Earl was convincing because he wanted the kid to be with a responsible adult for a week or two, while the shock of summer break wore off, to keep him out of kid trouble.

My logic was simpler. I knew that I would have three trucks loaded with trout fingerlings for the Lehigh River gorge.

The railroad tracks had recently been torn out and the area had become a state park. Railroad cinder banks in the gorge are steep and high. Three trucks full of fingerlings translate into a very long day carrying fish, and it was June and getting warm early in the day. I was afraid if I had to carry them all myself, and you get no sportsman help when the fish are not of legal size, my fat melting would salt the water to where the trout wouldn't survive.

We met the trucks at White Haven at 10 in the morning and the sun was already getting intense. We would have to hustle all day to prevent the tanks from heating up and the trout being stressed or, worse yet, dying. So hustle we did. Two buckets at a time, down over the bank Russell went, with me cheering him on from the top. Now and then, when it would look like he was going to drop over from exhaustion, I would hand him a can of soda pop as he topped the hill and waited for the next bucket to be handed to him by the driver.

I was having a time of it in the heat, too. This was before they bought us air-conditioned cars to sit in. The day went uneventfully, as Russell ran buckets and I pointed out outstanding geological features of the gorge or a soaring osprey. He was interested in nature, music and tales of yore. Anything that got him a break. I could tell looking at his railroad-dust-blackened face that he was having fun. The sweat was making neat little streaks in it.

As we neared the last four or five stops, I pitched in and helped him with a bucket or two. I didn't want the blisters that had broken open on his hands to become too sore. I had trucks coming tomorrow, too. Finally, with the sun setting and the fish gasping what little oxygen was left in the tepid tank water, I started cheering harder as Russell descended the banks with two buckets. The buckets now dragged the ground, since his arms had stretched several inches during the day.

We only had a few buckets left to go and he took them and started his running freefall to the river. Then it happened. From in the cinders, a root caught hold of his foot and sent him in a headlong pitch down the slope. Fish flopped everywhere, cinders adhering to their slimy little bodies. Russell rolled to a stop just short of the river, black cinders sticking to his sweaty body, head to toe. He was a sight.

After getting the fish picked up and thrown into the river, where most of them showed signs of surviving, he climbed up to the car. I kiddingly suggested he walk the 17 miles back up to the road and I would have his dad pick him up there. I explained I didn't want the patrol vehicle to get all grimy. Russell showed signs of becoming an adult by reminding me I didn't have a gun with me and he still had enough left to commandeer the car and drive home himself.

Ahhh, to be young again and get to go stocking!

FISH CHARIOT ON FIRE

Dedication takes many forms. This incident is inserted to show that while we try to always have fun with our job, there are serious moments and the Fish and Boat Commission employees from all divisions come through for the sportsmen when they have to.

One foggy morning, I was enjoying a rare day off. It was back in the days when you usually didn't get many days off during the spring. I was lazing around the house, having breakfast and doing nothing in particular. The phone rang. I answered and it was the Pennsylvania State Police. "You have a fish truck in trouble out on the interstate. Can you go?"

I saddled up the Matador and headed for Tank, on I-80. When I got there, I was greeted by a fish truck sitting on the berm. The back axle was missing and the white paint was all blistered and soot covered. The state trooper on the scene and the truck driver met me. They explained that the driver had gotten beyond his exit in the fog and then made a mistake. The mistake resulted in colliding with a brand new, empty school bus. The driver of the bus was unhurt, but the bus was nastied up.

I then was informed that our driver was hurt and had burned his hands and face quite badly battling the resulting fire. After some convincing, I assured the driver that with my previous hatchery experience I could keep the pumps running and save the fish and he should go for treatment. The police notified the hatchery and they immediately rolled out another truck. Upon its arrival we off-loaded the fish onto the new truck and had the wrecked truck towed.

The driver had been taken to the hospital by the troopers. It would have been easy for the driver to worry about himself, rather than the slimy cargo, but he didn't and 3,500 trout were returned to the hatchery for later stocking. The state police certainly deserved credit for helping the sportsmen that rainy April day, too.

THE LOVELY LEMON GATE

One buried truck, a career does not make. The Nescopeck Creek soon became a special challenge to me. The finest trout water in Luzerne County's southern half was in that stream. It was a fine, big creek in public ownership. Both very good reasons to try my darnedest each and every time stocking was scheduled to get fish into it. Over an eight-year period, I was confronted with rain, snow, heat and who knows what all. Another problem was gaining access. Sometimes it was state park property and sometimes it was game lands.

Now, we do cooperate as agencies, to an extent. The park people that ran a nonexistent state park did not like to call attention to their little sanctuary. But, ultimately, they did cooperate. Game people, at that time, kept thinking of my stocking access roads as their rabbit paths and linear food plots. They would stomp and snort when I would take a truck in and it would rut up the road. I tried to convince them that the rabbits didn't mind if the grass was growing in ruts instead of flat ground. It was never easy. Thankfully, there were some good people in both state agencies who cooperated and made the stockings possible by slipping me gate keys or actually opening them for me.

It was on just such a day, when the "Nesky" was low and clear, that I decided to take the truck across the ford at the Lemon Gate. Bob was driving and had strict orders, as usual, not to get the truck stuck. I assured him that I had crossed the creek in the Matador and turned around in the far field. It was all solid.

Bob was a motor-head and balked at getting his wheels wet, but finally gave into persuasion and the threat of riot by the stocking contingency. Across the creek we went and popped up on the far shore and began stocking. The creek was extremely low and the roads were dry. We stocked on through to the big field, where he would have plenty of room to turn around.

I swung the Matador in a loop, with him following. Stocking trucks have a little wider turning radius than cars. I saw him making his swing and knew I should have mentioned the spring in the middle of the field. As soon as I was on the road, I stopped and looked back. The truck was rocking and bucking and slinging mud. In the blink of a gnat's eyelash he was sitting on his horizontal spare tire and saddle tanks. No amount of pulling and tugging with 4WDs was going to extricate him from the quagmire he had settled in.

I was much smarter by now. I didn't even think about getting dirty. I just walked back and said, "Leave 'er sit there." The response was certainly not printable, but struck me as funny. Bob stood shaking his head and worrying out loud about the hell he was going to get when he turned in the towing bill.

"Not to worry," I assured him. "We now have preferred customer status."

I drove out and bought us a coffee, while my helpers went for the big red tow. After we drank our coffee, the truck arrived. In no time we were out of the mud and on our way down the creek. The stocking was completed and the tow was only twenty bucks. The tow driver said that one wasn't even a challenge and, besides, he liked getting to drive all those gated game lands roads.

You might think that this story should end here, and you're right, it should. But it doesn't. Since the Nesky is a high-pressure stream, the very next week to the day another truck arrived and we were at it again. A light mist was falling and Dave was the driver. Now Dave and I had gone to Fish Culture School together before I got into the wardening business. He was fun there and always fun when he was driving.

We started down the creek and soon made it to the Lemon Gate, where I swung off the road and opened the gate. The Game Commission hadn't noticed the hole left from last week's "rescue-pade" yet, and the locks hadn't been changed. As I unlocked the gate and swung it out of the way, Dave met me, shaking his head. "No, I can't. They'll fire me. All I heard for a week is not to let Steiner talk me into getting off the pavement."

I understood where he was coming from and showed as much compassion for his position as I could, while I talked him into driving in. I finally got him moving with an assurance that I had found a solid, uphill turnaround that he could drift out of, if he got stuck. He was uneasy, but followed the Matador in.

We stocked our way into the field with no problems as usual. The fish were handling well in the light mist and a beautiful, reasonably remote piece of water was getting stocked. We finished the load and I showed him the turnaround. He got out and looked at it. It was an old logging road that had been graveled. I don't know how I had missed using it the week before. It had some leaves over the gravel, but he was satisfied. He revved up the motor, popped the clutch and the truck walked right up the slope and was expertly guided onto the gravel roadbed. He was now sitting at a 90-degree angle from the road we had come in on and was uphill of it. It would have been a tight swing, but entirely make-able.

Dave wanted to get up another foot or two to make the swing in reverse a sure thing. He began backing and the wheels stuttered sideways on the wet leaves and, in a flash, he was off the gravel and buried to the axle.

The coffee tasted good on this rather cool day, as we waited for the big red tow truck.

SAVED BY A TOYOTA PICKUP

There is no feeling of helplessness like that of directing a stocking truck driver around a treacherous turn as he backs up and watching him go the opposite direction you are signaling. The more frantically you wave, the harder he cuts it the wrong way, and then it is over. You have a truck in to the axles. Not everyone is as good with rearview mirrors as they should be.

It was just such a maneuver that stuck a truck in the Nescopeck game lands "rabbit paths" one day. The driver missed making the turn by a few feet, but a few inches would have been too much. When he went down, it was with both rear duals in wetlands off the edge of the road. It was sunny and solid on the paths and I couldn't believe that I was going to have another truck towed out of the Nescopeck. By now, it wasn't even funny to me and most things are.

I had a friend along who drove an old Toyota Land Cruiser. He worked in the woods, skidding logs. He stopped, got out and looked, and decided that he could get the fish truck free. I didn't believe it, but was willing to give him a chance to avoid another expensive tow. He hooked on with a nylon sling and slammed forward, rocking the truck, but not popping it. He looked again and told us to get some rocks. He said that when he hit it forward the next time, if she rocked, we should throw the rocks in the tracks behind the truck. He did, and it did, and we did and in a matter of a half hour he had pulled off the most amazing recovery I had ever witnessed, saving me embarrassment and the Fish Commission a towing bill.

These guys, volunteers that you know in passing who use their resources and know-how to get a tough job done for the commission, are the unsung heroes of our stocking program. Trout fishing would only be under bridges without them

LEAKY WADERS

Float stocking the Nescopeck Creek was a way of life for me for nine trout seasons. It was beautiful water, totally in public ownership. If I got trout back into the game lands, I was creating a wilderness experience for people in an urban area. I felt obligated. After all, a lot of sweat and toil goes into making these fine stocked fish and they deserve to at least be caught somewhere that is pretty.

Bob, my deputy, and a young friend, Floyd, used to float stock the lower end of the game lands periodically for me. I would load the box and they would pull it downstream and net a few fish out here and there. It made real fishing possible, rather than the "one-hole limit." You had to earn them, and most sport fishermen appreciated the effort that went into spreading out the trout.

One cold April afternoon, I met Bob and Floyd and they were ready to go. Floyd had a "brand new" pair of waders that Bob had bought on sale for him to use. These were chest waders, since the creek was a little high and often would go over hip boots.

I loaded the float boxes, bid them farewell and cautioned them to "be careful." As the hours passed, I unloaded the truck at easier access points and then returned to their pickup truck to await their getting out of the woods. Darkness was nearing, and I wanted to be sure they were out of the water safely. They soon appeared through the dimming light and spitting snow. I noticed right away that Floyd was walking stiff-legged, and I stepped out of my Matador with a flashlight, to assist them along their way.

What greeted the beam of the light was a sight. Floyd's new waders were split from ankle to ankle around the inseam, with not a thread intact. Whatever glue had been used on the waders had not taken hold, and as they began their journey downstream, the seam had slowly parted with every step. Not wanting to abort the mission, they stuck with it, even though Floyd ended up wet-wading.

He was a sight, though. At six-foot-three, 200 pounds and a shaggy head of hair, Floyd normally was the picture of robust male youth. Today, however, he was a shivering mass of kid, with a pink face, blue lips and a large, loose-fitting rubber skirt. I'll always remember him that way.

WATCH OUT FOR THE CHUTE

Getting trout into scenic areas to provide a quality fishing experience can have its consequences. One such effort started innocently enough. I was a young warden in a new district. As I studied the map, I noted that one of my stocked trout streams, Nescopeck Creek, ran through the state park for several miles without crossing a road, making a pocket of "wilderness." At the time, this was a nonexistent state park. The land had been bought by the state, but it was not developed into any recreational facilities. In fact, they were still busy tearing down the last few houses.

One sunny day in early spring, I walked into this stretch to check it out. It was incredible. It had big pools, large boulders and a sandy bottom. Anyone who has ever dreamed of trout fishing in a remote setting has dreamed of this kind of water. I was excited. My new district had an added bonus I never would have believed.

I began asking my deputies and others how the previous warden, an older, heavy-set fellow, had stocked this area. I was dumbfounded by the answer I got. "He didn't. Can't get a truck in there, the ground's too soft." I explained over and over that you didn't have to get a truck all the way in, just the fish. Many persons scoffed at the idea, but a few bought in.

From this nucleus I built a stocking crew. The first attempt would be to get the fish truck in as far as possible behind Lake Francis, then run the trout down to the creek, via manpower, to a float box, and then float downstream to the Lemon Gate. The day of the stocking, it was cold, Woolrich-coat cold, and the creek was near the top of its banks. Too high for waders, but I would not be thwarted in my effort to get fish into this incredible stretch of stream.

I showed up with my personal 12-foot johnboat tied to the top of my Matador and two float boxes on my deer rack. We put the boxes in the boat and slid it on the snow to the creek. My two-man boat crew included Bob, a young deputy, and George, an employee of the nonexistent state park. They were wearing chest waders, hunting coats, stocking caps and life jackets. The frozen logging roads had afforded the fish truck reasonably secure footing and we began to load.

It was then that I first heard the question. "What are they going to do when they get to the chute?"

Admittedly, I hadn't walked the whole stretch but, after all, I was a WCO and I know water. I knew just looking at this stream that, while it had nice, deep holes and boulders, it fell slowly and could not be dangerous.

"No problem. This johnboat will skim right through it," I responded.

"What chute?" Bob asked. He had never seen the stream before that day.

"Pay no attention to him," I encouraged. "He's just an old man that worries too much."

Bob rolled his eyes and cinched down the belly band on his life jacket in a display of trust in me.

They were underway. It was apparent from the beginning that the trip was going to take a little longer than expected for the float stockers, since the float box became a sea anchor when loaded with fish. I would just drink an extra coffee while I waited.

The sun had appeared and was warming the late morning air as we walked the 300 yards back to the fish truck, parked on a logging road at the top of the hill. It would follow me out. The 4WD vehicles ground their way along the road behind the Matador, which was slinging mud. I drove several hundred yards and rounded a turn, then watched my mirror. No fish truck.

I stopped on the first solid ground, which I determined when I didn't see mud flying out behind my car any longer. The 4WDs slid to a halt in a heap and we sat and listened. Cursing is all we heard. We looked back to see a cloud of blue smoke and mud. The truck was down on its saddle tanks and the driver was venting his spleen about the quality of vehicle he drove, the state of government roads and, I think, possibly my poor judgment.

Efforts to free the belly-deep truck went unsuccessfully, and the trout load was in jeopardy of becoming fertilizer. We had tried three and four of 1976's best 4WDs attached to the mired white monster, but nothing would budge her. She was in dire straits; becoming a fossil was nearing reality.

Fortunately, we were not far from I-80 and a garage of full-size tow trucks. Expensive tow trucks. The driver was in a dither. He had been told to be cautious and feared repercussions from the higher-ups. I assured him that towing would be better received than having to tell them their truck had gone the way of the dinosaurs in the La Brea tar pit. After convincing him that the truck was history as it sat and so were the fish without drastic action, we sent for the cavalry.

In short order, an industrial tow truck arrived with chains and backed in. He jockeyed into position as the snow had melted and made more mud on top the frozen earth. He dug and chugged and finally hooked onto the fish truck. The big tow shuddered as the winch came taught and started to slide backwards, leaving ruts. Next we cut a few logs and dug a few rocks and blocked the tow truck wheels solidly, driving wood wedges behind the logs and rocks. The tow truck shuddered and then began to slowly stand on its hind wheels.

At liftoff the driver disengaged the clutch and bounced down. Next he cabled to a white pine of huge girth that was conveniently just in reach. With both cables stretched tight and everybody but the two drivers hiding, he engaged both winches. The big pine shuddered and tilted, the tow truck lifted from the ground, suspended momentarily by the cables, and then dropped. The fish truck popped from the mud.

With a few more tows, we eventually got the fish truck to the pavement and signed a healthy bill. The adventure was worth the price. I promised myself that I would never take a fish truck on those roads again ... until they dried out. We began quick-stocking the remainder of the load, while the trout still had a little kick left in them.

Eventually we got unloaded and went for coffee. I signed the driver out and wrote a note accepting all responsibility for the towing bill and attached it and sent him on his way. Then and only then did I think about the nagging words lingering in my head, "What about the chute?"

I hurried back up to the game lands and began to drive into the pickup point. My float stockers were not there yet. I walked a short ways upstream and then retraced my steps to the warm car. I sat patiently, drinking coffee and chuckling about having averted creating a fish truck fossil. I knew there would be hell to pay when the bill hit headquarters. I also knew human nature enough to know that, after the shouting, the rookie officer that buried the truck would be forgotten.

Now it was getting dark. I was starting to worry, so I drove up along the road again. There, staggering out of the woods, carrying parts of a badly destroyed float box, was my float crew. They were soaked to the hide, scratched, bruised and otherwise "well-adventured." From under their dripping knit caps came the comment, "Pay no attention to him."

I knew then that Bob had had the excitement he had expected and that I had promised when I talked him into taking a day off at his mundane routine of fixing cameras. I tried to con him and George into buying me a coffee for sitting around and waiting so late for them, but they didn't bite. Something about their money being all wet and no good. I then insisted that they let me buy. They quit chasing me and we headed for the diner.

There they explained that this normally placid, 50-foot-wide stream had unexpectedly rounded several turbulent bends and then narrowed between two large boulders to about ten feet wide. The water was sucked through like draining a bathtub. The Chute. The float boxes, acting like sea anchors, caught and stood the johnboat instantly on its stern. The water surged in the back and squirted out the front like a pressurized fountain, taking them with it. They were flung into the deep, rock-strewn pool to flounder refreshingly in their life jackets and waders.

Bob explained that the life jackets float you just about nose deep when you're properly equipped with waders and hunting coats. Just when they feared the worse, chunks of the johnboat began bobbing out of the tiny pass between the rocks. For a while they had thought it would come out intact and they would have to continue their outing.

They dumped the trout that were left in the float box when it came floating out, scooped up what trout they could from flooded puddles along the narrow spot, where the boat explosion had thrown them, gathered what gear they could carry, and began the walk out through the woods. I tried to tell them about the "real adventure" I had had getting the truck out of its near grave, but they were not very good listeners. All they wanted to do was talk about themselves and their lives and how surprised they were to still have them.

As I dropped them off at their cars, I rolled down the window and we exchanged parting comments.

"We will never again help you stock one more fish," they threatened.

"It certainly was fun, wasn't it?" I replied.

"You are a lunatic," they joked.

"Someday we will have to see if we can find the chute that old guy was talking about," I returned.

The Matador whinnied as it peeled rubber hitting the pavement. The rocks they had thrown at it fell well short.

THE FLOAT BOX, THE PREACHER AND THE DEPUTY

Fish stockers come in two varieties. Those that want to put all the fish in one hole and those that want to put them out individually, so they can't see each other.

The preacher was a young fellow and of the second order. He asked to float-stock his favorite section of Wapwallopen Creek to spread the trout out. Sounded good to me, and I just happened to have a float box or two.

When I showed up, the weather was sunny but bitterly cold. The preacher had his float box in the water waiting and he stood by in his hip boots. I loaded his box and cautioned him that he should have help; the water looked plenty strong that morning. He assured me he would be alright.

I finished the stocking and several hours later was surprised to see the young preacher's car still sitting along the road where it had been to start. When I stopped, he came shivering out of the bushes, almost incoherent.

He was so cold he couldn't get into his car. He had fallen in just around the bend and had been trying to get warm out of the wind along some hemlock trees for several hours. We got his car started and him in it and warmed enough to drive, and then went and got the runaway float box.

Deputy Al was helping me that day, and he had a plan. He would do the float-stocking in-season. Two months later the water was a foot or so lower and the weather was 70 degrees warmer when I pulled into the starting site. Al was standing there in a wet suit. He was determined not to get cold. He didn't.

BLIZZARD, SUGAR CREEK STOCKING

The upper mile of Sugar Creek in Venango County is a fine piece of water. It is one where the stocked fish supplement an already nice population of wild brown trout. It is known throughout fly-fishing circles for its grannom caddis hatch. These insects hatch in numbers that are equaled few places on earth. They make whole bridge piers appear to be crawling. For local tourism-related businesses, the fine fishing of Sugar Creek is a source of income that they are neither aware of nor understand. Each year, hundreds of fly fishermen try to be there for those few mornings when the caddis flies come in droves and the fish, even the big, old holdovers, lose their caution.

I felt I owed something to these guys, since I am one of them. I rounded up a crew of hardy, young "soldiers" and convinced them to float stock an inaccessible mile of the creek. Since I made it sound like high adventure, they rallied to the cause. The first year or two the effort was uneventful and all went well. Then came the third year.

Mark and Erik, two young deputies, teamed with Scott, an artist friend that is an avid fly fisher, to take on the challenge. The weather forecast didn't sound good: "A blizzard moving through northern Ohio should hit Pennsylvania at first light."

I called the hatchery to see about canceling the stocking, but they felt they could beat the bulk of the storm. It was snowing, but not all that hard. The fish were coming from Corry, in the lake-effect snowbelt, where eight inches of new snow is treated like "frost" is treated everywhere else in the state.

I had the crew get ready and I drove to the meeting point. The snow came harder now and the forecast sounded more and more forbidding: "Up to three feet of snow will fall in the next twenty-four hours, making roads impassable, causing trees and utility lines to fall. Travelers are advised to get where they need to go and stay there."

The truck was an hour late and a foot of snow was now on the ground. Visibility was down to 20 or 30 yards. Bundled like bears with waders, the youth of today insisted on seeking adventure, with my encouragement. I loaded the float box and cautioned them about frostbite, hypothermia and all the other nasty things that cold can do to you. It fell on deaf ears. The float box and float stockers disappeared down the creek, around the bend into the alders, and I was left to wait and worry.

The fish-truck driver and I finished up with the load, and I assisted in getting the truck out of a ditch, which the driver could no longer see for the deepening snow. He was headed back on a usual hour drive that was destined to take nearly four. Visibility decreased to a few yards, as the wind picked up. I waited by the creek for the float stockers. Where three hours ago there was slow-moving, winter-black water, there was now a total covering of slush ice.

Slowly, in 4WD-drive-low, I drove around all the possible emergency "exits" from the stream. Still no helpers. The temperature was dropping, night was nearing and the weather was getting worse by the minute. I first checked their Jeep at the exit and then went over the stream again. If I turned the car off for more than a few minutes, the windshield would have several inches of snow on it. Periodically I would clean my car off and the Jeep, and then kick the new snow down and move the car to keep the tracks broken. There was now well over two feet of the white stuff.

As evening grayed the skies, I looked up a logging road through the pines and saw motion. There, walking like zombies, came my young adventurers, waders caked in ice an inch thick, moustaches and hair frozen in a wet, white crust. Through blue lips, they greeted me with smiles. They were soon in the warm car and thawing. Scott went home since he lived close by, and my deputies stayed at my house for the night.

"Northwestern Pennsylvania has just been hit with the worst blizzard in one hundred years," the radio greeted me the next morning. Three young men will tell their grandchildren about breaking ice for a mile down a creek to stock trout during that storm. The trout will be caught by businessmen, doctors and lawyers and folks from all walks of life from Pittsburgh and Cleveland on a sunny April morning, fishing the grannom hatch, and local motels, restaurants and gas stations will make a little extra cash and never know of the heroics of the three young float stockers. Trout fishing makes men crazy for sure, but sometimes it is a good kind of crazy. It's the kind of crazy that comes with high adventure.

FORM-FITTING JEANS

Spring trout stocking attracts all sorts of people, short ones, tall ones, fat ones, skinny ones, men, women, ugly, pretty and of all ages, some with beards and some without. This early March day was no different.

The snow lay over a foot deep, and the light mist that was falling made the day bone-chilling and the footing treacherous. As usual, the short ones, the tall ones, the fat ones and the skinny ones were there to watch, but of no help carrying buckets. Only a few hearty souls were grabbing buckets at each stop along the East Branch of Sugar Creek, in Venango County.

As we got toward the last stops, where the stream banks steepened, we were down to just several middle-age fellows, myself and the one guy's 18-year-old daughter in a pair of form-fitting blue jeans. The kind, if I had been a young, single warden, I could not have helped but notice.

As the buckets were filled and handed down from the truck, the young lady with the jeans I hadn't noticed once again grabbed a bucket and started down over the bank. She was taking her time, so she didn't slip and upset the buckets. I grabbed the last two buckets and started down over the bank right after her.

My strides were longer and I was only a step or two behind. My right foot sunk deeper in the snow than her footprints, due to my greater weight, and my toe hooked under a tree root. I pitched forward, narrowly missing bouncing my head off the back of her jeans, and landed on my nose in the snow, not hurt but ending in an easily ridiculed position, trout flopping everywhere. There was a great scampering and soon the fish were all safely extricated from the snow, put in buckets and hurried to the creek.

There are those that were there that day who tell this story and are convinced that had I been watching where I put my feet and not the distraction in front of me, I would have never tumbled. I can assure you, though, that I never noticed the blue jeans.

ON THIN ICE

I went across the frozen puddle on the railroad grade in my Blazer, without a problem. I watched the fish truck behind me. The front end came across and then the back end dropped and, in a heartbeat, the truck slid into the boggy area on the uphill side of the old grade.

I thought for a second the truck was going to roll, but each time the water sloshed it seemed to just settle back in place. The driver, Rube, got out and I suggested we waste no time in calling a wrecker to tow us out. But Rube said he could get it. I, for once the conservative side of the argument, felt that we still had a truckload of live fish and the less time spent fooling around, the better.

Rube wanted to try to extract the truck. With an assist from the stocking help, he was able to get a set of chains on the high wheel and enough weight on that side for traction. In a half hour, he had walked the truck right out of the hole. I was always impressed with the talent some of our drivers demonstrated under adverse conditions.

LIKE CATCHING TROUT IN A BARREL

Stocking fish is very weather related. With few exceptions, you stock whether there is weather or not. So it was one day in my district. With trout coming into the county almost every day, rain, no matter how heavy, could not keep us from our mission. The mailman had nothing on us.

To some kids, fishing doesn't come easy. A school teacher deputy of mine, Dick, had a camp along one of our lesser-fished trout streams. His property was open to public fishing, so he would take a few of his underprivileged students to the camp for a hot dog cookout and day of fishing.

Policy at that time dictated that we not disclose the day of stocking. So naturally I would not disclose this information. However, Dick would call and ask if Tuesday would be a good day for a weenie roast.

I might answer, "No, Thursday's weather looks better."

When we made the camp stop, we would be met by eight or ten youngsters who would forever remember the day they were lucky enough to be at a weenie roast when the fish truck pulled in and they had fishing rods along.

For years this system worked well, with each kid almost always catching his or her first fish. But then enter the torrential rain. When we pulled in the driveway on Hemlock Creek, the rain was blinding. The driver and I elected to take a hard-earned break on the porch of the camp and wait for the deluge to subside. It wouldn't let up. Two coffees apiece, camp coffee, the kind with the grounds on the bottom like pond mud, and still the rain poured down. The 55-gallon barrel under the downspout gushed over with rainwater. The kids were anxious to see the fish.

The driver, with a schedule to keep, slipped into his raincoat and I put on mine. Then a strange thing happened. The ground, all wet and muddy, had become slippery. The only fishermen around were the six kids and the teacher, standing forlornly on the porch, watching the creek water turn brown like our coffee and destroying their hopes of a fishing memory.

As the driver handed me the first net full, I was caught off balance and the weight of the flopping trout shifted my center of gravity. As a reaction, I plopped the net into the rain barrel to take the weight off and protect my aging back. Some fish escaped into the barrel before I could regain my balance and carry the rest to the stream.

When we pulled out of the drive, we could see six youngsters that never got a break fishing for "fish in a barrel," over the porch rail. That night a phone call informed me that each kid had caught a trout, their first, and the rest had been netted out and placed into the stream.

EAST SANDY TRESTLE

When they began tearing out the railroad tracks and ties along the rivers and streams, I saw unlimited potential for spreading the fish out when we stocked. I would always run the rail bed to make sure it was passable and had a turnaround, before leading a fish truck onto it. Although I am adventurous, I certainly didn't want anyone hurt or any valuable equipment damaged. I did, however, like to surprise the drivers with a little adventure when they didn't expect it.

We were scheduled to stock East Sandy Creek in Venango County for the first time since coal mine pollution had wiped it out years ago. The stream had made a remarkable recovery and would sustain trout now in the lower reaches. I swung the trucks on the rail bed off Route 322, where I had gained access permission, and I intended to take them right down to the end. It was preseason and the rail bed had ice in spots, but should not be a problem.

Everything was going like clockwork. We were running right along. One stocking stop out of one truck, then the next out of the other. The fish were handling well and I had lots of help for the steep banks along the grade. I didn't have to carry a bucket. It was too good to be true.

Then we came to the first railroad trestle. I just kept rolling. I had been over them all earlier in the week and knew they had supported trains before us. Once we were out on it, me and both trucks, I stopped and jumped out shaking my head. I walked back to the first truck and said in my best deadpan: "I felt her give. We are going to have to back off."

This, of course, would take time with 20 cars tight behind us and no turnaround for miles. I let them sweat it and then said, "Let's chance it," jumped back into the Blazer and drove on across. They reluctantly followed. I don't think the drivers thought it was quite as funny as I did.

When rail beds are available, they allow even distribution of trout. The rail bed along this stream has since been gated and only certain stretches can be accessed by the fish trucks. Fortunately, there are still a few high trestles we can get over to keep it fun with new drivers.

THE REARVIEW MIRROR

Some guys are very one directional. I mean everything they do one way seems to work just fine, but when they try to do something another way, well, then it goes awry.

Jimmy retired from a "real" job and then went to work helping me as a deputy information and education officer. He also liked to stock fish. In the years that he served, he probably helped put a million fish from the truck into buckets and handed them to waiting bucket carriers. This is a sloppy, thankless job, but one that someone must do.

When he was helping, Jim always drove his own car, since sometimes he would have commitments and have to leave early. Or if we got done early, he would return to the stream and catch a few trout before driving home.

His work career had left Jim a little stiff in the neck and he wasn't able to flex like he did when he was a young man, say, like when he was 60. So when he drove his car, he relied on his mirrors. Remember the part about being one directional? Jim was only good in forward.

One day while picking up supplies at the region office, Jim put his Blazer in reverse, checked the mirrors and backed into another vehicle with the whole office staff watching through the window, unable to get his attention.

Shortly after that episode, we were stocking the East Branch of Sugar Creek, and Jim backed up to turn around after the fish truck and I had moved to the next stop. When he didn't show up on top of the truck during the next couple of stops, I figured it was more than the call of nature, so I went back to check. There was the Blazer, buried to the grillwork in a roadside bog. Jim had backed up to get turned around.

Not 300 yards from where we pulled Jim from the mud preseason, we were stocking in a mowed field later in the spring. Jim began to back up and hit the only telephone pole in the whole field dead-center with his rear bumper. The best part of all three of these episodes was that the only thing that got hurt was Jim's pride.

Getting trout from the Fish Commission hatchery truck to the stream or lake sometimes meant jumping on top and handing down buckets of fish for sportsmen and sportswomen to carry. Incredibly, I never, in a million trout or so, saw a bucket dropped during this process.

CHAPTER 3:
Guys and Gals in Green (Fish)

Fish and Boat Commission officers, both salaried and deputies, are a hardworking lot. All law enforcement consists of immense periods of waiting and watching, followed by a short period of interaction with a fisherman, boater or a person violating the laws that protect and pay for fish and insure boating safety. Close bonds are formed during the waiting time and many tall tales are told. Some will make you laugh and some will help you understand the job. One or two may even turn your stomach.

THE FAMOUS CLEVELAND SLED DOG ASSASSINATIONS
Anybody that ever attended the Cleveland Sport Show knew Big Joe Kopena. He was there for 20 years working the Pennsylvania Fish Commission booth. The second time I worked there, in the late 1980s, Joe had gotten very big and docile.

Fifteen years before, a bad batch of dog food had poisoned his team of sled dogs and the company had sent a vet to pull the award-winning dogs through. The vet stayed with Joe a week or two in his bachelor pad near Tionesta. A friendship was struck and, before long, Joe was doing dog food commercials dressed like Nanook of the North.

The commercials were all the rage, especially among wardens. Everyone picked on this bull of a man with a little china heart, especially us. The ads gave us another good-natured shot at Big Joe.

Two incidents developed off this scenario. The first was at the Autoport Motel in State College, at a law enforcement meeting. Ten or twelve of us were sitting around, telling stories. I was the junior and the instigator. Joe got up to go to the men's room and we quickly summoned the cute little barmaid, a college girl that said she was majoring in acting, to our table.

"You want to make ten quick bucks?" Jonesy asked her.

"Depends," she said with caution, looking at the old, leering duffers around the table.

"His name is Joe Kopena." George motioned to Joe, disappearing into the men's room. "He made a dog food commercial with his team of sled dogs. Just ask him if he's Joe and tell him you loved the commercial and the money is yours."

She turned away, carrying empty beer steins, as Joe returned.

In about 15 minutes she started. She would walk past and look at Joe and then let on she was trying to get a better angle, and be nonchalant if he caught her staring.

"I think she is sweet on me," Joe offered.

"Must remind her of her father," I quipped.

Soon she would go past again and give him "the look."

With exquisite timing, she approached the table. She stood behind George and looked at Joe.

"You're Joe Kopena! The guy in the dog food commercial with the huskies! I love that commercial and those dogs!"

"Well, young lady, since you are so nice and beautiful and all like that, I'll tell you what I'm a-gonna do," Joe said, rising from his chair. "I'm a-gonna go to my room and get you a picture of me and them lovely dogs and autograph it for you."

And away the bull of a man went.

"Here's your money, honey," George said, sliding the collection we had taken up to her.

"You were wonderful. You'll have a great acting career."

In came Joe, walking on air, like Jackie Gleason. He was waving the picture and doing his, "Hey, hey, hey, Joey Boy hasn't lost his old charm" routine.

He put his bifocals on and inscribed the picture and signed it and handed it to her. She took it, thanked him and walked to a customer at the other end of the bar.

The laughter from our table was a roar. Joe turned and realized for the first time it had all been a setup. His big face flushed, and you could see the rage about to boil over. I was in a corner with no place to go and knowing I was as good as dead. The rage slammed against his face in a flush of red and he turned and stomped out of the bar. Everyone breathed a sigh of relief.

Joe stayed in his room the rest of the week, trying to mend his fractured heart. The one his friends had broken for him. I felt bad. But not bad enough to keep me from orchestrating this next, similar, event.

Ten years had passed from the previous incident, and I found myself detailed to Cleveland with Joe Kopena to work the sport show. It was the last evening of our stay, a Saturday night, and things were winding down. It was all over. I took a stroll away from our booth, down past the tourist agencies from several southern states. I was looking for information on an upcoming vacation and figured the tourist booths with the pretty girls were as good a place as any to get it.

As I entered the aisle, they looked at each other across the corridor and raised repeating gum band guns and shot me all to hell. It was a good laugh and an inspiration.

One girl came from behind the booth and began picking up rubber bands. I said, "I have an idea."

"What?" she said, obviously bored with the show routine.

"That big guy in our booth, over my right shoulder, do you see him?

"In the green sweater?" she asked.

"That's him," I answered.

I stepped into her booth and told her I would watch it while she went up and "got" Joe. She sidled up to him with a pretty smile and loaded gum-band guns tucked into the folds of her plentiful "Southern Belle" outfit.

"Aren't you Joe Kopena?" she asked.

"Why, yes, ma'am, I am. The one and the only Joey 'Big Boy' Koo-pena," he said, batting his eyelashes flirtatiously.

I watched around the end of the booth.

"Are you the same Joe Kopena that did the dog food commercial years ago, with the sled dogs?"

"Yes ma'am, that's me," Joe said with a grin in his voice.

Drawing both rubber band guns with the speed of Wyatt Earp, she proceeded to empty them into his massive, sweatered chest saying, "I hated that commercial!" Then she turned and fled.

Joe knew who had gotten him, but it was too late, the show was over.

MOON-SHOT

There are few persons that made this job worthwhile as much as my fellow officers. Every day I spent with a fellow officer was an adventure or a chuckle. I can't help but recall some of the better chuckles.

Jonesy was a big old farm boy that grew up in Braddock. How he ever got to be a big old farm boy living so near Pittsburgh is beyond my comprehension, but when he arrived in Tidioute to spend his working years, he immediately became a big, lumbering, storytelling local.

As a rookie, I looked forward to working with Jonesy. When I got a Sunday assignment to go over and meet him and work for the day, I couldn't wait. I was on the phone with him in a few minutes to arrange things. He had me laughing in no time and we agreed that I would be at his headquarters, his house, at 8 a.m. As an afterthought he said, "Bring Lin along." My wife, Linda, was a deputy at the time, and we would be working boats somewhere, so it would be nice to have a third person.

Sunday morning arrived and Lin and I traveled to Tidioute. We rapped on the door and rapped on the door, but no answer. Finally, after some real pounding, the shower window opened and Jonesy hollered, "Go on in and have a seat." His wife and boys were at church, and Lin and I settled into his living room.

Now to appreciate this tale, you must understand that Jonesy's house was L-shaped. You entered at the short end of the "L" and, by taking ten more steps, could look down the hall toward the other rooms. Linda sat with her back toward the rest of the house, against the inside wall of the "L."

From my seat, I could see through the rest of the open spaces of the house. Lin and I sat drinking coffee we had helped ourselves to and looking at the Fish Law and regulation books, so we would be sharp when working with the veteran. I had just taken a mouthful of hot coffee, when the bathroom door swung open. Drying his back with a towel, and a towel only, Jonesy strode five or six steps toward me and began to give directions for hooking up boats, loading gear etc.

Before I could swallow my coffee and point to Lin, Jonesy passed the "L" corner and was smack in the middle of the living room. The astonishment smeared all over my face finally caused him to turn and look behind him. When he did, his eyes bugged out. He let out a hoot or gasp, jumped and tried to cover up with all the haste and modesty of a school girl accidentally entering the wrong locker room. But it was too late. Lin had been mooned. Jonesy scurried off to get in uniform and Lin and I sat laughing, unable to finish our coffee without spilling it.

CAR CLEANING

I am not a big fan of flatulence tales, but one such incident in my career merits mention. It was in the middle of an all-day session and we had three or four hours to kill before we were to go to the pistol range to qualify with our duty weapons. The organization that was forever reminding us that we were grossly overweight as a team had once again badly overfed us. We had a large salad bar, then a regular hot meal for lunch, with dessert and lots of coffee afterward.

Four of us couldn't sit around and waste this beautiful sunny day, so we piled into Officer Beaver's two-door Blazer and headed to Lake Wilhelm for a patrol, which was really an excuse to take a break and enjoy the midday hours. Officer Parise and I had climbed in the back seat and Beaver drove with Jonesy as co-pilot. Beaver and Jonesy were large men, both well over 6 feet tall and over the 250-pound mark. Frank and I are shorter, and Frank was thinner.

We drove along, talking about the spring patrols we had run and just enjoying a chance to be friends. I was enjoying a chew of tobacco in the backseat, holding in my hand a quart-size, clear-glass pollution sample bottle as a spittoon. Frank smoked a cigar and, at the time, Beaver and Jonesy both smoked cigarettes.

It was hot in the back seat since the windows did not wind down or even open. As we cruised, Jonesy sort of rose up and released a large amount of gas he had generated after eating a "hog's load" for lunch. Trapped in the hot back seat, with no air except Jonesy's, I began to puke. I have a reasonably weak stomach anyhow, and as I filled the jar with lunch, the more I saw in the jar the greater the urge was to keep filling it. Beaver swerved the car off the road into a parking lot and jammed the brakes, as the bottle began to overflow. Everyone was out of the car gagging; I continued to throw up.

After I had regained control and emptied my jar, I pulled a handkerchief from my pocket to wipe my eyes of tears and my face of lunch. Only then I did I realize that Beaver had pulled into a restaurant parking lot, directly in front of a picture window full of patrons. It took several days before I could chew tobacco again, and I never rode in the backseat of a two-door Blazer with Jonesy in the front again. I drove over that way just the other day and noticed the restaurant is closed now. I'm not sure how long ago it went out of business; I'm afraid to ask.

MADDIE'S LICENSE

Fishing license aren't terribly expensive when you figure the cost per day, but there are also those persons that don't fish that many days and figure it is better to take a chance. Wardens are always preaching to their deputies to be alert and observant. People will try to get away with things to beat the cost of a license. There was a year that the license paper went from a light yellow to a dark golden-yellow. Madeline Jones was a deputy and wife of the fish warden for Warren County and the mother of their three boys. With George racing around the house in his preseason frenzy and three boys in school to chauffeur and care for, Madeline realized that trout season was now upon them and the boys wanted to fish. George would be working and she would have to take them. So, while she didn't have time to go get a license before the season opened the next morning, she did have some Easter egg dye in the house. It worked perfectly and the license was dry by morning. The dyed license worked so well, she just used it all year. Husband George, the ever-observant officer, never noticed. Years later she showed it to him, after the statute of limitations had run out.

BOOKLET COVERS

I have cited only two persons in my career for not having their licenses with them. There were other circumstances that caused me to make those decisions. Generally, I gave them five days to prove they had a license before I did any paperwork.

Bartley, our officer in Pike County, did not have that reputation. He was hard-nosed law enforcement all the way.

A friend, Pat, had picked up my wife and me to go ice fishing in the early pre-dawn, and we had driven over an hour north on snow-covered roads when it dawned on me.

"We don't have our licenses with us, Pat. We'll have to get replacements."

"You know the fish guy, he'll let you send him proof you have a license," Pat responded.

"I could be king and it wouldn't make a difference with him," I said. "Bartley is by the book."

We stopped at a sporting goods dealer and I was reminded that I needed the original license number if I was going to get a replacement. I didn't have it. I certainly didn't want to ruin a day's fishing for my friend, so as we neared another bait shop, I told Pat to pull in.

I bought several license holders and picked up several regulation booklets. The cover was always the same color combination as the license, had the same fish picture and was about the same size. I had a plan. I knew that Bartley would pull in, use his spotting scope to look for licenses and only then, if he didn't see one, would he walk out on the ice to check.

I tore the covers from the booklets and put them in the holders and we pinned them on. We headed out onto the ice and sat so the licenses were readily visible.

It was a little over an hour later when I spotted the patrol car sitting on a rise and the scope working. I figured, "We'll see how this works."

Bartley sat for nearly an hour watching, like any good officer, and then drove away. We caught some nine and ten-inch perch that day, but I was nervous all afternoon.

HUCKSTERING TOMATOES

When you get to a new district, not every deputy you inherit has your work style. He or she is used to working with a different district officer, and it takes a while for them to adapt. Sometimes it is you that must adapt.

One deputy I inherited in the Luzerne County district I both admired and despised. He held to beliefs of favoritism that should be afforded him as a deputy. This did not sit with me. But he had a work ethic that was typical of the area at the time. Forty years ago, social handouts were not as readily available, nor were they expected. Especially in the little hardworking coal patch towns of the northeast. The area was settled along strict ethnic lines and had remained that way. There were no rich people in the patch towns, just proud people. They would do anything legal for a dollar, before they would ask for help.

It was a deputy from this background that showed up one day at Lily Lake, with the back of his old station wagon full of flats of vegetable plants.

"What's that Al?" I asked.

"Peppers and tomatoes," he responded.

"What are you going to do with them?" I continued.

"Sell them," he said.

"When?"

"Before I go home."

"I thought you were going to patrol," I said.

"I am," he responded. "I figured I would follow you with my car and sell the tomatoes when we stop."

"You can't huckster veggie plants in uniform," I told him.

He was heartbroken, but got a few hours' pay for his day with me on the boat. Then I left him to huckster his plants as I moved to another location.

COZY'S BLACKBERRIES

Some officers are fixtures in an organization such as this. Others become institutions. Officer Shearer was a legend. "Old Cozy," as his wife and the older officers referred to him, was a naturalist first and a fish warden second. He was happier when showing a youngster or a young officer the ways of the woods than at any other time. Since I was a young officer that was happier when learning the ways of the woods than at any other time, I tried to ride with Old Cozy every chance I got. I learned about mushrooms, wild asparagus, wild plums, watercress, marsh marigold and the list went on and on.

Many were the times those first two summers when I worked as an "extra" out of the regional office that Old Cozy's light-green state car would stop at the office. He would make an excuse to the boss why he needed my assistance. Then on a back road, we would slide to a stop and he would get out and motion me to follow. Down through the woods we would go to one of his secret spots. He always had a plastic bag hanging out of the back pocket of his baggy Lee work greens.

In short order we would have a bag of wild goodness that we would secret in a cool spring or keep in the car, depending on the weather. Old Cozy would talk about our find all day, explain how to prepare it and revel over it like a kid who found a fresh dollar bill would talk about how he was going to spend it. Mr. Shearer, as I respectfully always called him, had an enthusiasm for wild foods only equaled by his enthusiasm for identifying other wild things, critters, flowers, birds and all. A day with him was an outdoor education delight.

So that early August morning when we were cruising a dusty back road, the car's sliding to a halt didn't surprise me. I knew we were in for an adventure. Old Cozy bailed out of his side of the car and around the hood and motioned me to stay put. I thought, "Oh well, he must have been caught short."

I sat patiently awaiting his return from the woods. After some 15 or 20 minutes, he came lumbering back up through the roadside bushes like a big, old satisfied bear. I looked at him quizzically. He just grinned. Then I noticed the blackberry stains all around his mouth. Before I could ask any questions he began, "Nothing much better than blackberries with the morning dew still on them. I checked them a couple of days ago and they were just about ripe. I knew there weren't enough to share."

I have never disliked a man that was honest. Old Cozy taught me much about the woods that I have enjoyed for nearly 50 years now. I have a few patches of berries I don't share, either. Seldom a day goes by that I pick a mushroom or enjoy a wildflower that I don't think of this fine man.

STICKY MIKE

Mr. Shearer, for all his wonderful traits, had one that was somewhat hard to get use to. He had a friendly, spirited way of talking and telling tales that I can only describe as foundry mouth. Words that are used in coal mines and foundries and heavy construction projects were not meant for the sensitive ears of the general public. When the general public is a couple of secretaries and anyone with a receiver turned onto the police channel, it becomes embarrassing for the officer.

I was that officer. Mr. Shearer had retired and I had spent nearly nine years in the Luzerne County district, when to my surprise Venango County became open. I would get a chance to bid on it and return. As luck would have it, I was awarded this fine district.

Learning trout streams and dirt roads is a lot easier when you have a good coach, and I knew where there was one, Mr. Shearer. I called him and for five or six years he was my copilot. I enjoyed his company and his stories and, having somewhat callused ears, even got to appreciate that while the language used may have been foul to some, it was only meant to be colorful and certainly never meant to be offensive.

One afternoon as we stocked fish in the upper reaches of the county, I received a desperate radio call from my deputy to wait for him, he wanted to talk. I hate to slow down fish trucks, but I did, thinking that the deputy had run into a tough case. When he jumped from his truck and walked around to my side of the car, he was smiling from ear to ear. He motioned me to step from the car so no one would hear.

He then informed me that my radio microphone must be stuck in the on position and I was broadcasting Mr. Shearer's war stories loud and clear to half of the free world. I certainly hoped that I was out of range of the region office. I assumed I was, since they had not tried to call me to turn off the show. After dropping off Mr. Shearer at his house, I had to deliver reports to the office. Upon arriving, I was met by two smirks from the office girls.

"Mr. Shearer certainly has some stories," one said.

That certainly answered my question as to how far my radio would reach. Yet the very next day, at half the distance when I needed something, I was unable to contact them. However, to the end of my career, I was constantly checking the "broadcast" button on the mike to make sure it wasn't stuck.

FISH WARDEN BADGE

Upon returning to Venango County after a nine-year sentence away from the area, I found myself with a list of 17 trout streams, nearly a hundred thousand trout to dump and only a map to work with. I looked for help and found it in a retired fish warden, Clarence Shearer. Mr. Shearer lived less than a half mile away from me. I remember thinking when I found a house to buy, "If the area was good enough for Mr. Shearer, it's good enough for me."

Mr. Shearer readily responded to my plea for help, and the next six or seven years became the finest stocking seasons of my career. I would pick Mr. Shearer up. He would be wearing leftover Lee uniform clothing and his issue Refrigiwear coat, which was probably too worn out for reissue when he retired in 1976. His old Fish Commission ball cap had a terrible time staying straight on his large, bald head.

We would ride the back roads, always being chased by a stocking truck that only seemed to catch us at bridges. Shearer would guffaw with the stocking help and we laughed. We turned a job that many of my coworkers look on as drudgery into a raucous good time. Often were the days I would find myself sitting at a late dinner with my wife, telling more Shearer stories. Stories about the Fish Commission that was. One that I was now privileged to enjoy through the stories of a master storyteller. I tried hard to repeat them as he had told them, but I knew they would be lost with his passing.

It was a late spring day toward the end of May in the last year of Mr. Shearer's bodily existence. He would pass away in a few months.

I had just dropped Mr. Shearer at his house after our last stocking of the year. I got home and was doing a little paperwork before going fishing, when the phone rang.

"It's Mr. Shearer," my wife called up to my office in the loft of our log home. I ran down the steps and took the phone.

"This is Shearer." I don't think he knew his own first name. "You ought to stop back down here, boy. I found something you ought to have."

The phone clicked, and then buzzed. Usually a call from him meant somebody had littered under his kitchen window overlooking Sugar Creek or he had a bunch of new mushrooms for me to try or something had fallen from the car onto his driveway when I dropped him off. I jumped in the car and was in his driveway in a minute.

The backdoor came open and his Dalmatian came charging out to greet me. Shearer cursed the dog and shouted at it to behave, the same act they did every time I pulled in the driveway. Finally, when the dog was calmed down and the garage cats had found their place at his feet, he leaned against the old maple tree alongside the house. I stepped from the car and he reached into his pocket. Among a handful of change was an old-time fish warden badge. He sorted it out with his other hand and gave it to me.

"Thought you ought to have this," he said. "You are the last of the good, ol' fish wardens."

I choke up now as I write this. I certainly did then. I couldn't talk, so I just shook his hand and smiled. It was the proudest moment of my career.

My wife, Linda, was one of the first female Fish Commission deputies. She and a few other ladies back then proved to the conservation agencies that women were not only equally good at all aspects of the job, but often better than the men. Many violators would just stand and shake their heads as the ladies wrote them a ticket.

CHAPTER 4:
Checkmate

Routine checks turn up the most unlikely things. You see some fine artwork and some not so fine artwork. You encounter old friends, friends of friends, friends of enemies and meet some real nice people. Well, most of them.

BOMBS BURSTING IN AIR

Where were you on July 4, 1976, at noon? There was a lot of ringing of bells, whistles and fireworks across the country. It was splendid, and I truly wish I could have been able to enjoy our nation's bicentennial celebration. But, as usual on this summer holiday, I was working.

I had launched the patrol boat and had been making my way along the shore of Lake Nuangola, when I chanced to encounter a rubber raft just before noon. As was normally the case in those days, persons believed that rubber rafts were just toys with oars, and they couldn't possibly get hurt in them.

I escorted this one to shore and was putting up with a verbal barrage from the parents of a pair of 20-year-olds when the big event came. I paused momentarily to observe the festivities and then finished the work at hand. I felt like a war correspondent on the front. I believe, however, that as I left I wished them all a happy holiday.

OLD TIMER CHECK

What every young warden strived for when I first hit the field was to be recognized by his peers as a warden that would walk far and work in the dark alone. It was like being accepted into the fold when you were compared to one of the tough old wardens of the past.

The first year I came on, while working with our officer in Warren County, I met a Game Protector by the name of Dave Titus. Dave was thin and wiry and walked long and hard. He was a graduate of the very first Game Commission class. He was respected throughout the woods of Warren County.

It was an evening in mid May when Linda and I decided to take a walk from the campground at Chapman Dam and try to roost a turkey for the next morning's hunt. With no worry of getting lost, since we were walking along a Game Lands access road, we continued on until almost dark.

We were nearly three miles from the campground gate when I noticed a motion in the bushes near the creek. I stopped Linda with an arm extended in front of her. We stood and watched in the fading light.

Out of the brush came a thin, slender man. I showed my credentials and asked to check his fishing license and his creel for short brook trout. He carefully kneeled and laid the contents of the old wicker basket on the road in front of me. After he arranged the moss, he placed two or three just-legal brook trout on it. I measured them and told him he could put them away.

As we stood and I was making small talk about hunting gobblers and fishing, he spoke. "You did a good job young man. My name is Dave Titus, retired Game Protector. I have fished up here for nearly 40 years and this is the first time I've been checked. Keep up the good work." The three of us walked out to the gate together talking about his career back in the early days.

THE BULLHORN

If you count yourself among my friends, it is likely you should expect to be the object of humorous verbal abuse. I seldom play practical jokes, because to be really good at it takes planning, and I am more the spur-of-the-moment type of jokester. When an opportunity for a quickly designed and deployed practical joke arises, I try not to muff it.

You can imagine my delight when early one evening I spotted my 6-foot-tall, 350-pound friend mesmerized by a rise of trout, totally focused. I hid the Matador and sneaked across the bridge into Lake of the Four Seasons, a development on the banks of Nescopeck Creek, so I would go undetected.

As he cast relentlessly to the many rising browns and they continued to snub his offerings, I eased ever closer. Soon I was but a mere six or eight feet behind him, in a small clump of willow brush. I deemed the time proper to check his license, since friends are not exempt from licensing.

"How they hitting?" I blurted through the bullhorn set at its loudest and then hit the siren button. It was a sight to behold. His 350 pounds of wader-clad self came straight up out of the water. He ran in place for two or three strides and then was only able to catch his balance by jamming his new fly rod into the mud. He picked up his hat, shook the water off it and began to curse.

Tears ran down my cheeks as I easily outran him to my patrol car. He was hindered enough by the waders that I was able to make a clean getaway. He suffers from an irregular heartbeat as I write this. Doctors blame it on cigarettes, overweight and genetics. He blames it on a bullhorn.

AIN'T THAT RIGHT, NOLFIE

The hours and days before trout season are always a treat. One minute you are sitting, having a leisurely breakfast with your wife, and the next you have saddled the pony and are ready to ride, all because of a phone call. This bright, sunny April morning was no different.

The call came from my trusted friend, Bob Nolf, the Game Protector. He had received a call from a neighboring Game Commission officer that had seen some guys with fishing equipment and tents entering the woods near Wapwallopen. Since they were heading up along a stocked trout stream, and it was still a full week before the season opened, the officer had called Bob. He had been in a hurry and hadn't done any checking; they should still be there.

"How many?" Bob had asked him.

"A whole gang," had been the reply.

Bob contacted me and we did a cruise-by to assess the situation. It was at a small, steep, heavily wooded hollow with a rather large waterfalls on the creek. There were eight or ten cars parked along the road. We figured they would be camped near the falls.

Since the woods had very little leaf growth yet, we were able to get to a vantage point and size up what was going on. We watched for an hour or two and decided there were about a dozen young men in their late teens and early 20s. They had a few axes stuck in a woodpile and fishing rods everywhere, but none were yet in use. As we watched, though, a large bag of garbage from the previous night was thrown into an old foundation about a hundred yards from the camp. The two guys that carried it went back to camp. We watched a while longer and decided they weren't going to fish in the amount of time we had left to invest, so we planned our approach.

It was a fish case, so I would be the attack man. Bob would be backup. Twelve to two are not necessarily favorable odds in the best of conditions. In a deep ravine, with no radio contact, the odds were even less than that. It was time to maintain one's superior bearing and out-maneuver the violators.

I put a chew in and strolled alone into the camp, spit next to the fire and made small talk.

"What's up, fellows?" I queried.

"Nothing," come the reply from the five or six awake around the fire.

"An awful lot of fishing gear without a season for nothing," I replied, then continued, pointing at the two litterbugs, "I'll need to see some ID from you two guys."

"Why us, man?" came the reply from the thin, tall kid with a bandana holding back his long brown hair. His homemade tattoos told me he wasn't an honor-roll student. He had misspelled Mom. I decided that, of the bunch, he would be the barometer of the trouble level.

Once I had the two IDs in my possession and pocketed them, I explained the littering violation and the field acknowledgement of guilt. The "chosen two" didn't like it, since it was everybody's beer cans, but they would be heroes and take the rap if their buddies would pitch in some money. All was going smoothly and the preferred ending was coming into sight, and then I had to push my luck.

"Guys, while I'm here I'm going to check your coolers and tents for fish, so I'll need you to bring everything outside the tents and wake up your buddies."

So far nobody had noticed the six-to-one advantage around the fire they had. I should have just taken the "chosen two" to the car and written the paperwork, but I just had to check for early fish. And since the car was about a half mile away, I figured I might as well do it now, while I was here.

As they unraveled sleeping bags, wine bottles, food, fishing gear and their friends, it dawned on the skinny fellow that with each new person that crawled out of a sleeping bag, the more advantage they had.

"I got an idea," he offered, as I looked through the last cooler. "Why don't we just kick your ass. You got a lot of nerve coming in here to our camp all alone and telling us what to do."

"Alone? Why, whatever gave you the idea I was alone?" I answered.

"You're bluffing," he quickly shot back.

"I'm not alone. Am I, Nolfie?" I called out.

Fifty yards away, from behind a tree, Nolfie stepped into view, .30-caliber carbine with a banana clip reflecting the morning light, mirror sunglasses and all. He stood for a few seconds and then disappeared again behind the tree. The two kids climbed up the hill to the car and paid their fines, while their buddies tore down the camp ... under supervision.

HOMEMADE LIBERTY BELL LICENSE

It was ice fishing season, early in 1976. I was working the ice on Lake Pleasant with Jim Carter, the warden, not the president. Everything was going well, and when I checked a young fellow I didn't look closely at his license. I had seen the Liberty Bell, that year's license's featured artwork, which I trained myself to look for, so I just made small talk with him about fishing. As I walked over and got back with Carter, something in my head kept saying I had missed something.

I told Carter to wait a minute, and I went back to the kid I had just checked. When I looked at his license more closely, I realized what had caught my eye. It was a homemade license. He was very proud of the attempt, knowing he had nearly foiled justice. I complimented his artwork as I wrote his ticket and impounded the license.

JOHN BARLEY CORN'S LICENSE

The tailwater of Francis E. Walter Dam was always one of my favorite places to fish and to work. It was just down over the hill far enough that people thought they could get away with anything. I had the two essentials to work the area. A spotting scope that allowed me to watch what was going on like I was right there with them and a key to the gate, so I didn't have to walk up and down the hill all the time.

It was a rainy Sunday afternoon in midsummer when I got to watching three fellows fishing and drinking beer from quart bottles. Eventually they broke a bottle against the rocks. Since I couldn't see a fishing license on any of them, I decided to wait them out at the top. Who knows what else they might do?

There was only one car in the lot and it was parked tight against the concrete overflow of the dam. I pulled right up against it and went for a walk, as I awaited their arrival. Eventually they made their way up over the dam and down the ramp to their car. I began checking licenses and explaining violations. The license I couldn't readily see was produced, but it didn't look right. I took it in my hand and out of the faded license holder and discovered it was made out to a "John B. Corn."

I asked the person with the license who John B. Corn was. He said it was him. I asked for identification and he said he had none. I had also noticed the license was homemade with colored pencils, but hadn't played that ace yet. I went to the radio and radioed in the vehicle license plate to get a real name, since he said it was his car. It came back as stolen out of Wilkes-Barre. I stepped out of the car, staying behind my door and ordered the three guys to go over and stand away from their car and keep their hands where I could see them.

I then notified the dispatcher that I had this stolen car and its operators and if the Pennsylvania State Police would like to handle the case, I could use the backup. In minutes the sirens were blaring as troopers arrived from both sides of the dam. When the first officer stepped out of his car, I recognized him and he recognized the culprits. He called them by name and they came over to him. He asked me what I had in the way of violations. I told him.

Then I spoke to the defendant and asked him, "Who is John B. Corn?"

"A friend of mine. He loaned me the license," he responded.

"You borrowed a homemade license?" I said.

"Yeah, he couldn't afford one either," he returned.

All along I had thought John B. Corn was actually John Barley Corn. It turned out, I guess, that it was a real name. I didn't pursue it any further because I didn't think the charge of loaning a license would stick if the license was homemade.

The state trooper asked me what the defendant owed and I told him. He told them to start digging. If they didn't have it, they were going for a ride. The littering and licensing fines were paid on Field Receipts. He then issued them a citation on the stolen license plate charge. The car's plate had been reported stolen, by them, off another of their own cars!

COUNTERFEIT LICENSES

"Hi. This is Neil, Chief of West Hazleton," the caller said. "Can you come up to the station? We have a bunch of counterfeit fishing licenses."

"Be right up," I answered.

I had previously in my career uncovered two homemaders, but "a bunch of counterfeit licenses" sounded like I was going to be in on a good one.

When I arrived, Chief Neil explained that they had been called by a manager of a manufacturing plant in the local industrial park. Seems the plant had an agreement with the union to routinely check lockers for drugs, etc. In doing so they had uncovered nearly 60 counterfeit fishing licenses. They didn't know what to do, so they called the local police.

After consulting Neil, it was agreed that I would talk to the state police, since this was counterfeiting of a state document. Considering the price of a license, it was like forging seven dollar bills at the time.

The state police sent over two detectives, Starsky and Hutch. I don't remember their correct names, but can see them to this day. Starsky was a tall, Clint Eastwood type and Hutch was a short, refined, trench coat type detective. We reviewed what I had and headed over to the plant.

After talking to the manager that found the licenses, we discovered that the plant manufactured boxes with printed color pictures on them for packaging. The managers figured the machine that had been used had the capability of making up to 4,000 licenses an hour. They also gave us a list of persons known to associate with the young woman whose locker the forgeries were in.

Starsky and Hutch went over the list with the manager and decided that there were some tough characters on that list. The girl would be the weak link. She would be interviewed first.

She was invited to the state police barracks and ushered into a large room usually used for briefings. It was quite friendly, as rooms go. She was given a seat and you could just see her resolve to not tell and get her new friends in trouble. She had just started working at the plant about six months ago, after graduating high school. Both Starsky and Hutch questioned her nicely about her age and high school and a few other things and got her to relax, as I sat quietly in the corner.

Then Starsky, who had been facing the wall, turned briskly toward her with a menacing look and took several quick strides closer, stopping just short of running into her. She backed away as far as she could in the chair. She couldn't run. I jumped at his maneuver, but I was behind her and she didn't see me.

"The counterfeit licenses were in your possession. Counterfeiters go to jail in Pennsylvania. Do you know what happens to pretty young girls like you in jail?" he growled. "You're trying to cover for your foreman, Stan, aren't you? You're sleeping with Stan."

It was over. I would have confessed. She just bawled and sobbed. I felt bad for her. Her willpower had crumbled under the assault by a superior power. Her friends were all going to jail with her. She had given them up to the law.

The way it shook out was that about ten of them had decided to go up to Joe's Camp on Pine Creek or one of those trout streams in the north-central part of the state. There were eight guys and two girls. The other girl was hardened, we found out in the interview.

I believe this trip was planned to harden the weak link, as much as to fish. They were going to buy a few fishing licenses and pass them around at the camp when someone wanted to fish, but then decided to put their skills and the company's equipment to work.

Since they could reproduce from a photograph and mix the inks, they were able to do perfect licenses and run them twice to get both sides. They had done the deed in less than an hour. Someone even realized that if you made them all with the same serial number, they would stand out. So they blanked out the number and ran the fake licenses through another machine designed for serial numbers.

When all was done, there were only two differences in the counterfeits and the real thing. The real thing has perforated sides for tearing out of the book by the issuing agent. The forgeries were razor-stamped cut. And the numerals were different. The real thing had round-top threes and the counterfeits had flat-top threes. I looked all year to find any on fishermen, but found none. I believe the whole stash was intercepted, as the young girl had told us.

Her testimony was good in court, putting the guy who came up with the idea behind bars for a short stay and getting probation for everyone else, herself, included.

FOOT RACE WITH A SOLDIER

Foot races are generally fun. I was always a pretty good runner, despite the fat roll that I had cultured for over 30 years.

I was checking a lone fisherman at the tailwaters of the F. E. Walter Reservoir, having walked down, mainly for the exercise. When I got there, the guy didn't have a license, but thought he should get a break since he was a Marine Corps veteran. I told him that I also was a veteran, but it didn't exempt me from the law.

"Marines are special," came his reply.

"I was in the Coast Guard. Now, they were special," I said.

"A Marine will kick a Coastie's butt every time," he countered.

Before I could get the situation under control, it was starting to look like a scene I had seen in a bar in Rockaway, New Jersey, one night during my military career. I decided it was time to use my strong suit, running.

"I'll tell you what I'll do," I offered. "If you think you Marines are tougher than us Coasties, I'll race you to the top of the dam, right up over the rip-rap. If you win, there is no fine. If I win, when you get to the top you shut up and pay the fine. Deal?"

"Deal!" he said and took off for the top.

He had an early lead, but the sun was wearing him down fast. I had set a pace I knew I could maintain. Soon I passed him and was standing on top, enjoying the view, when he finally labored up. As I stood at the car hood writing the ticket, he stood with his wallet out. At least he was good to his word. Then, after catching his breath, he spoke.

"That wasn't fair. I had chest waders on."

"The Coast Guard entrance test is harder to pass than the Marine one," I replied.

After I collected the fine I said, "Don't forget your rod and tackle box."

"I left it down below," he remembered.

"Yeah, I know," I said as I got into the Matador and drove off into the sunset.

CHEERLEADER JACKET

The pretty young girl had been fishing with her friends at the mouth of Stewart Run. I asked her name and age.

"I'm Joanne and I'm only 15," she said.

"Where do you go to school?" I followed.

"Oil City," she replied.

"I think your name is Carly, you go to Rocky Grove High School and you graduate this year, which makes you at least 17," I offered.

"How did you know?" she asked.

"You have your cheerleader jacket on," I replied.

LEMON GATE GIRLS

The Nescopeck Creek or "Nesky" was a wonderful remnant of the past. It had only survived because the Game Commission had purchased the property the stream ran through for a State Game Lands years before the development push was on in Luzerne County. The many tributaries that flowed down from the mountainous hillsides kept the "Nesky" clean and cold. What little adverse influences that existed were minimal.

I stocked trout in several places in the Game Lands, but the easiest to stock and easiest for fishermen to access was the Lemon Gate. It was an access road that lead back through the woods for about a half a mile and then crossed the creek at a ford. Downstream from the ford was a nice pocket. Any trout you dumped at the ford quickly moved downstream to this first good hole.

The hole had an overhanging oak whose root system provided a shaded pocket. Within a half hour of stocking, the hole would be full of trout without ever dumping a bucket there. Most fishermen couldn't figure out that the trout had moved. They just thought they disappeared, I guess. They would watch us dump several hundred trout at the ford, and then begin fishing. Two hours later they would still be standing there and complain that we hadn't stocked enough trout.

It was a spring day in the middle of my tour of duty in Luzerne County. At the time Linda and I had two dyed-in-the-wool fishing buddies. Mae and Chris were both juniors in high school, and after several fishing trips with us the girls had become fanatics. Every day when they got off the school bus, they would be knocking on our door to see if one of us could take them fishing. I decided on a plan.

I made arrangements for Linda to take the girls to the hole just below the ford at the Lemon Gate. I would be stocking that day. When the truck arrived I did the area in the normal sequence and was happy to see that the girls had arrived before I got to the ford. I stocked and talked to them, but dumped no buckets in the hole, only at the ford, and moved on. I had previously told them to be patient.

When I returned an hour or so later to check on their fishing progress, I was dismayed to find the hole surrounded by old guys. The girls had stood their ground and were catching a few fish. The old guys stood glaring at the stream, not understanding why their heavy lines weren't catching fish in the clear water and the girls occasionally were.

While the girls didn't seem to mind the encroachment of the old guys, I did. I figured the girls deserved a peaceful evening by themselves, without being surrounded by a bunch of tobacco-chewing miners. After all, Chris and Mae studied hard all week and Linda kept busy writing. So I devised a plan.

I casually leaned up against a tree, smiled and winked at Linda and held still. I would stand there a few minutes and stare at one of the three or four old guys, and they would get nervous and reel in and walk up the creek. I would walk up, check them, and then go back and silently lean against the overhanging tree again. Soon another would leave and I would repeat the procedure. In a half hour the girls had the place to themselves and eventually all limited out, a first for the two young ladies.

I never could figure out why a staring warden makes people nervous when they haven't done anything, but I know it works every time.

That night when I arrived home, fish-cleaning lessons were going on in the kitchen sink. I thought the girls would be all bubbly about the great fishing. They were happy, but the conversation was all giggles about something else.

"Did you see those guys slink away when you showed up?" Mae asked. Then they giggled.

"Yeah," I said. "That was pretty funny."

"When we got there we told them to be careful, the warden was looking for us and they didn't want to be seen with us. When you showed up it worked perfect."

It wasn't a fair thing to do. But then neither was crowding out two young girls just learning to fish.

HELICOPTER CHECK, LEHIGH

The Lehigh River above Francis E. Walter Reservoir is a great backcountry stream that, because of the terrain and vegetation, is for the most part inaccessible. I have always liked inaccessible. I made special efforts to get trout into this stretch of river by whatever means it took. They were floated in rubber rafts and dropped from helicopters.

To drive in and fish was nearly impossible, so most of the access was by boat. Fishermen would take their boats up to the mouth of the river, and then walk a mile or so upstream along the shoreline and fish. They were treated to an experience that was as remote and beautiful as many of the famous Canadian rivers.

I was faced with a bit of a dilemma, though. I really should patrol the area if I was going to be stocking it, so I had to devise a plan. I could boat up and walk the shoreline, but that meant I needed waders to get back and forth across the river and I would have to leave the boat unattended. I didn't like that, since it only takes one person to set a patrol boat to floating when no one is near it. That would have meant a lot of rock climbing and laurel bush fighting to get back to the car.

It was then that I remembered an old adage that I once heard from one of the old-timers in this profession. "You don't have to check them all. You just have to make them all think they are being checked."

On a sunny Saturday morning, I paid a visit to the Pennsylvania State Police chopper pad and talked to the fellows on duty. After a coffee, they warmed up the bird and I got a front-row seat. We were over the remote stocked area in minutes and, as expected, there were quite a few fishermen since I had stocked mid-week.

The helicopter pilot got down to within a hundred or so feet and handed me the mike for the public address system. Flipping a switch, he gave me the nod.

"State Officer," boomed from the bird as it hovered. "Please hold up your license."

The first guy seemed startled, but complied by waving his hat and pointing to it. Every fisherman within earshot got into the act and turned so we could readily see their licenses. Soon we had checked the 20 or so fishermen on a four-mile stretch of river and were on our way back.

I thanked the pilot for the interagency cooperation and jumped in my car and headed for the launch ramp at Walter Reservoir, where all the fishermen on the Lehigh during the air check would return. I couldn't wait to hear what they had to say.

RIVER CHECK

Sally was a Fish Commission deputy when she and her husband moved to Luzerne County from Montgomery County. Having a female deputy caused a few problems back in those days. I told the guys they didn't have to work with her if their wife didn't want them to. All they had to do was bring me a written excuse from their wife. Things got back to normal in a hurry,

Sally was an excellent person and a pretty good deputy, even though she had worked several years in a high-conflict district. Now, in Luzerne County, she began to adapt to working "Steiner style." As I had been warned, she soon became the most reliable law enforcement soldier in the force. Sally would go to all ends to solve a case and bring a culprit to justice. She wasn't afraid to work.

Since her schedule required her to be home most of the day, I worked often with her after darkness set in. It was rainy and dreary at the end of one patrol and we were heading in. Sally had been talking about her chances of ever getting hired as a full-time conservation officer. I had been encouraging her to try. We pulled into a private boat ramp at Wapwallopen, on the Susquehanna River.

"Nothing here," I said, although I could plainly see a lantern ahead of me.

"Out there is a lantern, boss," Sal responded.

I knew I had her hooked. The lantern was on the downstream tip of an island in the Susquehanna River, 50 yards out. I knew the river in that area. It wasn't much over your waist; I had fished it in the winter in waders. Now it was May and the water temperature was up in the low 60s.

"Sure would like to know what they're doing," I offered.

"Me, too," she replied.

"One of us ought to wade out," I said.

"Aw, boss," she said, knowing where I was leading.

"We'll be getting you home first. You'll be dry by the time I get home," I assured her.

"Aw, boss."

"We don't have to check them. But a case like that sure would look good if you could talk about it at an interview, if you get into the hiring procedure."

"Aw, boss."

She grabbed her light and waded in.

A half hour later she came back, dripping. She stood outside the Matador for a few minutes, so the seat wouldn't be quite so soggy for the deputy that was riding with me tomorrow, and then got in.

"That was Tommy and his dad from up the river. They're regulars here," she said.

"I know. I talked to them on the way over to your house to pick you up, before they waded out."

"Aw, boss!"

ADDENDUM: Officer Sally Corl retired as Supervisor in the Northeast Region after a 25-year career with the Fish and Boat Commission.

PAUL NEWMAN

Sally's husband had died. He had never recovered from injuries suffered in Viet Nam, and she was alone in the big house on the mountain. She worked as a deputy a lot that summer to keep her perspective and was doing fine as we headed into Labor Day. She was still a young woman, which I often forgot when patrolling with her. To me she was just another deputy, and a darn good one.

We were working Hickory Run, where the creek comes down through the state park, when she came toward me with a young man in tow.

"Boss, we got to talk."

"Yeah, go ahead."

"He sure is pretty," she said.

Now I will admit that I noticed a resemblance to a young Paul Newman. He had piercing blue eyes. But since I had always been more attracted to pretty girls, I hadn't paid much attention.

"What did he do?" I quizzed.

"Fishing without a license," she responded.

"Would you rather I wrote the ticket?" I offered.

"He's broke. I thought maybe I could pay the fine for him," she said, kidding.

"He has a nice hunting knife strapped on him," I replied.

"I'd sooner hold him in custody on the mountain until he can pay," she returned.

"We'll just take the knife."

When we explained that we were going to take the knife, he produced the money and paid and was sent on his way. I guessed, however, that I had gotten a dose of role-reversal boy talk, just to see how it must have been for her working with all guys all the time. I'm sure I deserved it.

ROLLING OUT OF A BOAT

If you have never ridden in a jet boat, you have missed a rare experience. Jet drive units are made to lift the boat while propelling it forward. Thankfully, the act of lifting causes some energy to be lost, and you don't travel as fast as the horsepower would indicate. Thinking like a normal cop, you would reason the faster you go, the more bad guys you can catch. Thinking like a jet boat "river cop," the faster you go, the farther you fly when you finally do hit something.

Now the real thrill in these jet drive outboards is that the shallower you run the boat, the faster you must go to keep from hitting anything. The faster you go, the greater the lift. The first jet I had took about three inches of water to keep from hitting. The second one took about half that.

Judging the difference between an inch of water and an inch and a half at approximately 30 miles an hour is an art form and, for the most part, after more than a decade of river work I was a master. In fact, it is believed by some of those who rode with me that I used Zen to make the boat go where I wanted it to go.

Deputy Greg was one of the few habitual riders that really seemed to be relaxed when I was tooling along in the jet over gravel bars in the upper river. While some deputies sat clutching the gunwales, Greg just seemed to sit back and enjoy the beautiful scenery that appeared around each bend of the wild and scenic river.

One hot, sunny summer afternoon, we noted a group of fishermen on a little island below Kennerdell. Having run that section of river often, I knew it was shallow going into the island. I usually just waved at anyone sitting there or behind the island toward the east shore. It was possible to get there, but having to stop in water that shallow would cause us to bottom out. We then had to get in the river to float the boat. We had to start it and begin to rev it in forward gear while hanging on. When it began to lift we rolled in and got it under control. This left our river boots wet for the day.

For some reason, on this particular afternoon my warden's intuition told me this was a good bunch to check, and I throttled right into the island. My side of the boat had a small console and windshield, but the deputy seat had nothing but deck the whole way to the bow.

As I barreled toward the island and prepared to shut the boat down at the last second, I hit bottom and the boat stopped right now. I was thrown against the console, but received no injuries. When I noticed Greg, he was rolling up the deck toward the bow like a cannonball. He came to a halt teetering over the bow, none the worse for wear, but certainly not in a position that a law enforcement professional likes to find himself.

"I got the boat," I hollered. "Go on in and check them."

Greg stepped off the bow toward the island and immediately found himself immersed in water nearly to his armpits. After checking the fishermen for violations and finding none, we refloated the boat, did a wet entry, and headed down the river. I am sure there are four fishermen that still talk about the day Steiner catapulted his deputy right into chest-deep water, gun belt and all, just to check them.

LILY LAKE CANOE

Why trout fishing season starts at 8 a.m. and the rest of the seasons start at midnight has always been a mystery to me. Think of the fun we could have with tangles, hooks in fingers and such if you could start trout fishing at midnight. I think we are missing something.

It was drizzling lightly when I picked up Sally at her house to ride patrol the night bass season opened. I had thrown the canoe on top of the Matador. She looked at it questioningly and climbed into the car.

"What's up?" she quizzed.

"Thought we would do a little moonlight canoeing," I offered.

"I love it," she answered.

We slipped the car into the parking lot at Lily Lake and eased the canoe off the top unnoticed. It was still an hour and a half until starting time, and there were already forty boats on the lake.

We left the shore quietly and headed up to the east, paddling ever so slowly and quietly. We never spoke. As we approached a boat, Sally, in the bow, would lay down her paddle and I would maneuver us alongside until she could grab hold of the fishermen's boat.

"Good evening fellows," she would whisper. "How're they hitting?"

We would check safety equipment and then licenses and containers that could hold an early bass. None were found and soon we had checked most of the boats, having made believers out of nearly all of them. Something about not seeing a warden until he or she is practically in the boat with you keeps guys honest for years to come.

About five minutes after midnight we checked a boat with a 4-pound bass, stone dead, in a bag under some line. We knew we had been beat, but also knew our activities would keep many law abiding for a long time.

NEVER ANY PATROL

I was learning to fly fish so was naturally interested in the speaker as he told about the many hatches on Little Sandy Creek. His presentation was excellent and his photography better, but then there was that one remark. During the presentation he felt it necessary to state, "The problem with the fishing on Little Sandy is that there is no law enforcement. You never see a warden there."

I sat quietly, biding my time. Several of the club members had snickered at the comment. When the presentation was over and the crowd had dissipated, I approached the speaker and introduced myself.

"Nice talk. Your slides are excellent. I'm Bob Steiner, the Waterways Conservation Officer responsible for patrol on Little Sandy. I was disappointed that you feel there is not enough patrol there. I certainly make it a point to check there as often as I can."

"I fish there a lot and have never seen you or I would have recognized you in the crowd," he said, indicating that he was doubtful I patrolled there much.

"I patrol often without checking everybody. I just stand back and watch and if all appears on the up-and-up, I move on," I further offered.

"I would have seen you," he responded.

"Well, you have a very nice program there," I complimented once again as I departed.

In the back of my head I had decided to prove a point. I left as he left and noted his vehicle make and color.

It was around mid July, when the only thing that hatches is tiny bugs, that I noticed his car. I grabbed my binoculars and set out to find the doubter and prove a point. I soon located him on the Trestle Pool, just off the west bank, fishing to a pod of rising fish along the east edge in a little eddy. I knew he was engrossed in his fishing since he was casting "far and fine," as they say. With flies size 20 and smaller, you must watch closely as you fish or you will miss the action.

Cautiously I slipped to the bank's edge, which had a large cherry tree on it, leaning slightly over the water. I leaned against it. He was down in the water below me, in waders. His backcasts were just going under the overhanging limbs in front of me. I watched at length and kept count of the fish he caught.

Finally, an errant breeze tossed his fine tippet into the limb at my feet. He shuffled along the creek bottom until he could reach the fly. It was in the leaves less than five feet from my well-polished, green river boots. As he focused through his bifocals to unhook the fly, he startled, nearly falling. My boots must have come into focus, too.

"How long have you been there?" he recovered and asked.

"Well, you've caught eight browns and a rainbow since I first leaned against this tree, and you have changed flies twice. You are a fine caster. Have a good day."

"Yeah, well, uh, thanks," he replied.

I think he got the message.

CANDY-STRIPED MITTENS

One blustery Saturday in buck season, I had donned my full uniform and an orange vest and gone for a walk on my favorite local Game Lands near Hazleton. We called it the Oley, after the little run full of wild trout that flowed through the main hollow. It was a big piece of ground nearly two miles between access roads.

I began to hike and check hunters. Late in the morning, I came to a big man sitting huddled up against the butt of an old oak. I recognized him as The Gutter, my stocking helper. He was known for being as big and rough as they come.

"Steiner, I'm not going to tell anyone that you checked me way up here on this ridge. They wouldn't believe me," he chuckled as he stood to tower over me. He was shivering from the cold.

"Good," I responded. "I'll make you a deal. You don't tell anyone that I checked you way back here and I won't tell anyone you have red-and-white candy-striped mittens on."

He looked at his hands sheepishly, shook his head and laughed.

ADDENDUM: It was the night before the Pennsylvania bear season opener, seven or eight years after I had left Luzerne County. Linda and I were staying in a motel in Bradford to hunt, 150 miles from Hazleton. We had eaten a nice meal and I walked into the very dim bar to pay the bill. A loud, gruff voice from the darkness said loud and clear, "You're a stinkin' old fish warden."

I couldn't see into the darkness, my eyes were slow adapting. But I knew the voice.

"You're a stinkin' old Gutter," I responded.

The bar fell silent, except for that big deep laugh. I knew I was right. Linda went to our room and I had a few beers with an old friend, a long way away from where we were both supposed to be.

HANGAR LIGHTS

It was late at night in midsummer. We were working the Allegheny River, just above Foxburg. There is a good pool and some rocks to fish from on the west side there. As we came across the Foxburg bridge, we noticed several lanterns located on the rocks.

We went up the river, turned around and came back and parked close to where a family keeps a pontoon plane. They run it up into a hangar 20 feet above water level by cables and pulleys, when it is not in use.

As we worked into position with binoculars to see what was happening on the rocks, the whole world lit up. One of us had triggered the motion sensor on the hangar lights. From then on when we eased in to check anyone on the rocks, we learned to avoid the hangar. It is tough to sneak up on somebody in the dark, when you have half a dozen spotlights on you.

WAKEUP CALL

One evening on Justus Lake, I sat until 2 a.m., seeing the flash of an occasional cigarette out on the lake. It was obviously in a moving boat. I determined I would cite this boat for a violation, even though he was the only boat on the lake. After all, he was six hours past due with his lights.

When he arrived at the shore and I began the check, I saw a beautiful 8-pound walleye on a stringer and got distracted. We talked about the fish and he told me he had released two others just like it that weren't hooked as deeply. He was one very happy fisherman. I couldn't stand to ruin his day, so I gave him a warning and a lecture on the danger of his actions and sent him on his way.

TORNADO WORM CAN

Just after moving to my new log home in Venango County in the spring of '85, a devastating tornado blew through northwestern Pennsylvania. It missed my house by less than a mile and left many persons dead and many others homeless. It leveled acres and acres of forest habitat. Timber stands one evening turned into tremendous clear-cuts the next. It was both awesome and horrendous.

Weeks went by until all the secondary roads were cleared and life's routines got back to normal in the areas affected. The summer was spent by timber salvage crews getting what useable lumber out of the twister's path they could. During summer, the briars that regrow first in clearings in the western part of the state jumped from the ground and made the tornado-hit area an impenetrable thicket.

The following opening day of trout season was unseasonably warm and nice. Fishermen were out in record numbers and fishing pressure was heavy to the extreme on the stocked trout streams. As I patrolled during the day, I kept trying hard to turn that first case of the year. It just wouldn't come. I thought of the training the old timers, like Mr. Shearer, Wilbur Williams and others, had given me ten years before.

I decided the trick today would be to show up somewhere the scofflaws weren't expecting me. I headed for a wild trout stream, Beatty Run, that ran right through the heart of the tornado blow-down. Logs were still jumbled across the creek. Any trout in this stretch had lived a pretty much unmolested life last summer. I drove by the Beagle Club property to a rather remote stretch of the stream, and there I found an old flatbed truck parked in a pull-off along the water.

Tracks in the dust indicated that the fisherman had headed downstream. So did I. After several hundred yards of parting briars and crawling turtle-like over downed logs, I spotted a coffee can sitting on a log. A one-pound coffee can is the official bait container of the once-a-year fisherman, and I thought it would behoove me to sneak in and watch for a while.

I sneaked to within a few feet of the coffee can and found the fisherman crouched on one knee, doing a very nice job of fishing under the brush downstream. I leaned against a tree snag whose top had been torn off by the big wind, watching. The coffee can was right at my waist a foot in front of me, on the log. I couldn't back out undetected, so I would have to watch and make my check when the fisherman first noticed me. I stood dead still.

After several attempts, a small brookie stripped his worm from the hook. He stood up and came back to the can, where he reached in to get a worm, rooting in the leaf debris in the can. Suddenly his eyes focused on the gun belt and badge and he jumped backwards several feet as if snake-bit.

I did a routine check and moseyed off through the briars as though this was an everyday patrol. I am sure that somewhere, in a bar or in front of a campfire, the circumstances of the day he got checked in the tornado blow-down while fishing for wild brook trout gets repeated. You don't have to arrest everyone to keep them honest. You just have to let them know you can surprise them when they don't expect to be surprised.

LIKE AN APPARITION

Campfires the night before trout season along lakes and streams have for years attracted kids of all ages. Like moths to a light, the kids would come, stand around the fire and shiver and shake and think they were having fun.

Oftentimes it was the romance of it that was the lure. Other times it was a few underage beers. Generally, though, I think it was just being a kid.

Campfires have a mystical effect that, when properly used, can be a lot of fun. Children and adults stand and stare at the fire and their eyes become accustomed to the light. That light only reaches just so far, depending on the size of the fire. Right at the edge of that light is the zone I claimed for mine.

As the kids would be staring into the fire the night before trout season, I would ease into my zone and stand still until one person would look across the fire and past their friends. Their eyes would adjust to the decreased light and focus on me and my uniform. Before they could lock on, I would step back behind a tree and use the shadow to fade out. They would inevitably whisper to someone and suddenly they would all snap around, but I was gone.

I always thought it worked better than actually surprising them, most of the time. If there was a violation, I would generally just stand behind those with their back turned toward me, until the focus was on me, and then I would state, "State Officer," and why I was there. Both were very effective tools.

SLIDE-BY CHECK

I had received a call from my friend Tom Young. He was on his lunch break and had walked out on the trestle at Little Sandy Creek, in the Fly Fishing Only Area. There were two guys there, using meal worms on their flies. They never saw him and were still there, he said.

I drove with the speed of wind and arrived at my favorite hiding spot in the center of the project, just above the trestle pool. I eased out onto the trestle and watched, as first one man and then the other reached in his vest and pulled out a container of mealworms to spice up his flies. Once I was sure they both were in violation, I decided that I'd better get on them quickly, before they could run. I started down the loose cinders alongside the abutments of the trestle. My feet went out from under me and I went sliding right on by, in uniform.

Seconds later I was on my feet and had them surrounded. They both gave me the mealworms without a hassle and paid their fines.

Two years later I had a cadet officer, Ted Kane, working with me. I sent him upstream with instructions to meet me later at the Trestle Hole below. I walked down along Little Sandy and checked the fishermen. I had an idea who was there and what was going on, but found no violations. Ted eventually followed down, not realizing I had already checked everybody.

What happened, I didn't expect.

Ted caught up to me with a fellow walking ahead of him that I had just checked. Ted had watched him try to ditch some mealworms after I missed finding them on him during my check. Cadet Kane got good grades that day for making an old warden look bad.

A LITTLE CANOE FALLOUT

Generally, if you work or play around the water long enough, you have to expect to get wet. It became company policy, toward the end of my career, that all officers must wear a life preserver while working on the water. I certainly jumped at this excuse to begin wearing one. From time to time I had elected to wear one, but often felt that it didn't look proper with the uniform. Once it was mandated, I began to wear it.

The end of May a few years back, I was working with a new deputy. He had one very admirable trait. He could keep a straight face, no matter how funny things got. Perhaps he was just too dumb to know things were funny.

This particular day, we had been patrolling downstream from Franklin and finding little but a few canoes to check. As we rounded a small island, a canoe sat anchored and fishing. As soon as I spotted the craft, I killed the motor and began to float down to it, rather than power in.

The check of licenses and creels was routine, until we got to the part about personal flotation devices. The canoe had none. The older fellow in the boat was a gentleman and began to try and apologize his way out of getting the inevitable ticket.

At first the younger fellow in his mid-20s, in the back of the canoe, sat quietly, but his eyes told me a storm was brewing. Finally, when it became obvious that I was going to write a ticket, he threw a tantrum about how he was a good swimmer and had been in canoes on the river since he was six years old and had never once tipped one, and they were only 25 yards from the shoreline and on and on.

He worked himself into a frenzy and then, magically, somehow, managed to fall out of the canoe without tipping it enough to throw his buddy out. He surfaced, standing about chest deep, and climbed back into the canoe. The dump in the water seemed to do him a lot of good, because he sat quietly from then on.

Through the whole scene, my deputy sat and never cracked a smile. While I wrote the paper, he just held onto the bow of the canoe. After we had left the scene and rounded the next bend, he looked over at me and grinned. That did it for me. I had to stop the boat and get the giggles out of my system.

CHAPTER 5:
Trouting Culprits

Trout culprits are those folks that think trout are like dollar bills. They learn how to miscount, conceal and pilfer the things until they get good at it. Stealing trout is like robbing a convenience store. It is still a robbery, but not a bank robbery. Fish wardens specialize in seeing all the slight-of-hand tricks, the deceptions and the miscounts. They try to make the robbery more like robbing an inconvenience store.

OPENING DAY BONANZA
It was a frosty opening day the third or fourth year I was in Venango County. I had a hunch where I could turn a case, so I walked from my car at 6 a.m. to watch a fishermen's campsite. When nobody was stirring from the tent by 7 o'clock, I reasoned I had guessed wrong and returned to my car. It was still early and I could try somewhere else.

I looked over my notes. There was one that I had gotten from a deputy's wife. A girl she worked with fished a hole on Lower Two Mile Run each opening day, with her dad. They were disgusted since there was a group of guys that always started fishing early. I had written it off as only a few minutes early, like most tips, but decided I was close and it sounded like as good a bet as any.

Cloud cover rolled in as I drove the few miles and rain began. I parked four or five hundred yards back from the supposed area and, after donning my rain suit, approached the creek through the woods. I skirted along several stocking points, without seeing a soul. The cold and now the rain, which was becoming heavy, must have held them back I thought.

I was between the creek and an old railroad bed as I closed on the site of the complaint. There the creek passed through a gap left from the long abandoned railroad bridge. The bridge was gone, but the abutments still stood.

As I neared, I slowed my pace and climbed the ten feet or so to the top of the rail grade. Just as I could begin to see the hole, I spotted two fishing rod tips, obviously fighting trout. I strode to the height of the grade and was dumbfounded. There were 12 adults and one youngster, all fishing. I spoke loud and clear. "Good morning fellows."

I hesitated until they all looked my way. I slowly looked at my watch, then continued, "Its 7:20. Lay down those fishing rods." They did.

I was shocked that they hadn't scattered like a covey of quail. I dropped down over the bank toward them and grabbed a white bucket with several trout in it. I began picking up stringers and demanding licenses. They all cooperated. Now there were only two adults and the kid left to get to, across the creek. It is a small creek, but I still didn't want to get wet.

"Don't just stand there. Get your trout and get over here," I ordered sternly.

They complied. I couldn't believe the way this was going. The rain was pelting now, so I jumped up on a stump and made a short speech. Using my best group speaking technique, I explained their options as a field acknowledgement of guilt or a citation. I finished with, "Walk up that path to your cars and wait there. The first one paid will be the first one that gets back to fishing."

I headed cross-country to my car, with a bucket of flopping trout. I expected a few of the violators to be anxious, since the contents of the bucket indicated that fishing had been pretty good. But when I got back, they were all in line.

I pulled in and invited the first one into the state car. It was the father with the kid. I got out and asked the other 12 adults, ranging in age from 30 to 50, if anyone had a problem with me letting the kid go. There were no objections. I also assured them they must tell me exactly how many trout they had caught, and the total had better be the same as in the bucket when I was done. If not, we would have to handle this in another way. I wasn't sure just what that other way would be yet, but I would think of something.

I was on a roll. As each got in the car, I had him find his license in the bunch, produce another ID, and tell me how many trout he had caught. I was in a writing frenzy. I had called for a backup, but nobody heard me except the boss at the office. He came out, but couldn't find me; he was on the wrong creek. He had only been in the area a few weeks and had gotten lost.

I had written eight of the dozen when I ran out of field acknowledgement forms. They had all indicated they wanted to pay. These guys were getting antsy, since now it was after eight o'clock and some of their buddies were already fishing. I offered them citations again, but they just wanted to pay and get it over with. So I once again improvised. I gave them each a business card and told them to go ahead and fish. But when I beeped the horn when I got back, they had to get up there and take their medicine.

I drove home, had a coffee, got more forms and then returned. I beeped and up they came, all paying in turn. One had limited out, including the two trout that I had. He had been afraid to catch a legal eight knowing he had two illegals earlier. One fellow turned out to be a second offender and had to forward more money, since his fine tripled. However, when he got the note, he immediately replied with the difference.

Everything went fine that opening day, and I added another case later. This certainly was an exceptional opening day. Had I not thrown that handwritten tip from a sportswoman on the seat that morning, I would probably have headed another direction. Sportsmen that care and get involved make it all happen. This turned out to be a grand slam in a homerun season. The fellows that had started early made things go easy once they were caught. Had they not cooperated, I would have probably had to spend all day staking out cars from a post in the wet woods. By cooperating, I got to go have lunch and coffee and they got to get on with their fishing.

YOUR BOYS WOULDN'T LIE

Oley Creek is a gem in a rough setting. It is a Class "A" trout stream that crosses under I-80 three times and runs between the traffic lanes for nearly a mile. When I was the warden in Luzerne County, it was stocked with 500 brook trout in its upper reaches. The water was so shallow some years that the fish would all end up in a few pools created by stream improvement devices I put in with the Bishop Hoban High School environmental class.

One opening day, I had worked elsewhere without detecting any violations, so I headed over to the Oley Creek to work. I had a friend, Ken, along as a partner, while my deputies worked in pairs elsewhere. We parked at the gate and walked in, a break from all the road miles. We came upon a man in his 30s fishing, and he had a stringer with sixteen trout on it.

I quizzed him on his luck and he explained that he had caught seven and the boys had caught nine between them. The boys were right down around the bend at the next hole. I motioned to Ken to stand where he could watch the guy, and I moved down the stream to talk to the boys. They were about ten years old, fishing with the intensity that only youngsters that age can generate.

"How many didja catch?" I asked.

"I got three." the oldest volunteered. "I only got two." the other piped in.

"Naw, you guys are better fishermen than that," I chided.

"Nope, only got three." the oldest reiterated.

"Two for me," stated the youngest as his smile soured. "Are you guys sure? It looks like you got good bait," I pushed.

"That's all." the oldest confirmed.

Now I'm not a math wizard, but I right away ciphered that five from sixteen makes eleven. Eight is the limit and eleven is three too many. So with my new-found information, I confronted the father with the truth. He assured me the boys were lying. I looked him square in the face and said, "I don't believe those boys were brought up to lie. But if you want them to, they will get their chance under oath in court, because I am citing you for three trout over the limit."

"I'll pay, I knew better," was all he said. He signed and paid and went away, knowing that maybe he couldn't count or maybe he gave into temptation, but he had two fine sons that certainly didn't lie.

LAKE FRANCIS AND THE NEW YORKER

My deputy John's wife, Sue, was a rabid angler. She loved to catch fish more than most guys. So it came as no surprise to me on the opening day of trout season to hear that she had taken their son and daughter to Lake Francis to fish.

Lake Francis was stocked with trout and would be nice, clear water, despite the heavy rains. No streams ran directly into it. It had a valve that could control incoming water. When the creek got muddy and threatened to deposit silt in the lake, it was an easy matter to simply shut off the valve. When the creek cleared up, you could crank it open.

Lake Francis also had a valve on the outflow to regulate the discharge. Going out to the valve was a railed catwalk, designed for limited people-traffic for working the valve. I always thought it looked fairly dangerous. The state park had posted signs making it off-limits for fishermen.

Now, Sue, for all her wonderful traits as a dedicated fisherwoman, had a few minor flaws. She was born and raised in the Bronx, had a New Yorker's regard for posted restrictions, and she talked funny. She also had a terrible time identifying fish.

Her husband, John, had just become a deputy, and despite my urging him to fish with his family on opening morning and then give me a hand, he insisted that he work. I had him and several other deputies undercover at Lake Francis that morning. Eventually, I showed up at the lake and began to take a walk around, checking licenses and such.

Things were going fine, until one of the other deputies told me that someone was fishing out on the catwalk. Through my binoculars, it looked like a woman and children. I made my way there, continuing to check as I went. When I got to the catwalk, I was surprised to see it was Sue and her kids.

I walked out and said, "How you catchin' them, lady," as if I didn't recognize her, though I drank coffee with her and John several nights a week.

"I got two trout and a panfish," she replied, pointing to a stringer attached to the shoreline end of the catwalk.

I looked into the crystal-clear water and saw two bass and a crappie on the stringer. Now bass were out of season. Rather than make a commotion that would attract the attention of fishermen nearby, I just reached under the water and released the bass and they swam away from the stringer.

I walked back out to her and whispered, "Those were bass. Remind me to bring a color fish I.D. book over tonight when I come for coffee."

"Thanks," she said. "I'm sorry. I didn't mean to embarrass you."

"You hadn't hurt the fish. I would have given anyone a warning," I answered.

In her case I knew she had made a mistake and was not trying to get away with anything. As I turned to leave, I asked her to respect the park signs, which she did by moving. She said there was no room at starting time and she had wanted the kids to have a chance.

Then she stopped me again as I went to leave with, "Bob, please don't tell John."

Now I can do a lot of things, but I can't keep a secret. Especially one as funny as this. I figured John and the other guys and I would have a good laugh over it. When I got to the deputies, I signaled each of them to meet me at the car. Since nothing seemed to be happening, we stood talking for a few minutes.

With John standing there, I told the catwalk story, thinking it pretty funny. Suddenly John spun and headed down to the catwalk, fuming. Soon he and his family were loaded in the car and headed home. It had badly embarrassed him and I thought I had heard him stating that, "You will never fish again."

I thought he had overreacted and wished fervently that I had honored her request to not tell him. However, since I caused the trouble, I figured it was my part to end it.

I took the fish identification book over that evening. I sat with the family and explained the differences in fishes and how to tell them apart. When the chance presented itself, I apologized to Sue. I was assured it had only been a momentary storm and had blown over. John was trying so hard to be an all-star deputy and the situation had embarrassed him. I still felt I owed Sue and the kids something for the discomfort they had suffered when John had gotten upset.

Later that week I was stocking Lake Irena. I made a point of keeping my stockings so secret that my deputies didn't even know when they were going to be. Once they were over and the fish in, I then would and could, by policy, let the word out. The weather was beautiful. I called Sue after John would have gone to work and the fish were in. I told her the lake was stocked and she and the kids ought to get up there right after they got home from school. I would meet them there.

I rigged their bass-fishing equipment with light leaders, bobbers and kept them baited with minnows from a bucket I had brought. They hammered the brook trout. Sue was busy cleaning a fresh trout dinner when Earl walked in from work. To say the least, he was amazed at their fine catch of a dozen or so trout. Sue did not tell him I had coached.

Before long, she and the kids had equipped themselves with trout gear instead of the heavy bass gear they previously owned. I would have coffee with her and John, and when he would leave the table for anything she would say, "Think I'll take the kids fishing this week at Lake Irena."

I would reply, "Thursday afternoon is supposed to be real good for fishing."

She would never let John know when the stocking was. She knew if word got out there would be more competition for her and the kids. She jealously guarded the secret. John even once accused me of telling her when the stockings would be, but I denied it. And I never really did. It would have been a violation of policy. I figured I kept their dad from taking them fishing. So, I reasoned, it was my duty to be sure they didn't miss the fun. Any day from that day at Lake Francis on, when you would see Sue fishing, she would have her tackle box sitting on the ground, holding a fish identification book open to the page with trout on it.

TROUSER TROUT

It was a typical in-season trout stocking day on East Sandy Creek, at Van. I had met the trucks and had managed to find fifteen helpers, which is about what is needed for this creek and its two trucks. I split the crew and sent the first truck on its way, and began to stock right below the bridge on Route 322, my first stop.

I was standing idly by the truck, jawing with the old-timers that had seen the truck from the highway and stopped. The buckets had been handed down and run to the creek. We were ready to move, when one pickup truck pulled out and headed up on the highway.

"Just a sightseer," I thought. About then a friend and helper, Scott, came running up and grabbed me aside, pointing at the exiting truck. "He just dumped a bucket of fish in the bushes!" Scott exclaimed.

I tried to get a look at the truck, but it was gone. Scott went on to tell me that a worker was standing at the gas company across the creek, leaning against a tree and eating his lunch as he watched us stock. He had hunted turkeys before work and was still in camouflage. He had seen the guy dump the trout and hollered to Scott.

I couldn't believe someone would actually dump trout in the bushes. I figured that since the water was up, it had just appeared that way. I went down through the brush and, sure enough, there were twenty or thirty flopping, sand-covered trout. I told everyone just to leave them alone and hastily made a plan.

Greg was with me. He was training to be deputy and had his own truck. I grabbed Greg and told him to switch cars with me. I carry all my paperwork in an unmarked gym bag. I grabbed it and got rid of everything in Greg's truck that looked like the Fish Commission.

I told Greg to go stock the fish, and if he wrecked the car I would just say he had stolen it and hijacked the fish truck. I then jumped in his truck and moved it several hundred yards up the road, alongside the first gas company building, so it looked like a worker had parked there.

I jumped out and headed up into the woods on the opposite side of the road from the dumped fish. I worked across the hillside, until I was directly above the fish. With the binoculars I couldn't see the fish, but could see where they were.

Before I could begin to wonder about my setup, the truck came back in. He drove by slowly and pulled up to Greg's truck, stopped, got out, and looked in. He then drove back past again and looked like he was going to pull out onto Route 322. He backed up to a wide spot, then turned around and pulled in the only parking spot along the road. I had made sure nobody would stay to fish.

He got out, sat on the tailgate and put on his hip boots and vest, then pulled out a fishing rod and rigged it up. I was beginning to wonder if it was the right guy, when he pulled out three white plastic bags and shoved them in his vest. He headed right for the fish. As he walked to the fish, a distance of about thirty yards through streamside brush, I slithered to a position right across the road from his car, at the base of a mammoth white pine.

To my surprise, I could see his every move with the field glasses. The first bag of fish went in the top of his right hip boot, the second in his left, and the third in his vest. He immediately turned and headed to the truck. As he rounded the tailgate, so did I.

Before I could say a word he blurted, "Boy am I glad to see you."

I must have looked like I was in a daze. I thought I was the last person he would want to see.

"I dumped those fish and then drove away. I had this plan and I knew it was wrong, and I came back hoping to catch you and confess. When you weren't here, I was going to leave, but decided it would be immoral to waste the fish, so I carried on with the plan, knowing I would have to live with it on my conscience for the rest of my life," he told me. "I've never done anything like this before. In fact I have fished very little and was overcome with the moment. I just retired and have been hoping to fish more. I don't know what came over me. I make enough money on retirement I could have bought that many lobster. I should pay a double fine."

I was really in a daze now. However, soon I came out of it and did the paperwork and collected the fine of nearly $300. I didn't accept the double payment.

When the time came, I recommended that his license not be revoked, and it wasn't. However, six or seven years have gone by, and I have never seen him fishing again. I think I'm actually sorry he didn't stick with it. It really is a great sport for retirees.

TROUGH CREEK WOMEN

I was trying to fish at Trough Creek State Park. The water seemed off-color everywhere, so the evening turned into more of a tour of the area. When I stopped one place in the park, I noticed two women on lawn chairs, fishing, and a guy fishing below a little dam. I walked down just to see how they were doing. The longer I watched, the more I wondered where the older woman was from. It was obvious her accent was not that of a local. Not even a ridge runner from the Raystown area sounded that much like a "Grit."

So I asked. "Where you from?"

"Tuscaloosa," came the reply.

"I thought so," I said and I mentioned the difference in the way she talked.

Since I was on vacation and not in uniform, I was carrying my badge in my shirt pocket. I showed it to the lady, and then asked to see her fishing license. Now it should be known at this point that I wasn't planning to cite her, just have her go get a license and show it to me. But then she lied, and I don't like liars.

"I wasn't fishing," she said.

"Ma'am, I stood right here and talked to you while you cast, retrieved and even missed a fish that tugged on your line," I said.

"No sir, I wasn't fishing."

By now the son-in-law decided he had better become a player. He walked up and started to butt in. That sealed the situation. I was either going to get the fine money or watch her put it in an envelope and in a post office box.

After the normal "she doesn't have the money" and "we don't have the money" speeches, the son-in-law went to his car for a checkbook and wrote a check for the fine. As I finished the paperwork and began to walk away toward my car, the guy thought he had to get one final shot in.

"You asshole!" he called after me.

I was about 50 yards away, but heard him. I did a complete military turn and started to stride right back at him until I closed the distance to a few feet.

"What did you call me?" I asked indignantly.

"Not you. I meant her," he stammered, pointing at his mother-in-law.

I just walked away. I figured the price of having called me that vulgar term would have been insignificant, compared to the price he was now going to have to pay.

TROUT THEFT AND SHEEP KNIVES

A lady was killed, shot to death with her boyfriend, when they chased and stopped two guys in a car that were out joyriding and random shooting. The guys had shot at one of her dogs on her lawn. Her loss to her family was tragic.

She raised trout in her spring-fed "swimming pool" for our local chapter of Trout Unlimited, which was one of the Fish Commission's trout-rearing cooperators. The fish were stocked for the public to catch in places open to unrestricted public fishing. It was a good program.

Previously, an old friend of hers had visited and seen the trout. Knowing when she worked and that the kids would be in school, he revisited with an uncle and helped himself to several of the brood fish at the site.

He hadn't realized that one of the kids was home from school sick and heard the dogs barking, saw the dastardly deed, and called mom at work. Mom called me at home and told me where the guy lived, about an hour away.

I picked up Jay Waskin, then a rookie officer working out of the regional office, and headed for the perpetrator's house. When we arrived, we realized he was in the butchering business. In his garage hung several just-killed sheep. As I approached, he stood holding a long knife, wearing a blood-soaked apron. On the counter were several other butchering tools.

I walked right to him and introduced myself. When he heard who I was, he laid the knife down and went and got the fish from the freezer. They weren't frozen yet. He settled the case, as did the other fellow who was living right next door.

On the road back to drop Jay off at the office, he asked me if I had been scared walking right up to the guy with a knife in his hand.

"Did he have a knife in his hand? I really hadn't noticed."

I hadn't. I had been locked on accomplishing a task and just hadn't noticed. Nobody would stab you for a fish, would they?

DOUBLE LIMIT

John, a game deputy, called me one evening after I had stocked Pithole Creek and said he had seen a prominent businessman, Bob Richards, take a limit of trout in the morning and had helped him clean them. I thought it odd that he called just to tell me that, and then he continued.

"I talked to a friend, Lou, later at the Pulaski Club and he said he watched Bob catch a limit, too, and he helped clean them," he added.

I thanked John and made my plan for the next morning. I was at Bob Richard's place of business when it opened. He acted surprised to see me, but cordially invited me into his office. I wasted no time.

"Bob," I said, "you caught a double limit of trout yesterday. I'm here to do the paperwork."

"I did not," he responded indignantly. "John and Lou will testify for me. They're my witnesses."

"No, they won't. They're my witnesses," I countered.

"Well, I caught them early when John was there and waited to clean them when Lou was there later. I went home for lunch and returned with the seven fish, caught my last one, then cleaned them. Lou helped me."

"Bob, trout don't grow new guts. John helped you clean eight and then Lou helped you clean eight. Now do you want to settle or have a hearing?"

He settled the case. Friends of mine told me that for over a year he had my picture from a local sportsmen's booklet as the center of his office dartboard.

PENALTY BOX

It was trout opening morning at Lake Irena near Hazleton. The circus had come to town. In an hour the hundreds of fishermen surrounding the lake would cast their lines among the thousands of stocked trout and there would be flopping and splashing and hooting and hollering and then, in an hour or so, the opening day magic would be gone and the rest of the season would settle in. The one-day fishermen would go home and the all-season guys would have the water to themselves.

But not yet.

The hoopla was working itself into a frenzy. Suddenly a teenager came up to me and pointed to the back corner of the lake and said, "There's two guys fishing back there, now. They're an hour early."

I couldn't have agreed more. I was off at a jog. Well, a fast walk. Soon I was employing stealth tactics developed by years of sneaking in the house after curfew, when I was a kid. Suddenly I appeared, larger than life, on a desk-sized boulder, right behind the two "guys."

"How's luck?" I asked in a low roar.

"Catching a few, mister," the kid cranking in the battling brookie responded, then looked over his shoulder and whispered loud enough for me and his buddy to hear, "Cop."

"You guys know what time starting time is?" I asked, seeing now that I was going to have to improvise a punishment, since the court frowns on ten-year-olds in handcuffs.

"Eight o'clock," the one with big ears nearly frozen under his ball cap answered.

"Yep, you're right," I said, getting down off the rock so I only appeared three times their size. "Know what time it is now?" I continued.

"Ten after eight," they responded simultaneously, both pulling up their sweatshirt sleeves to show me their incorrectly synchronized watches.

"Funny, I got ten after seven," I offered.

"Don't you suppose all these other guys would be fishing, too, if it was eight o'clock?" I asked.

"Never thought of that," Big Ears answered.

"Guess we better quit, huh? Our watches must be wrong," added his buddy, Chunky.

"Let me show you guys what I think happened," I said, rolling up my shirtsleeve, pulling out the stem on my watch and turning it slowly until it was ten after eight. Their eyes just got bigger with each motion of the minute hand.

"Didn't it guys?" I interrogated. But they did not answer.

"I'll tell you what I'm going to do," I said. "I'm going to take your fishing rods and think about whether I should take you to jail or not."

I picked up their rods and reeled them in.

"What are we going to fish with?" Big Ears sort of squeaked, not sure whether he wanted me to hear him or not.

"Probably should have thought of that earlier," I replied.

I took the two rods and strolled off, leaving the two of them sitting there, pouting. Now I'm not one to beat up on kids, but I don't like them thinking they are going to get away with something, either. I figured a lesson learned by two kids at Lake Irena would be a lesson learned by every kid in Hazleton who liked to fish.

I strolled around the lake, carrying the rods, and listened to the comments from the fishermen, young and old, as I said I got some kids fishing before the season up lake. There was no sympathy for them.

As eight o'clock came, the "two guys" came running up to me, panting.

"Can we have our rods? Please, mister?" Chunky pleaded. "They'll have them all caught by the time we get to fish."

"You mean like you guys would have, if I hadn't stopped you?" I replied in my sternest voice. "I'll bring them over to you in a few minutes. Go back to your spot."

They walked away dejectedly, fighting tears, past lots of flopping trout. I figured the message had been delivered.

I returned the rods and watched a few minutes as the boys went back into action. In no time they were catching brook trout hand over fist. The tears had faded and smiles were beaming from ear to ear, like ten-year-old boys are supposed to on opening day of trout season.

"Remember you are only allowed to catch eight, and next year starting time is eight o'clock," I said as I left.

"Yes, sir, and thanks for not taking us to jail," Big Ears said over his shoulder, never taking his eye off the stout brookie he was furiously cranking in.

RING OF TROUT

I was returning home, driving up along Sugar Creek after stocking trout in it earlier in the day. A hatchback car was parked at one of the stocking points. I thought I'd stop and see how they were biting. I figured I might return and fish later, after I had eaten dinner.

As I walked by the hatchback, I noticed trout on a stringer laid out on a sheet of plastic inside, like the numbers on a clock. I counted ten. With the limit only eight, my curiosity was piqued. I found a fisherman downstream and began to talk with him.

"That your hatchback?" I asked, motioning toward the car.

"Yeah, that's mine. Problem with the way it's parked?" he responded.

"Looks fine to me. I was curious about the trout. Did you catch them?" I continued.

"My girlfriend and me," he replied.

"Where is she now?" I said.

"Took her kids up to the store for a pop and snack."

Just then I saw a small blue car coming from the direction of the store, signaling to pull in. I felt I might as well check her license. When she got out of the car, I walked over and started with, "May I see your license, please?"

"You didn't see me fishing," she responded sharply.

"Your friend told me you caught some trout," I explained.

"He's lying. I wasn't fishing. I don't even have a license."

I suggested then, "Why don't you take the youngsters with you and go talk it over with him. Either you were fishing without a license or he has too many trout."

A few minutes after the hollering subsided, the guy came walking up to me with his wallet out. I guess he either couldn't count or made a mistake and divided by persons and not licenses, when he tried to figure a way out of his predicament.

THREE SPECIAL CASES

New deputies are always full of enthusiasm. The testing and qualifying procedure is long and drawn out. Training is a time-consuming affair and, when their commissions are finally handed out, they hit the pavement raring to go. The natural resources of our state are better protected than any other state or province because of these dedicated men and women. They work a tremendous amount of hours, without pay.

Mike was one of these fresh deputy recruits. He had only been in the field a few weeks when trout stocking season began. He liked working the White Haven area, since he was familiar with it. One rainy afternoon, he was patrolling Wright's Creek when he spotted two men fishing for trout. The stream had just been stocked and the season was not yet open. Mike approached them and was met with a dilemma. They both were Catholic priests on retreat.

The situation soon grew way out of proportion to the crime. It all ended happily for Mike, though, as justice was dealt with. After many meetings, a local church offered to ante up the fine money from the "coffee" fund, the magistrate ended up a good guy for negotiating a truce, and we settled the cases on field receipts, which was our intention all along. Mike was a happy officer, having seen his first case go from a nightmare to a successful completion.

He did take some razzing from his fellow deputies, though. So when Mike radioed me from the parking lot of F.E. Walter Dam a few weeks into the season that he had apprehended a man with a double limit of trout, I felt relieved for him. This would establish him within the "pecking order" of deputies. Over-the-limit cases are hard to come by and are considered quality apprehensions.

When I stepped from the car to settle the case, I immediately knew that Mike wasn't off the hook yet. There stood Paul Charles. Old Mr. Charles was a sad case. He had outlived all his friends. He resided in town with his 60-year-old daughter and her husband, and neither had much time for him. So they brought him to the dam at 6 a.m. and he fished his days away, wearing an old pair of Keds high-tops, a Down-easter hat and battered work clothes.

The year before, I had given Mr. Charles a warning for a short musky and a bass out of season. I reasoned that he was getting old and forgetful. I often talked to him and knew much about him. I felt bad for him, but this was obviously an overt act and not an innocent mistake, as I had considered the other two incidents.

"Mr. Charles, you know me and you know what I have to do," I started.

Mike stood by, watching justice in action again.

"Yes," he replied. "You're Steiner and you have to fine me and take the eight extra fish." Eight was the limit then.

I was startled and relieved.

"How much is the fine?" he questioned.

"Its twenty-five dollars, plus ten dollars for each fish over the limit," I answered.

Old Mr. Charles pulled a worn billfold from the pocket of his soiled pants and said, "That's about one hundred and five dollars. Is that right?"

I responded, "Yes," as he paid me with five crisp twenties and a five. Mike was busy writing the necessary paperwork.

Mr. Charles continued as Mike wrote.

"When you gave me those breaks last year, I decided if I was going to keep violating the law, I better carry some money with me for when I got caught."

I was dumbfounded, but glad I was no longer being played for the fool. Mike, however, now had two cases to his credit, two priests and an 89-year-old man. The razzing not only continued from the other deputies, but intensified.

Memorial Day is a big event at Hickory Run State Park. Campers are everywhere, every picnic table taken and fishermen on every drink of water. The crew had split into teams of two and I was working with Mike. I knew in my heart today I would get the monkey off Mike's back.

"Check close for licenses and watch for nonresidents with resident licenses" were my instructions as I dropped him on a stream. "If you find any violations, just walk them down the stream to the first little dam to settle," I coached.

I then left Mike to walk the stream corridor, while I went to observe the fishing behavior at the dam near the campground. A half hour later, Mike arrived all a-puff and excited.

"I got one, a nonresident without a license," he exulted.

"Good work! Where is he?" I returned.

"He's coming. He's on crutches. He only has one leg," was Mike's reply.

The gentleman paid his fine, never knowing that his misfortune wasn't nearly as great as Mike's would be when we met the rest of the crew that evening.

WILBUR'S WIRE

I was fresh out of the training school and anxious to get on with it. Wilbur Williams had called me to assist with stocking Kinzua Creek in McKean County and to do some subsequent patrol. In the early years, there was no such thing as work hours. They were all either work hours or sleep hours.

We had worked long into the dusk of the late spring evening. Wilbur had me stake out the lower end of a "wired area," a special regulation section of stream that had been recently stocked. Fish were put into these areas with the thought that they would slowly work out and provide a fishery over a longer period of time. Some culprits thought that they were supposed to work out in fishermen's creels. I was to watch for such culprits.

Two vehicles remained along the road. A good bet as the shadows lengthened. I hunkered along a huge hemlock as evening settled in. I could clearly see the bottom 50 yards of the trout-infested wired area. Wilbur had sidled up to the upper end and maintained a guard on that end of the wired area. We had no radio contact. This was the mountains, and we were working as wardens had for a hundred years. I loved this kind of patrol.

I heard voices coming up along the stream from the open fishing area below the wire, and soon six or seven persons, obviously a family, came past me at a distance of only a few feet, in single file. When they got to the wire they detoured around it as required. I reasoned they couldn't all be in one car and fell in behind them silently. I had toyed with speaking to them, just for the shock effect, but stifled the urge.

Suddenly I saw two forms along the wire on the opposite side of the creek. I kept in line as we moved along another large pine tree, but stopped when I went behind it, totally unnoticed by either group. There I stood watching, as first one and then the other of the two young men ducked under the wire and began to fish. Only their white rods were visible to me now. They had fished for ten minutes or so and I was beginning to plot an undetected approach, when Wilbur made his appearance. He was not visible, but I could hear keys rattling on his belt.

"Williams!" one of the culprits hissed.

They sloshed across the shallow riffle and began to duck out from under the wire on my side. Before they could straighten, I had taken hold of their fishing rods and had shouted, "State Officer!" in identifying myself. Two more surprised young men I have never seen. They shook with fear. As they tried to dig out identification, they dropped everything. Then they were taken to the cars, where they were written tickets. They drove away, still not in control of the shakes, when last we saw them.

TRACK STARS

I ran track as a kid. Not well, but I ran. That was many years and many pounds ago. I still can remember running, but remember is about all I do.

It was a warm and sunny Friday afternoon before trout season. Tomorrow at eight the highlight of the Fish and Boat Commission's year would kick off. I was on patrol with Denny, a deputy of like age and build. We were trying to keep the kids honest, since they had the day off from school.

We were cruising out the Buxton Road along Prather Creek, when Denny said, "There's kids fishing."

I stopped on the berm and told him to stay with the car. I figured they had spotted us, so I exited running. I had nearly 120 yards to go through a weed field to get to them and expected them to be long gone when I got there. Much to my surprise, they stood and kept fishing as I closed the gap. I charged out of the field and into the thin strip of woods. When they heard the sticks snapping and cracking, they dropped their rods to run. "Stop! State Officer!" I bellowed.

They had only gotten a step or two each and then they froze. I backed them all together over to the creek and began to gather identification. Denny arrived and gathered rods and trout from the leaves along the bank. We eventually sorted out the mess and trooped them all up to my car. As they walked ahead of me, I realized they all had Titusville school track team sweatshirts on. Since they were all juveniles under 18, I was going to take them all to their homes and let their parents pay the fines and sign the paperwork. They didn't like the idea, but didn't see where they had any choice.

One by one we made the deliveries and collections and I was left with one young fellow in the car. He couldn't get out without knowing the answer to a question that was gnawing at him.

"What would you have done if we would have scattered and run?" he asked.

"I would have run about another three steps and then dropped dead," I replied.

He grinned. "We wouldn't have wanted that to happen."

He suffered the wrath of his mother like the rest, but then asked, "No, really, what would you have done?" as I was departing. He had talked freely in the car and had been a pretty good kid, so I leveled with him.

"I would have let you go, but I would have been at the very next track meet with your coach," I said. "I'll bet he would have helped me cure you guys of running on an officer."

"I'll bet he would of, too." he said. "I'd be doing laps until I was eighty."

It is good to see that track coaches haven't changed.

CLEMENTINE

In the old days, back when supervision and policy seldom entered into our judgment, I took a friend on patrol with me. He worked in a foundry and wanted to see what "real work" was like. We had some good times during the week he rode with me. He said it was one of his best vacations. That was funny to me. It had been one of my hardest weeks of work.

We had just stocked Wright's Creek in Luzerne County. I had all the hotspots laced with "undercover" deputies, as was the practice then. When we got done stocking, I would go sit out of the way and wait for the deputies to report in. In short order, Jim and Mike showed up and told me that a man wearing a brown sweatshirt and driving a light green pickup truck had caught a limit of trout and put them in a cooler behind the seat of his truck. He had then moved to another hole and walked back into the woods carrying his rod.

My vacationing friend, Lenny, and I drove to the area and headed in along the creek. We were both in plainclothes, too. I had worn mine under my official stocking coveralls. With rods in hand, we got to the creek, but could see no signs of the guy. I sent Lenny downstream and I headed up to a hole that had received several buckets of trout. I told Lenny if he saw the guy to just whistle and I would come down.

I then camped on the hole full of trout, anticipating the return of the scofflaw. I had an oversized jig on and just sat at the hole with the jig lying on the bottom amid the 20 or 30 trout. As long as I let it lie still, the trout showed no interest and I could look like a "goober" fisherman and watch the action. Nobody fished the hole I was sitting next to for a half hour or so, then I heard a man whistling. He was walking along the creek and whistling, "Oh, My Darling Clementine."

It was Lenny, and he was walking a step or two behind the guy that we were looking for. I stifled a smile and Lenny walked on, whistling, as the guy stopped and began to talk to me. Suddenly, the scofflaw spotted all the trout in the hole and began to fish in earnest, as though I wasn't there. Quickly he caught eight more trout, while I had not a hit. I made small talk with him about what he was catching them on and he offered me some bait.

"No," I insisted. "I'll go to town and buy some." I told him I was hungry, anyhow, and I would eat and return.

I walked from the woods with him until we got to the vehicles, then I badged him. I explained that he had caught eight trout in front of me and had eight in a cooler behind the seat, which he had caught in front of two of my deputies. He confessed and wanted to pay the fine, a hefty $105. While he and I were standing at the hood of my car, me to the side and him in front, filling out the paperwork, my two young rookie deputies pulled in and parked in front of us.

"You got him. Good," said Mike as he exited the vehicle. He understood my blank stare meant, "Shut up," and ceased his remarks. He was excited. It was a good case and he knew it.

As I wrote, Mike jumped back in his truck, explaining that he had to get to work, but he was obviously still riding high on the adrenalin of a good case. He shoved the Blazer into gear and popped the clutch, but instead of going forward it came roaring backwards, toward us. I screamed and it slid to a stop, inches from crushing the defendant's knees between Mike's rear bumper and my front bumper.

Mike then left without a word. I settled the case and apologized for Mike's remark. Nothing more was said by the defendant. He had taken his medicine like a true sportsman. I did call Mike and give him hell though. I explained to him that if he had crushed the guy's knees, we would have probably had to let him go without any fine, and cases were hard to come by.

OVER LIMIT, BROKEN ROD, SUGAR CREEK

Be inconspicuous. That is the first rule of undercover work and, I imagine, the first rule of poaching. I know for sure the opposite happens. If you attract attention to yourself, once attracted it isn't going away.

I was new to Venango County and not everybody knew me. I had decided to work the open, grassy areas at Cooperstown on Sugar Creek undercover before everyone knew who I was. I was just fishing and watching the day of a stocking, when I heard a commotion upstream. A young guy in his late teens had a real nice rainbow on and lost it right at the shore. He slammed the rod to the ground, breaking it. Then he picked the pieces up and threw them out into the creek. They floated directly to me.

I reached for the pieces and threw them on the bank. Then I watched. I knew I could learn more by watching. Shortly the teenager went up and leaned against the tire of a truck that was parked on the field along the creek, instead of along the road. That answered that question.

I was starting to think about citing him for one or the other, littering or parking on the field, when he got up and walked over to the edge of the stream and hoisted a stringer of five trout and returned toward the truck. I timed it so I would arrive at the same time as he did.

It was well choreographed. He had just opened the cooler to reveal another limit of eight trout inside. "Who caught the ones on the stringer?" I asked.

"My brother."

"Who caught the ones in the cooler?" I continued.

"I did," he said.

"Thought you might want this back," I said, extending the handful of broken rod parts.

"Screw it, I quit fishing. Throw them away," he moped.

I laid the rod parts on the back of the tailgate and he pitched them against a post along the field. He wasn't going anywhere, so I went up the creek to where he had been fishing. Finding a guy that resembled the one at the truck, I started a conversation.

"How's luck?" I quizzed, as I eased into the water next to him and cast.

"Not bad. I got six," he said pointing to a stringer on the shore behind him. "And my brother up there just lost a big one."

I caught a fish and then moseyed on down to the truck. This time I started the conversation a little more officially, beginning with the badge being shown.

"State Conservation Officer. I'll need to see some identification. You are parked illegally, have littered the same rod twice and have caught 13 trout and killed them, young man. You are going to receive some citations."

Since he was only 17, I wrote only the over-the-limit case and wished him a safe journey, after explaining to him that his temper tantrum had called attention to himself.

A few days later the payment came in the mail, with an apology, handwritten, for his behavior. It read: "Dear Officer Steiner. Sorry for the way I acted on Sugar Creek. I really didn't want to get caught. Sincerely, John."

BOYS WILL BE BOYS

Back in the old county, my first district, Luzerne, I was scheduled to put on a fishing school at Crestwood High School on a Saturday, just before the trout season opener. My parents had driven out to visit. I asked Dad to come along and watch me in action, teaching youngsters how to fish.

To my surprise, only two young red-headed boys showed up. They had been to a similar program I put on the week before in a neighboring school district, so I begged off.

Since I had just stocked Wapwallopen Creek in that vicinity, after we loaded all the gear back into the Matador, I suggested that we go do a short patrol. I had suspected someone would figure out I was teaching and would not be patrolling and would take advantage.

I swung up along the creek, where it ran through a housing development. I hadn't gone very far, when I noticed two teenage boys fishing. They may not have been 16 yet, but they certainly were old enough to know better.

I hid the car and began a slow sneak through the backyards and alders to the creek. Conveniently, the boys were standing side by side, so when I grabbed I got both of them by the collar of their shirts. They surrendered immediately, having been scared to death when I bellowed, "State Officer!" at point-blank range.

I led them to the car and laid their fishing equipment on the hood, then walked them up through the development for five or six blocks in front of the car. All their buddies saw them.

When we arrived at the first kid's house, I left the other kid standing by the car with my father guarding him. Actually, he was just talking to him. I carried the fishing rod as I accompanied the first boy to the door and told him to get one of his parents. I was met by an irate father.

"The kids were just having a little fun. Don't you guys have anything better to do? Can't you find any real crimes? My kid wasn't fishing. You have no proof."

He continued loud and boisterous. I just turned and walked away with his fishing rod in my hand, headed for the car.

"Where are you going with that rod?" he shouted after me.

"I'll need it for evidence in juvenile court," I replied.

I had been meaning to give stern warnings and release the kids into the custody of their parents for discipline. Now I had changed my mind.

I started to back out the driveway with the other kid ready to resume his walk in front of the car, he being more shaken than before having heard "juvenile court" mentioned.

The father of the first boy hollered for me to stop.

"I'll pay it, but I'll have your job," he said.

I settled the case, requiring the father to sign with the kid, and told him I didn't think he could get my job.

"To get this one you have to pass a Civil Service test and you, sir, are not civil."

And I drove away.

I just couldn't wait to get to the other house. I figured a phone call had beaten me there when I saw a large, robust woman standing in the doorway, glaring at us. As I exited the car, the woman opened the door and said come in.

"Here we go again," I thought.

She wheeled around and grabbed the kid by the shirt and bounced him off a wall. As he was getting up, his mother shouted, "You're 'going to wash a car' my ass, you little liar!"

She unloaded a right hook that would make most prize fighters proud. The kid took it as a glancing blow, but knew he was licked, not being allowed to fight back. He stayed down.

I talked the lady back to sensibility and she and the boy signed the papers and paid. I was assured he would be paying this fine back "all summer." I guess there is a lot of interest on twenty-five dollars when you have to come up with it quickly.

When I got back to the car, my dad was smoking his corncob and grinning.

"What's so funny?" I asked.

"I thought that was you I saw bounce off the wall through the window," he replied.

LAST DAY OVER-THE-LIMIT

Over-the-limit cases are tough to come by, even when you just stocked. I don't think they happen that frequently and when they do it is generally a case of a guy getting a limit, then relocating to another stream and catching another limit in another officer's district. I think a few guys catch a limit early in the morning, take them home, then return and catch another limit in the evening. Occasionally guys will pass fish and help fill someone else's limit, which is also unlawful. Usually, a day or two after you stock, the chance of getting an over-the-limit case becomes extremely remote.

It was the last day of the extended winter trout season on Oil Creek, at Drake Well. The February day was warm beyond normal, and Oil Creek had defrosted weeks before. I had a meeting with the people at Drake Well

Museum for something or other and had arrived early, so I decided to work on my tan and go for a walk on the flood-control dike that contains the creek along the museum property.

As I got slightly below and behind the museum, I noticed an old-timer fishing. I had seen this guy fishing several other places late in the year, so I just stopped to watch. I was remembering that he was the first guy I saw catch a fish in Venango County, when I moved in. It had been the December before, and he had been landing a seventeen-inch rainbow under the bridge at Sugar Creek.

As I stood and watched, I remembered that he was a minnow fisherman and fished them "strung" with a front hook and a trailer hook. I watched him cast to an overhanging willow and suddenly set the hook. He reeled in a smallish trout and placed it in a plastic bag and in his vest. He checked his bait carefully and cast again. Again he hooked and landed a trout. This one was a little nicer. I almost cheered, but didn't want to spoil his enjoyment by startling him. He landed this trout and put it on the stringer that hung from his belt.

A new minnow was rigged, and he cast again. Again his bait was smacked immediately, and he landed another small trout, which he placed in the plastic bag in his vest. He continued casting. I realized now that I had better pay attention, so I got out of the open and behind a bush along the bank.

It took a few casts this time, but despite the fact that the stream hadn't been stocked since late May the year before, he was onto another good trout. The battle lasted a little longer and he hooked it on his stringer. He spent another ten minutes casting, then began to work his way to the shore.

When he arrived, I asked, "How's luck?" acting like I had just arrived.

He hoisted the two on the stringer and said, "Need one more for a limit."

"Don't the two in your fishing vest count toward your limit?" I asked.

"I don't have any other ones," he replied.

"I'll have to check your vest," I responded, motioning for him to turn around. I looked in every nook and cranny and couldn't find those fish. Yet I was sure they were there. I had him take it off, and on a diligent search I found the two eight-inch trout tucked in a side pocket in a bread wrapper.

Reluctantly he paid the fine. Then he smiled and said, "I'm still way ahead."

I'll bet he was too; he was 72 years old. I am sure, however, that I was either the only officer or one of very few to ever get an over-the-limit of trout case on the last day of the season.

FINALLY, A SHORT TROUT CASE

Opening day of trout season is overwhelming. There are so many good guys out there that it is hard to single out a culprit and make a case. You run yourself to a frazzle and seldom come up with anything in the way of an actual "trout" violation. I liked to spend part of each opening day in some out of the way place, checking the fishermen that fish for native trout, with the hopes of keeping them honest.

This day had been rainy and the stocked streams were swollen to the banks. Opening day fishing was less than good. I began to prowl the native streams. Along Route 62 is a little stream we call Whitetail Run. It is only four feet wide, but it holds a few native trout in its short existence before it reaches the Allegheny River.

As I paralleled it, I noticed a car parked, so I got out and began to sneak along the bank. I worked my way downstream and eventually came on a fishing pole leaned against a hemlock. From the shadows I skirted the stream, watching diligently ahead with my binoculars. Soon I saw an old man and a young boy, about eight years old. I watched as they fished and landed a brook trout. I could tell from where I was that it was not the required seven inches long. The old man took it from the hook and put it in a fabric creel that was lying on the bank, after some fussing with it. The kid beamed. I was going to be a party pooper, I was sure.

Silently and cautiously I made my approach. I asked, "How's fishing?"

The kid responded right away, "I got a native. It sure is pretty."

"And I believe it sure is short, too." I replied.

The kid just looked at me. Grandpa immediately began to produce the trout. I measured it and found it to be three-eighths of an inch short of the required seven inches. I asked the old man for his license. As I began jotting down the pertinent information for a citation, the old man spoke. It was the same old line about how he wanted to teach the boy right and never would teach him to cheat and on and on. I listened patiently as I wrote.

Finally, after I had all the information I needed, I asked him why he hadn't measured the fish. "I did," he replied. "On the new fishing creel I just bought him."

"Show me," I said, handing the old man the fish. He did, and the fish measured about 7-1/8 inches. I measured again with my ruler and the trout was again short.

I pondered the situation and then I struck a deal with Grandpa. "The fine is $25," I said. "Now you can buy two mighty nice tape measures for that. You agree to buy one for you and one for the boy and I won't have to ticket you. Fair enough?"

"Fair enough," he agreed. Then I turned to the boy and gave him my card and told him to put it in his pocket and if Grandpa didn't buy him a good tape measure, to call me. Gramps must have come through. I never got a call.

CHAPTER 6:
Warmwater Culprits

Most tourist fishermen have no clue about seasons and required sizes for fish. Ignorance killed the last passenger pigeon and nearly got all the buffalo. It is, therefore, no excuse. If you are going to drive a car, you need to know the rules. Same goes for using a fishing rod. Some of the fines helped pay the freight when license sales dwindled. They bought the trout, gassed the patrol cars and paid my wages. When I caught you violating, you had to be really good at convincing me that you were just oblivious or you were cited.

WALTON JONES

My only brother, Scott, is four years younger than me. As a child he had a dire medical problem that landed him in a coma for eight or nine days. His roommate, Walton Jones Jr., was a youngster who never gave up hope. He never let his own medical problem bother him, though it too was very serious. He continually reassured my parents, "Not to worry. He's a kid, he'll make it." The doctors didn't think so.

When this was all going on, I was 15 and interested in girls. Since I wasn't allowed in the hospital and had to go to school, I hadn't really been apprised of the seriousness of my brother's situation, nor had I noticed.

Finally, during week-two of the ordeal, my parents sat me down and explained that I would probably never see my brother alive again. He had gotten progressively worse, and the doctors said he only had a day or two left. The little roommate didn't believe it. "He'll make it," he kept repeating to my mom and dad as they sat holding Scott's hands and hoping beyond hope.

A medical miracle then took place. The doctors treating Scott left for the weekend for a conference and talked to an old-time country doctor that knew advanced lockjaw when he heard about it. That doctor flew in from Texas and in two days had my brother out of bed, dribbling a basketball in the halls. "Told you he'd make it!" greeted my joyful parents as they walked into the hospital expecting the worst and saw Scott up and playing.

The story has been told again and again in our family and the little roommate, though of a different race and creed, has served as an inspiration to never give up. As I strived to beat the odds of gaining this job, I had thought of the "never say die" attitude I had heard of so many times. I often had reflected, as I got older, of what Scott's roommate's attitude had meant to my brother, my parents and me. Walton Jones, Jr. comes up in conversation even now, nearly 60 years later, at regular intervals.

Imagine my surprise and chagrin when I greeted a rental boat at the shoreline of Pymatuning Lake one late spring evening and found a cooler with several very short walleyes. As I further checked, I found several other infractions of the Fish Law. Upon asking the operator of the boat for identification, I was handed a driver's license. It was Walton Jones, Jr. He was very indignant and arrogant, obviously well to do. He paid the fine but assured me the ticket had been given only because of racial bias and not because there had been three violations.

I never reminded him about Children's Hospital. I don't think he would have cared. I returned to my car a little dismayed with the outcome. My folk hero had died that day, and I was the guy that killed him.

WHITTLING AWAY

It was in those early formative years one lovely Sunday morning, when I began to work along the north shore of Pymatuning. Officer Beaver had taken his family to church and would meet me later in the day. I was just taking my time, learning my way around and trying to check everyone I could find.

Somewhere along the way I noted a family picnicking at a picnic table. The table was set with a nice buffet, and the father was carving a watermelon with a butcher knife. I took note but paid no particular attention. In front of them were several rods fishing and a fish basket tied to a shrub at water's edge.

As a formality, I asked who belonged to the fishing equipment and could I check the basket. "Go 'head," came the reply.

As I lifted the basket, I noted several short walleyes in it. I asked to see the man's fishing license and he started to resist when it became evident to him I was going to issue a ticket.

I had my back to the water and was down over a four or five-foot bank. Before I could get up over the bank, he started preaching at me with his butcher knife as a pointer.

"No man is arresting me for those fish. Another guy came along and asked me if I wanted them and I said sure, just put them in the basket. I never even saw them."

His every other word was being highlighted with a down-stroke of that knife. I was still ten feet away, not nearly far enough if an attack came. The whole speech had gone into slow motion. My ultimate bodily defense mode had kicked in. I started to think clearly. One side of my mind was setting up a retreat, while the other side set up an attack. I could see the anger welling up in his face as he continued to wave the butcher knife.

"Sir, you will have to lay the knife down. Lay the knife down alongside the watermelon. Lay the knife down," I repeated in a calm monotone.

It seemed like I repeated it 25 times until it sank in, and he realized he had forced me into a fight or flight situation. He also must have realized I was armed, and while I hadn't cleared the holster, I certainly had brushed the long "cruiser" style coat from over the handle of the .38 Chief's Special.

As soon as the knife was on the table, I was up over the bank and on level ground with him. I asked him to step away from the table, which he did. I calmly, in a monotone, again requested his license, which he produced and I went to the car and wrote the ticket. He paid on the spot. I have to confess that this was the first time I went into the "total focus slow-motion" mode that helps you elude panic. I can only think of a time or two in my career when this mode was achieved.

I met Beaver for coffee before we headed out for the afternoon patrol.

"How'd it go?" he quizzed.

"Nothin' special, just a man with a couple short walleyes. He paid once I got him away from his family and his butcher knife."

LILY LAKE GUARD RAIL SETTLEMENT

The electric company had several little ponds around the county, for what reason I never knew. They were posted against fishing, but were heavily fished by the locals. Word was out you never got chased.

It was raining cats and dogs and was reasonably cold on a Sunday morning in mid-May. My in-laws were visiting, so naturally I was looking forward to work. As I went to get into the car, I had one of those weaker moments and asked my father-in-law if he wanted to ride along. This wasn't frowned on quite so much back then.

He agreed. We had an uneventful morning of traveling from lake to lake in the Mountain Top area of Luzerne County. That was when I noticed the old car sitting along the road. It was just a heap of rusted-out fins. I knew that fishermen used this road as a back way into a cove on Fenner's Ice Lake. I got out, put on my yellow raincoat and pants, and headed down in the pouring rain.

As I sauntered toward the shoreline, I noticed two guys standing out in the water, fishing with waders on. One was fighting a fish. I leaned against a tree and watched. He landed the short bass, pulled a bag from the front of his chest waders and put it in, then replaced the bag in the waders. I let them make a few casts and then continued to saunter toward the shoreline in plain view.

"How're they hittin'?" I asked, startling them both.

"Just tryin' to get some bluegills, but it must still be too cold," was the reply.

"You guys mind wading in, so I can check your license?" I asked.

They turned and complied. They still thought I hadn't seen anything. Once they had stepped up on shore, I asked again to see their licenses. One admitted he didn't have one and produced an ID from his wallet. Once I had that, I reached and grabbed the top of the plastic bag sticking out of the waders. I then found one in the other set of waders, too. The catch was something like seven or nine short, out-of-season bass.

I hiked them to the car and got out of the pouring rain and wrote the tickets. One came to ninety-some dollars and the other was around fifty. The guy with the low fine paid on the spot and badmouthed a little, but nothing really excessive. I figured he was madder at himself than at me. The guy with the high fine asked for a couple of weeks to get the money, since he was on some social program, although he looked perfectly healthy to me when he was fishing.

I granted him the time, and we agreed on a meeting place at the Lily Lake parking lot, two weeks from that day, at 10 a.m. I was there waiting when the rust mobile came rolling in. I did the necessary paperwork, which was a three-part field receipt that you filled out on the spot, and handed him his copy once I had the money.

He pocketed the receipt, then he started, "You mind if I tell you what I think of you?" he asked.

"No, go ahead. You spent enough money to be entitled to an opinion," I countered.

"I think you are a no-good sonofabitchin' prick!" he responded.

He then turned to leave, forgot the guard-rail wire was right behind him, and it took his feet right out from under him. He landed on the dirt road access to the parking lot, the wind knocked out of him.

I leaned over, decided he was all right, just mouthy, and said, "I guess the Lord agrees with me and the fine," and walked away.

FRENCHMAN, BELL FISHING

Walter Dam drew tourists from all over creation. You never knew what to expect next.

As I looked through the binoculars one day, I noticed that the kayak club was holding a school off the ramp. These folks, at least the regulars, were my friends. I had a patrol kayak, and they knew that and respected my effort to learn their sport. They also were trying to overcome bad publicity that was drawing battle lines in the Lehigh River between them and fishermen. I had worked to make the river a place that both groups could enjoy simultaneously, without getting in each other's way. They would help me any time I asked, if they could.

Kayakers are an unusual group, if you look at generalities. Back then they were usually rich kids with lots of play money, trying to act like poor Europeans. That is not meant to be derogatory, only to set the stage for what was to happen. Many of this group was from New York and Philly, where they did business things or taught school or whatever during the week. When the weekend came, they let their hair down and kayaked.

On the opposite side of Walter Dam, on the high over-jutting rocks along the water discharge tower, I noticed a lone fisherman. As I looked him over for a license, I noticed something unusual. Something I had only seen once in an old sporting magazine. Between the tip and first guide on his rod was a little silver or brass bell, suspended from the fishing line. It was an audio strike indicator, rather than a bobber. That was very clever and very European. I figured he had to have been with the kayakers and just got tired or wasn't really interested, but had come up from the city with someone else that was attending the school.

I stealthily approached from above, like I was hunting mule deer in the rock ledges of the Rockies. I watched him cast and retrieve and then made my final ascent through the rocks to him. After I dusted myself off from the crude landing, I asked the routine question. "How they hittin'?"

"Je ne parle pas Anglais."

I knew I had a problem. The two years I had taken French in high school were now filed under ancient history. But I did know it was French. I motioned with both hands for him to wait there.

After scurrying up over the rock ledges like a well-fed groundhog, I jumped in my car. I quickly drove down to the boat launch, where the kayak school was underway, and found one young woman that I had talked to a few weeks before. She was the lead instructor. She had told me she had taught French in a suburb of Philadelphia. She had spent several years in France.

I told her I needed her help. She got out of her kayak, told the class to take a break, and got into the front seat of the Matador. I drove to the upper parking area and asked her to follow me. That she did. She still didn't know what the problem was.

When we got to the guy with the fishing bells, I turned to her and said, "Would you ask him in French if I could see his fishing license?"

There was quite an exchange between them, and then she turned to me and said, "He says he doesn't have one. Says he wants a break. He knew he needed one, his friend told him before he left the lodge and told him where to get one and how. He says you should give him a break. I think you ought to arrest him, he knew better."

She had done a better job than I had thought she would. I had figured she would back out and leave me stranded. Not everyone is cut out for law enforcement.

I explained the field receipt option to her and had her explain it to the defendant in French. He hesitated and she flew into him in French. I knew there were expletives. He dug out his wallet and paid and signed the papers. She was even better at law enforcement than I thought.

THREE MUSKIE CASE

I never like to leave a deputy work alone, but sometimes you, deputy or district officer, find yourself all alone and forced to either take the case or let it go. Nobody likes to let them go, no matter what the odds.

My wife, Lin, was a deputy at the time. We had company this particular weekend, a couple with their two fishing fanatic kids.

It was decided that Lin and our friends would fish the tailwater of F. E. Walter Reservoir, and I would get there in the afternoon. As an afterthought, it was decided to have all the deputies rendezvous there around three o'clock and have our wives bring a picnic, and we would enjoy the afternoon with our families.

From around noon on, Donna, the kids' mother, was left guarding the food and two picnic tables with a view. Lin, Donna's husband, Mike, and the kids went down the trail to the stream and began fishing the tailwater pool. The other families began to straggle in.

When I arrived with the first shift of deputies, we went up on the top of the dam breast. When I swung the spotting scope on the tailwater pool, I immediately picked out Mike and the kids, but not Lin. Then I saw her. She had her pen out and was holding a stringer with three short muskies on it. She had three big guys cornered and was covering them with her ink pen. I am sure the first one that would have moved would have gotten it. She looked like a Chihuahua with three wolves at bay.

We unlocked the gate and rode to the fair damsel's rescue in the white Matador. She said it looked like the cavalry coming as the dust rose in plumes behind the catapulting vehicle on the access road.

The three guys had decided not to submit to a license check after she took their three short muskies, and she had cornered them where they had to either climb, swim or chance going past her. She was in civvies, with only a pocket badge and a pen. They paid in a hurry when the state car unloaded.

ESCAPING SHORT BASS

Every outlaw has his own way of thinking. They all think they can beat the system or they wouldn't be trying some of the stunts they do. But they all think they have thought of a new way to beat it. Few work and few are really new.

The patrol was ending and it had been relatively eventful. Deputy Dick and I were about to head the jet boat into the ramp at Franklin, when I looked up the river to the 8th Street bridge and noticed a johnboat anchored near one of the abutments.

"One last check," I smiled, looking for Dick's approval.

"Why not?" he responded.

As we closed the distance, I recognized one fisherman as the alleged marijuana kingpin of Franklin. This, understand, is not that lucrative of a profession here, as the guy also has to run a bunch of vegetable and Christmas greens stands in their respective seasons to make a living.

His boat was a small, 10-foot johnboat, and since it was loaded to capacity or beyond with two adults, I slowed my approach earlier than normal to keep from sinking the fragile craft. It was then that I noticed Hiram, the culprit, turning loose a cheap rope stringer from the side of the johnboat.

I hollered to Dick to grab the stringer as it drifted by us, but despite an arm wet to the shoulder, he barely missed it. He looked at me and said, "Two short bass." Since that was exactly what I had seen as Hiram was releasing it despite my shouted order not to, I pulled alongside.

"I need to see your license, Hiram," I stated.

"You can see it," he responded, pointing to his hat.

"I want to read it," I said.

"You can't arrest me for nothin'," he replied.

I was fast losing my patience and only upon my insistence was I handed the license.

"Hiram, I'm citing you for having two short bass in possession. I also need to check your life preservers."

"Ain't got none," he responded.

"Then, my friend, this fishing trip is over. You will have to take your boat to shore now."

Since the boat was only powered with an electric motor, it was slow getting to shore, but once there we got him off-loaded and I began to write the necessary paperwork for the two violations.

"I can't believe you are wasting my time like this," Hiram insisted as I wrote. "You ain't got no evidence."

"Hiram, my friend, we both know the magistrate reasonably well. We both have been in front of him eight or ten times. Now what I am going to do is testify, under oath, that with ten years of experience, it is my professional opinion that the two fish you turned loose upon identifying us during our approach were both bass and they were less than nine inches long, having measured hundreds in my career.

"Then I am going to call deputy Dick here to the stand, and he is going to state that his full-time job is that of a biology teacher and that is what his degree is in and it is a Master's. He will also state that he has been a deputy fish warden for over ten years and has measured hundreds of bass. Then he will tell the magistrate that he was within three feet of the fish and feels certain that they were both bass and much less than nine inches in length.

"You," I continued, "will then have a chance to explain that they were not bass and that they fell off the boat and they were plenty big. You will be able to recite your vast legal experience in front of the judge's bench. When all is said and done, it will be decided on the reliability of witnesses and whether or not I am recognized as an expert witness. It will be my word as a conservation professional, with deputy Dick as my witness against you as a professional petty marijuana grower and your witness. The judge will decide."

I had forgotten the other guy, considering all the jawing Hiram was doing and would have neglected to check him at all since I was focused, but then he spoke.

"Cain't arrest me for nothin'," he volunteered.

"'Where's your license?" I returned, suddenly remembering him.

"Right there in that car," he said, pointing to a rusted out, nondescript vehicle.

"Well, let's see it and the little book you got with it," I instructed.

He went to the car and unlocked it, got the book with the license still neatly tucked among the pages, just like he had bought it earlier that day. I took the book and the license and showed him in the book where it explained the "must be displayed on an outer garment" clause and that the glove box of the car just didn't qualify.

He was somewhat indignant as I wrote his ticket. I didn't really blame him, since it was less than a good case and certainly would not have been written under other circumstances. As I handed him his paperwork, I explained that had he just kept quiet, he would have never been checked.

The second fellow, John Smith, paid his fine to the magistrate as prescribed by law, but Hiram failed to even enter a plea. Eventually I had a warrant for his arrest and tried often to serve it at his mother's house, which was practically in sight of mine, but to no avail. Checking with my local contacts indicated that business had not been flourishing up north, so Hiram had moved south to the Carolinas.

I had to believe he would be back someday, so I just kept carrying the warrant. One day I heard through the grapevine he had returned, only to find that there were warrants out for his arrest for more drug charges. Soon he was incarcerated. I went to the jail and put a retainer on him. He would not be permitted to complete his stay at the big house until he cleared up the Fish and Boat charge against him.

When he was told this, he indicated that he would stay in, rather than pay. However, by the time release day came, he had found the money to pay both fines. I guess the facilities got a little tiring and trying on the soul.

Shortly before he passed away, Clarence "Cozy" Shearer gifted me with his original Pennsylvania Fish Warden badge. I treasure this memento of one of the last of the great old-time fish wardens. More importantly he gifted me with his friendship and a sense of how to enjoy the job. He saw to it that every time I shared a patrol vehicle with him I laughed until my sides hurt. Even when our mission of the day was serious, his synopsis of the day's events would cause me to chuckle.

103

CHAPTER 7:
Things That Go Bump in the Night

Night patrol throws a new light on everything. When I take a walk down the driveway at night I feel like large unidentifiable things lurk in the shadows, waiting to surprise me, scare me and harm me. When I went on night patrol looking to check fishermen, I became that large unidentifiable scary thing.

MID-RIVER CHECK

Deputy Mikey and I were patrolling at the Tionesta Sand and Gravel, on the Allegheny River. It was July and hot and muggy. Dark had just settled in and my shift was due to end. Policy dictated that you end your shift on time, unless you had a violation in progress. With just enough time to drive home, we took one more look around the Tionesta Pool. That is when we saw the light working.

We set up the spotting scope and were able to ascertain that there were four persons in the johnboat and they had several spears or gigs. They were working the shoreline with a light and periodically throwing one of the spears. We reasoned it through and decided it was an illegal frogging caper.

We figured they would work the bottom of the pool and then come back up our side to the car with the roof rack that was parked on the old boat ramp. We waited and watched. At one point, they speared a large snapping turtle. It was loaded in the boat, then they all got out. After much laughing and cursing, the turtle was discarded and they all climbed back into the boat. This wanton waste of the turtle was enough of a violation to justify further observation, so we continued.

At about midnight, several hours into the extended shift, the boat floated through the downstream riffle. We saddled up and drove along the river, spending the next three hours shadowing this illicit operation. Finally they neared the Hunter Station bridge. We found a large bullfrog talking along the riverside golf course. We got behind some sparse cover, where we could watch, and settled in. Though we saw them periodically throw the spears, they ignored the frog even after having it close in the light.

I could wait no longer. I had to know what was going on. If they didn't take the boat out here, it would be daylight where they next hit a road downstream. I needed a plan. I ran downstream along the golf course, back from the water's edge, while Mikey moved the car down the back road. I knew of a place where the river was shallow, just groin-deep, the whole way across.

I reached the shallow spot ahead of the boat and, keeping the light in sight, waded into the center of the river. The mist that was falling diffused their light as they drifted to me. I maneuvered directly in front of them and, as they floated within 20 feet, I spoke to them from the rainy darkness.

"Good evening fellows. State Officer. Lay down those spears. I'll need to check fishing licenses and safety equipment."

They startled audibly and then complied. I ordered them to shore and the wanton waste case was written. They were trying to spear carp, which is legal, but had been unsuccessful. All four, three men and a woman, stood by on the bank, shaking. That might have been because of the chilly dampness, but I tend to think it was the surprise of being checked in the middle of the Allegheny River, fifty yards from either shore, at 3 a.m., that made them shake.

LARGELY ON RIVER

Brent Largely loved to fish the Allegheny River for the big channel catfish and flatheads that inhabited the deeper holes. In the late '80s, the railroad track along the river was torn out and the old cinder grade became a fisherman's highway, opening up thirty miles of river that had always had limited access. Fishermen and squatters controlled the right-of-way for a few years, until Rails-to-Trails began to civilize it and gate portions. During the period of lawlessness, one of my favorite and most productive night patrols was along the abandoned rail grade.

One Friday evening, in a light drizzle, deputy Mikey and I started a patrol south along the river. We were about thirteen miles below Franklin, when I spotted Largely's car along the edge. I never hesitated, just kept rolling down the rail grade. A lantern was out on an island in the river. Obviously they had brought a car-top boat to get to the island. I was in a quandary. I sorely wanted to do a check, but knew that I would be very wet when I got there.

I began to snoop around one of the squatter camps, looking for a boat to "borrow" for a trip to the island. The squatters were all asleep, since it was nearing 1 a.m. I moved slowly in the light of their dying campfire. Suddenly I focused on a large pit bull, sleeping next to the fire, a step ahead. I quietly backed out, plan "A" thwarted.

Then I decided on another tactic. Since Largely hadn't seen the state iron and would not have been able to see the insignia anyhow, I crept up to his car. I shined my light into the window and all around the car. Soon a roar came from the island. "What are you doing there? Get away from the car!"

I continued to shine my light. Soon the three fishermen loaded gear into a boat and came across. Mikey and I turned off our lights and sneaked down the bank to positions behind trees near the water's edge. When they landed, they were greeted by two officers that stepped from behind trees. The ensuing check produced two violations which were paid. Largely at first flared up when his friend identified us as "game wardens," but immediately calmed when he saw me, saying, "That's Steiner, the fish warden. He's alright." Curiosity had killed that cat that night.

THE SACK OF WALLEYE RACE

One lovely drizzling spring Friday evening, Officer Beaver called and asked if I wanted to go up to Pymatuning Lake and help him guard some of the inflowing streams. They were full of spawning walleyes, and the bar crowd would certainly be trying to grab a few, by whatever means, around some of the bridges and culverts.

I couldn't pass up an invitation like that. I was just a rookie and needed the experience. Times like this you could get more experience in a few good days than you might earn elsewhere in a year. I saddled up and rode. For the most part, the fish are safe in the daylight. It is too easy to get caught. The experienced walleye poacher works under the cover of darkness. The weapon of choice is an inexpensive spear, one that when the race starts you can jettison.

The stage was set. After meeting Beaver and getting the game plan all laid out for me, we split up. We would very slowly start edging along Linesville Creek, toward each other. If we encountered a situation, we would try for the apprehension. If it turned out to be a runner, we would sing out in the darkness.

It was around midnight and we were on our third or fourth stretch of stream. From the brush below, I heard Beaver hollering, "Halt!" From where I sat, I could silhouette anybody running to my left in the nightlights at the high school.

I hunkered against the bushes, heart beating like a racehorse's before the gate flashes open, and then there he was. He had gotten around me in the shadows, but was sprinting across the practice field. I had always been a good runner, but I was turbocharged for my first real footrace. I felt like my feet had wings and I was gaining two steps to the culprit's one.

In seconds I pulled alongside of him and ordered him to halt or I would stop him. He was winded and stopped, hands on knees, head hanging, sucking wind. At his feet lay a feed sack of flopping walleye, must have been 30 or 40 pounds. He paid, but I always wondered whether I would have caught him if he had just dropped the fish.

SNAGGING WALLEYE IN A BOWL

Pymatuning Reservoir lies on the extreme western edge of Pennsylvania and part of it is in Ohio. It is noted for ducks that walk on the backs of carp as you feed them bread; "Murderer's Row," an abandoned railroad track near the goose sanctuary where gunners, not hunters, line up to sky-bust escaping geese; and crappie and walleye fishing.

Since there is no limit on crappies in the lake, or at least there wasn't for a long time, and no size limit either, they seldom caused any additional work. However, the walleye that ran the small tributary creeks in the spring were cause to take notice. Their delectable fillets were a great temptation. Something exciting was always happening at Pymatuning, especially at night.

At the time I was a rookie officer spending my time working out of the regional office at Franklin. Any good detail that developed, I was immediately in on. My wife, Lin, had signed on as a deputy and that certainly made for a great cover, a husband and wife fishing.

Warren Beaver was the fish warden there and he would call the office for a team to help him patrol for walleye snagging after dark and such. All the guys would take a turn going up and working with Beaver.

I recall this particular night there was a reasonably big gang of us. Jim Ansell and several others had been undercover at the spillway. The walleye congregated there and poachers would use the cover of darkness to snag them. A jig jerked through the water often produced a fish hooked in the side, face or tail. Once a snagger was caught, the cover of the arresting officers was gone, which was a problem.

The plan was simple. One law enforcement team would fish and catch someone. They would make the arrest and leave. Shortly thereafter another undercover team would arrive and do the same thing. There was a constant changeover of people, so the violators never seemed to catch on. Some nights we would use three teams in the same place, one after the other. Sometimes two guys would walk down ten minutes apart, to give the illusion of two singles.

Lin and I waited in the wings. We were in our early twenties and anxious for a chance to prove ourselves under fire. When the hoopla died down, we moved in and started fishing. It was now after midnight.

The fishermen's talk about what they would have done to Jim if they had known he was a warden was pretty funny. We knew it was just a matter of time until we would haul some culprits out of there, too, and they would be talking about us the same way. You would think after several nights of this they would get the message, but they never seemed to. Walleye fillets make men do strange things.

After Lin and I shuffled into position, I cast out a minnow and started paying attention. It was only minutes before the two young fellows next to us on the right began to jig with intensity, but they weren't in the right place. They couldn't snag a fish, no matter how hard they tried.

However, to our left on the corner of the bowl near the sanctuary wire, three guys were doing a lot better. They were in their late forties and looked pretty rough. They seemed to be onto a fish about every other cast. None appeared fair-hooked, as they quickly and secretively netted them. I would get the angle and see the snagged fish and let them continue. They soon had eight or ten, and I decided since they were drinking and had littered and were from Ohio, it was time to make a move.

I signaled Lin to get above me on high ground on the old railroad bed. When she had the high ground secured, I badged them.

"State officer!" I yelled, grabbing their stringers.

"You no-good sonofabitch, I'll kick your ass. You're not takin' those fish. We're not getting arrested."

All came rolling out from the group, as I gained a foot or two of high ground toward the bank top, then stopped and took a solid position before they could get smart and run. They had to run past me or swim.

I turned toward the two young guys who were trying to violate the law, but had been unable to due to lack of skill. "I'm deputizing you two guys."

I handed one the fish and told him to take them up to Lin and carry them to the car for her. Pointing at the biggest one, I said, "You stay here." I told Lin to call the other officers on the radio.

107

The three guys must have thought they were badly out-numbered at this point. There were four of us and only three of them and more of us arriving. They calmed down, followed me to the car, signed field receipts and paid their fines. They never noticed that we didn't have a radio and two of the four "officers" were unofficially deputized.

After all was taken care of, I thanked the two young fellows for their help and explained to them that had they been any better at snagging, they would have been standing in line to pay fines, too. They thanked me for the break.

GILLNET AT PYMATUNING

When walleye are running in the tributary creeks at Pymatuning, it is not unusual to see a hundred or so in short stretches of these small, shallow, brush-choked creeks. This makes them easy prey for poachers.

Poachers are generally an industrious lot. If they worked that hard at finding a real job, they wouldn't have to be thieving fish from recreational fishermen. But they sleep all day and thieve all night. Guys like this ensure guys like me will never have to work in a foundry. As long as there are fish poachers, the honest, law-abiding sportsmen will keep employing fish wardens.

It was getting on toward bedtime when I answered the phone. It was Beaver. He had found a section of gill net stretched across a small stream that was running full of walleye. He had been watching it, but was getting tired. He had a deputy watching it, but wondered if I could come up and take a shift waiting for the culprits to return.

Gill nets catch and kill their prey by allowing the fish to stick its head through the mesh. Then the fine web slides in behind the gill and keeps the fish from pulling out. Illegal netters need only to string the net from bank to bank and then disappear for a few hours. When they come back, they just untie the net and load it, fish and all, in a tub, throw it in a truck and are gone.

I arrived shortly before midnight and took an old portable patrol radio with me. I bundled up for a long vigil and snuggled in against a willow tree, not ten feet from the net. I sat marveling (as in jumping every time) at the night sounds of an early spring swamp. Young wardens never get scared; they get apprehensive. I was very apprehensive all alone in the dark. Occasionally I was jolted upright as a walleye, intent on getting upstream to spawn, became tangled in the netting and splashed itself to exhaustion. But nobody came for the net. As the eventless night went on, though, I got used to it.

In fact, I got so used to it that when Beaver woke me up the next morning at daylight the net was gone. I had slept right through its removal.

"BEAR" IN THE BRUSH

When your nickname is "Bear," not much more is necessary in describing you. I have always had at least one "Bear" sized deputy for special occasions. This story, however, is about a rainy night before trout season and my original "Bear" deputy.

We were patrolling Lake Irena, Bear and me, around midnight on Trout Season Eve. All around the lake burned the fires of the youth of Hazleton, partaking in the first rites of spring. Why you must get sick on cheap wine to celebrate spring is beyond me, but it had developed into a tradition. Smuggle a bottle of "Homemade Red" out of your dad's wine cellar (all homes in Hazleton have wine cellars; they double as coal bins). Hide it in your rolled up sleeping bag, grab a tackle box and fishing gear and head for the lake. Many kids never actually used the fishing gear, due to hangovers.

Around the lake grows a primeval northern barrens. It's a bit of Canada in the hard-coal region of Pennsylvania. The tradition dictates that you drink the wine, get throwing-up sick, shrug it off, make a half dozen illegal midnight casts for trout that are busy studying the game plan for tomorrow and won't bite anyway, and crawl in a wet sleeping bag and doze under the glow of the mall lights on the rain clouds. If you have read about Alaska, I am sure you can imagine that with that much wine you are seeing the aurora borealis. At daybreak you go home and sleep it off and leave the lake to the real fishermen.

It was into this tradition that I strode each trout season Eve for nine springs. I would walk around, get the fires out if it was dry, advise against littering and just exhibit a uniformed presence, because it was sorely needed. Generally my backup was my self-esteem or a rotund, little constable named Francie. But this night, I had Bear.

As I strolled from camp to camp, I made small-talk. Since the Bear seldom spoke, he usually just grunted, I let him shadow me a campsite or two back, staying out of sight to see what happened when I left. I thought maybe the early casters would challenge each other to catch a trout while they knew I was at the lake.

I eventually worked well around the lake. Up near one spring hole that always held trout, I was immediately thrown into a verbal confrontation with five or six drunks. These guys were beyond high school age, but probably had barely made it beyond grade school in reality. They were local ruffians that I knew to see, but not by name.

They cajoled and bitched and just generally got verbally uglier and uglier. Not wanting to retreat, but starting to think it would be a smart move, I figured I would play my ace if I had to. Finally the perfect lead came. "You're awful brave being out here at night, all alone at our lake, aren't you?"

"It's not your lake," I replied, "and I'm not alone, am I Bear?" I spoke loud and clear.

I was hoping the limb I had heard snap as they guffawed was Bear moving into an advantageous position in the dark.

"Gruuunnt," came the reply from closer than even I expected.

Flashlights were thumped and banged as they tried to focus in the thicket for the originator of the noise. Suddenly he came into focus, standing cross-armed and huge in the flashlight beams, and then as quickly disappeared into the black night. The problem had ended and all was cool.

When I got back to the car, I commented, "I know how big and powerful you are, but you looked ten feet tall standing in the darkness back there."

In one of the rare moments when he actually spoke, Bear responded, "I found a rock to stand on."

THE ABUTMENT JUMP

To be effective as a warden, you must come out of nowhere at all hours of the day and night, sometimes.

I had dropped deputy Mike off at his home in Oil Creek State Park one night at two or three in the morning. The world had seemed void of human life along the river for the last hour or so. The few fires that were still burning were catfishermen that we had already checked.

I decided to head up over Rynd Hill and home. As I came to the exit of the state park on Rt. 8, I noticed a car parked where Wykel Run comes into Cherrytree Run. I shut off my lights and parked and got out to see what could be going on. This area was always home to a big brown trout or two, since a deep hole had formed when the Pennsylvania Department of Transportation dumped riprap to ensure the stability of the bridge.

I eased up along the road and soon saw a young fellow in his mid-twenties, peacefully fishing. My eyes had become accustomed to the darkness and I could see a fish on a stringer in front of him, the fin showing above the water in the near darkness. He was intent on fishing and hadn't noticed my approach.

I stood on the bridge abutment, not eight feet directly behind him and six feet up. I watched for about ten minutes, and when I decided there was nothing obviously illegal going on and he was all alone, I decided the time had come to check his license.

I jumped from the abutment and landed in the soft sand and fine gravel, right next to him. I honestly thought that by now he knew I was there, having turned and looked up a couple of times.

Now 200 pounds of warden and hardware do not land softly. They make a pretty good thump. When I lit next to him, he about jumped out of his skin, shrieking something like, "Jeez-oy, don't hurt me, just you, you scared me half to death!" all in one word that took less than a second.

His license was fine and I exited. I didn't have to wonder long whether my entry had left a lasting impression on him or not. His cousin, one of my retired deputies, called the following day and was belly laughing. He said I scared the living bejeezus out of his cousin. The fisherman thought I had been air dropped.

ELEPHANT OF SURPRISE

The night was black. There was no color and no air moving. At midnight it was still tee-shirt hot. It was a great night to work the river.

I had several deputies with me as we patrolled the Oil City area of the Allegheny River. This pool always provides fishing action and subsequently law enforcement action. Tonight had been no different. We cruised Rt. 62 on the west side of the river, noting the location of the "bug fires." After checking a few fishermen behind the motel at the mouth of Oil Creek, we crossed the river on the bridge and parked the car along the street. Locking the car against vandals, since this is a somewhat vandal-type area, we slid down the bank to the railroad grade and began to move out along the tracks.

Creosote oozed out of the railroad ties and was tacky on our boots. Other than the snapping sound as we lifted our feet from the ties, all was quiet. Soon we were standing in the shadows above the first group of fishermen, three young guys. Their rods were propped in "Y" sticks and they sat back on the bank, quietly fishing, making occasional small talk. We watched for nearly half an hour until they all had cast and retrieved several times. We were sure, now, that they all needed to have a fishing license, if they were 16 years or older.

Through the binoculars, I focused on a stringer hanging in the slow current. In the lantern light, I determined that a fish was in possession and that it was a walleye, a short walleye. I set the battle plan. I would go the last 20 yards down over the loose railroad ballast in a freefall, digging my heels in to slow me enough to keep my momentum from carrying me into the river. The two deputies would stay in the shadows, alert to back me up or chase a "runner" if the situation developed. I felt I would have to get down over the bank quickly to prevent the walleye from being tossed.

I studied my course of fall down the cinder bank, then plunged over the steep incline with as much speed as I could muster and still maintain balance and control. I was nearly among the fishermen when their senses reacted to my sudden arrival. They jumped and bailed out of my way, away from the fish. Startled half out of their wits, they scattered a few steps before recognizing the uniform. One young fisherman, catching the breath which had left him at my sudden approach, blurted that I had been "the elephant of surprise." They all snickered under their breath. I quickly scooped up the stringer, only to find a smallish sucker, not a walleye. My eyes had played tricks on me in the lantern light.

A check of their licenses revealed no violations, so I climbed the bank back to my deputies. When they stepped from the shadows, they had trouble keeping their grins from getting away into full blown laughs. After we had gotten far enough from where the fishermen could hear us, one of the deputies looked at the other and repeated, "The elephant of surprise!" and a hearty laugh was had by all. That did it. I was often referred to by that phrase throughout the summer. I have since lost considerable weight.

CHAPTER 8:
Don't Drink the Water

Any animal dumb enough to use its drinking water for sewage and industrial waste disposal will not rule the earth for long.

WILKES-BARRE MINE TUNNEL

The caller said that the Susquehanna River had a sheen of oil on it near Duryea. I went up, looked and noticed that the "oil" was coming from an old mine tunnel. The floor of the tunnel was all flat concrete, except that in as far as daylight shined, about 50 feet, there was a divot out of the bottom.

I took a pollution sample bottle and walked up into the tunnel and collected a source sample and then one downstream and upstream. I began a search for a culprit, but could find nothing along the edge of the river that could be suspect.

The next day, my routine was the same. Again I took samples and, after arriving home, placed them in my basement, figuring they would serve no purpose until I located a suspect.

The third day I had just completed my sampling and frustration, when I got a radio call from our regional office, instructing me to go to the Department of Environmental Resources headquarters in Wilkes-Barre.

I was greeted warmly by the fellows I usually work with and then ushered into a board room. At the table sat all the high rollers in the water quality section of D.E.R. and the Chief of the Wilkes-Barre operations.

"Could we get you to quit sampling that Duryea site?" was the leading question.

I am not a dummy. There was a reason all the big guns were sitting there and the Fish Commission office had sent me in.

"Sure, why?" I asked.

"We'll tell you later, but for now, just quit," was the reply.

I reported the outcome to my supervisor as soon as I could get to the office in Sweet Valley. After a phone conversation with D.E.R., he instructed me to back off.

A few days later, I decided that a swing across the bridge a mile downstream wouldn't hurt anything. When I crossed and looked up, I was greeted with a sight that nearly stopped my heart. Moon suits, lots of them, hovered around the mine tunnel.

I turned the car around and headed into the area. I was greeted by men in respirators and white suits. Barrels of cleaned up absorbent booms sat everywhere and a perimeter was roped off around the tunnel site.

"I need to talk to the site commander," I told the perimeter guard. Soon I was ushered into a small trailer, the command post.

"What is so bad?" I asked.

"A bunch of stuff, but mostly cyanide gases," he replied.

I explained that I had sampled for three days and was in the tunnel.

"You're lucky you're not dead," was the response.

"Why did you guys let me in there if you knew what was going on?" I queried, more than a little mad that I had been considered expendable.

"Our field men were disguised everywhere around the site and we didn't want to blow their cover."

I left in a huff. My pollution sampling days had come to an end. That was D.E.R. work and they could have it.

Before the day was over, I was ordered to take a boat, meet WCO Bob Fasching and help stretch booms across the river. Once again, like lemmings following to the sea, I attacked the project. We got covered with the stuff and cleaned it from our boats for days. Hip boots were covered and stored in locked cars. I was a terribly slow learner.

Soon the operation was disclosed in the newspapers. A trucking outfit, nearly two air miles away from the site, had made a circle of empty tractor trailers around a bore hole in their parking lot. Tankers would pull in and discharge under pressure their lethal load into the mine hole. From there it worked its way through the labyrinth of underground mines to that mine tunnel, endangering nearly 200,000 lives above.

In the end, eleven men received jail and probation time and the fines paid by them and their companies amounted to over one million dollars. The Pennsylvania Fish Commission was forgotten in the settlement and received nothing.

If I take prematurely sick, these 11 people and those at DER and the EPA who stood and watched as I walked in, and took no action, will remember I was there.

CHERRY RUN SPILL

It was nearly midnight when Assistant Supervisor Cloyd Hollen called.

"Pennzoil has had a pollution. You better get over here."

It was unusual for an assistant supervisor to be out on a pollution call, but he said they had tried to call and couldn't get me. I hadn't been home, so the situation for Cloyd's being there was explained.

"I'm on my way," I said.

I got a uniform on, filled a Thermos with coffee and headed over.

When I arrived at Rouseville, I was greeted with a roadblock and knew it was something big. When I made my way to Cherry Run, a Class "A" Wild Trout Stream, I knew it would be a long night. Every little backwater was full of dozens of dead trout.

I found D.E.R.'s Gordon Buckley and we began an investigation. We tracked the source of the pollution to behind the truck terminal and then, using sophisticated electronic equipment, sniffed out the site. The stuff had been hosed over the bank. A trucker had just emptied it into the creek. It seemed incredible, but the only answer.

The next morning, we counted thousands of dead trout and other fish life, and then gave it up for a rest. We had interviewed a dozen truck drivers and figured one of them was lying. I thought I knew which one, but couldn't be sure.

Pennzoil was contending that due to the roadside accessibility of the site, it could have been anyone, not necessarily one of their drivers. This was an unusual negative stance for them, considering their environmental record.

We kept interviewing when the drivers came in the next day. While I could not come up with an exact "who," I was sure it was one of them and the rest were covering. I had witnesses to the site for two hours, an hour on either side of the spill time, and nobody saw anything unusual in there. Nothing but Pennzoil trucks.

The next morning was time for a move. I contacted the Attorney General's office and let them know what we had going. They were interested. Then Gordon and I headed for Pennzoil. Armed only with my Miranda Rights card, I approached the trucking supervisor. He panicked and sent me to the company C.E.O.

As the boardroom door swung open, I was met with a little bit of visual contempt. Although he was congenial, he was too busy for this. Mr. Miranda changed all that. I explained the seriousness of the crime and that it was certainly a Pennzoil truck and he was responsible.

"Can I make a call?" he asked.

"Sure," I said.

He left the room and I settled back with my coffee, awaiting the next volley. After a while, he came back.

"We have a company investigator flying in from Texas. He'll be here at 7:30. Could you meet him at the airport, drive him to the motel and brief him?"

"I would be happy to do that," I answered.

Several days later, the driver's head was delivered to me on a platter, and the Attorney General handled the paperwork. The guilty party did six months in jail and probation until fines were paid. That amounted to over $15,000 and community service. He was also fired.

ADDENDUM: Normally that's where this would end. But like Paul Harvey would have said, I thought you would like to know the rest of the story.

I was fishing the tailwaters of Kinzua Dam one day with my wife. We were talking to a couple of older guys that were there bait-fishing. I fished for an hour or so with them in sight, then I waded out to take a break on a rock with one of them. Nothing was hitting for me, and he had several nice brown trout. I thought I might learn something. Conversation eventually led around to his being retired. I told him I was, too, and that I had been the fish warden in Venango County.

"My son was scared to death by one of you," he started. "There was a gasoline spill that killed lots of trout. He was sitting in his office a day or two later, thinking it was all over and in comes this guy. Wants to talk to him alone. Sits him down and reads him his rights, just like on TV before you go to jail in handcuffs. Scared him half to death."

"That was me. Your son must be George," I said.

"Yeah," he replied.

I sat thinking about how officers nationwide had worried that the Miranda Decision was going to compromise law enforcement. It never did anything but make my job easier.

OIL SPILLER WITH A GUN

I got the call from my supervisor on a day off.

"There are six or seven D.E.R. guys being held at gun point on a pollution over on Sage Run. It's an old guy and he won't let them in to sample a pollution. They want you to come and back them up."

At the time I was working hard through my union to get Waterways Conservation Officers classed and paid correctly for what they did. My response indicated it.

"Let me get this straight. There are six or seven pay-grade 38s from the D.E.R. that want one lone pay-grade 34 to come to their rescue?"

"Now's no time to argue that," the boss responded.

"I'm on a day off. Send the State Police," I countered.

"Get a uniform on and roll," he ordered. The phone clicked.

I felt like Paladin, "Have Gun; Will Travel." I couldn't imagine what I was getting into this time, nor could I imagine why I was getting into it. When I got there, there was an old man in his late seventies leaning against the outside of a little building and a half dozen D.E.R. guys sitting in their vehicles across the road.

"What's up?" I quizzed the pollution investigation people.

"Looks like an old gas or kerosene tank has rusted out underground and is leaking into the stream," was the reply.

"What's this about a shotgun?" I asked before crossing the road.

"He said if we try to take samples and arrest him, he is going to go get a shotgun."

I felt better already. I walked across the street right to the old guy, loading a chew of tobacco as I crossed. I offered him a chew as I got near him, which he waved off. I asked him what the problem was. "Old tank's leaking. They want to arrest me."

"They're goin' to and I'm goin' to," I responded as I leaned on the side of the garage that was also holding him up.

"Why?" he asked.

"Because it's the law that the state legislators that you elected and pay passed. They hired those guys," I said, pointing across the street, "and me to enforce it. But if you help me out on this one, I will get you off on the low end of the money scale."

"You'd do that?"

"Sure, I like old guys."

"Thanks," he said.

I motioned the pollution team over. They took samples and had the old timer get a friend with a backhoe to remove the tank and seed the area. The price of that went toward the fine, so effectively it cost him only for the work. I whacked him a couple hundred dollars as required by law. He thought I was the good guy.

However, I can't understand why D.E.R. (now D.E.P.) thinks for one minute that they don't want to wear law enforcement uniforms and equipment and then continually call us for backup. Even park people are uniformed and outfitted with police gear. Surely, someone must realize that water pollution enforcement is police work, too.

DIESEL BEAR

The bad news is that one-half of the water in the Commonwealth suffers from some sort of industrial pollution, probably more. The good news is that about 50 years ago, people started to notice. I don't believe that politicians will be politicians for long if they ever roll back environmental safeguards to create larger industrial profits. I for one like clean air and water and abhor any politician that would sacrifice the lives of many for the greed of a few.

Over the years, I have been involved in investigating literally hundreds of pollutions. Many of them were cut and dried "I did it, I'll pay. How much?" sort of things. But some of them took a little more effort. It is the pollution cases I had to work for that make the best stories.

I hooked up with a Pennsylvania Department of Environmental Resources water quality specialist and went to investigate an oil spill in Cornplanter Run. Cornplanter Run flows from a mountain valley that is used by the locals as a dump. It runs past some old shanties and houses, through a short culvert-enclosed section and into Oil Creek. The upper end of Cornplanter Run and its tributaries are in an oil field.

Despite all that this stream has going against it, it holds a fair amount of wild brook trout. Some had died. We began the investigation by driving along the creek and in short order had identified the pollution scene. It had been caused by an overflow to a home heating oil storage tank when it was being filled. Nobody claimed to know when it happened or had noticed it at the home. The driver knew nothing, too.

We began to walk the damage zone. As the little run passed under a driveway and entered the creek, we came on the evidence we needed to prove the suspects were aware of the problem. The ditch had been dammed with rocks and an effort made to sop up the oil sheen. A large teddy bear had been anchored across the flow with rocks and logs. After taking photos of the scene, we set the bear upright on the culvert and took another photo, of the "Diesel Bear." It served to remind us to make the point in court that pollution, like forest fires, is not good for forest inhabitants.

NAMING BOWLER BROOK

Explorers of this continent missed very few landmarks as they traipsed around the new country, naming things. But somewhere along the line, about the time they got to streams less than ten feet wide, they just threw up their collective hands in frustration and gave up. By so doing, they left thousands of little tributaries unnamed. I have always wanted to name a stream, but never figured out how to go about doing so. Not until one icy night in the late '80s. Again, it was a pollution call.

I was called to the scene of a truck wreck on Rt. 322, just east of Seneca. A truck was carrying hot wax from one of the local refineries and failed to negotiate a particularly tough turn. The tank tore open, spilling a large part of the load onto the frozen pavement. The wax instantly solidified and blocked the road and the culvert and coated a beautiful little stream that fell through boulders and hemlocks into Hall's Run. The cleanup took the biggest part of the night and, as the word of the spectacular wreck spread, TV cameras began to arrive. Soon my Department of Environmental Resources sidekick, Buckley, and I were being interviewed over and over again.

We were smooth at explaining what the product was, how the cleanup was going and that it appeared that the small unnamed tributary had been spared real tragedy. A cute little lady TV reporter signaled for the lights to be turned on and another interview began.

"The truck driver lost control and hit the rock over there," my D.E.R. counterpart explained, motioning slowly, giving the camera a chance to pan in and out, "spilling the hot wax to the ground. It flowed through this culvert and into that unnamed tributary."

The signal was given to stop and the lights went out.

"Why are they always unnamed tributaries?" the reporter asked, turning to me.

"You want it named, we'll name it," I replied.

"You can't do that," Buckley pleaded.

The camera was on, Buckley hid in the shadows and I explained how "the truck had hit the rock, the wax had been released to the ground, flowed into the culvert and had entered Bowler Brook."

The camera and lights went out, the reporter smiled and thanked me for the interview and left.

"Bowler Brook?" Buckley quizzed from the shadows.

"Bowler Brook," I said. I pointed to a sign under a neighboring mailbox. It said "The Bowlers."

He looked at me again and I explained. "I have looked at lots of topo maps and never seen a brook in Pennsylvania. I thought we should have a brook."

The maps still have the little tributary as unnamed, but Buckley, the reporter and everyone that saw that newscast now know it as "Bowler Brook."

ANYTHING WILL SMELL BETTER THAN THIS

A call came from the region office. There was oil in the creek. A little tributary to Hall's Run, near Seneca. It was an overcast, muggy day in early September. When we arrived, the little valley reeked of fuel oil. Buckley was again my D.E.R. sidekick. We tromped along the stream, following it to a broken-down log truck in the woods. For four hours we worked in the fumes of fuel oil, without a fresh breath of air.

After we had sampled and photographed and tried to locate the owner and all the other things you do in a pollution investigation, we got back to the car. As we drew near the car, I could hear the radio calling me and hurried to get in, but missed the call. Before calling headquarters back, I took off my fuel-oil-covered boots and remarked to Buckley, "I don't know what they want, but I'll bet it will smell better than this job." I would have lost the bet. We spent the next five hours working at a tributary to Little Scrubgrass Creek, on a manure spill.

HOT WAX VIDEO

One of the big refineries in Oil City had a spill of liquid wax. Well, it was liquid when it hit Oil Creek, but the creek was cold and so was the Allegheny River. By the time the wax had gotten a half mile down the river, it had solidified on everything it touched. Rocks, bridge piers, logs, ducks and anything else in its way. Video cameras were just coming into their own, and a deputy of mine had one. I called him and, before long, Buckley, my D.E.R. counterpart, and I were starring in a movie about the hot wax spill at Oil City.

We had photos of sampling, environmental damage, the cleanup and much more. It got out of control. Before long, copies showed up within the agencies with credits and titles, etc. It became "The Hot Wax Video," but to the best of my knowledge never won an Oscar and never received a rating. The company responsible for the spill promptly paid when showed the videotaped sequence with the well-waxed ducks. I always thought the quackers should have received "Best Supporting Actor" nominations.

MY DAUGHTER WON'T TALK TO ME, I'M A POLLUTER

One investigation into a caustic release that killed trout in the upper reaches of Big Wapwallopen Creek led me to several companies. Both had simultaneously, without any preplanning, released substances with very high pH readings into the water. The net result was that after a good rain, the upper reaches jumped to a pH of 12 and fried fish for a mile or so.

The investigation was confusing because of the dual participants. It took some time to sort out who was responsible for what. Eventually justice prevailed. But not before the newspapers got hold of the story. Soon I was settling cases and doing the paperwork. As I went to settle the first case, I sat with the corporate executive officer who had been mentioned by name in one of the articles in the local newspaper.

"I don't mind paying the thousand-dollar fine," he stated, "and the publicity didn't bother me. But what really got me was when my fifteen-year-old daughter sat at the supper table and refused to talk to me because I was a polluter."

I accepted his check for the violation and went to the high school and bought my hunting buddy, the C.E.O.'s daughter's homeroom teacher, a coffee.

OIL HAWK, GRASSHOPPER PUMP

Sometimes ultimate success is so close, but fate denies it. I worked nearly daily with a D.E.R. oil and gas specialist, Doug Neely, for the first several years after arriving in Venango County. We became good friends and rode herd on the booming oil and gas well drilling business.

One day when I was off duty, Doug was checking a small spill and came upon a hawk covered with oil sitting nearby. While he tried to get a photo of the oil-soaked hawk, it got nervous and jumped and climbed to the top of a grasshopper pump and sat and posed for some time. Doug has photos of the dying bird, but they are not of the quality necessary for magazine and newspaper reproduction. I only wonder what the regulations would now be like on the gas and oil industry had I been there with my quality camera gear.

SIT DOWN BOY

The floods of the early and mid-70s ravaged the Susquehanna River valley. The Army Corps of Engineers at the time were deluged with cries of more dikes, higher dikes. Public meetings were held almost weekly in the Wilkes-Barre area. My boss, Bob Perry, suggested that he and I attend one of these public meetings just to see which way the wind was blowing.

I hadn't yet learned to plot an attack. I was still a street fighter and not a very smart one. So, when the cry came to dredge the river and dam it and dike it, I jumped to my feet in a room of several hundred people and erupted in a plea for environmental sanity. The grandmotherly little old lady next to me got to her feet before I could really get rolling and sharply elbowed me in the ribs, knocking the air out of me and back into my seat. She then turned on me with a vengeance and gave me a tongue lashing about homes and lives versus the environment and told me to, "Stay set down and shut up."

I told my boss that I thought the next time I would wear my uniform, but I don't think he heard me. He was busy holding his sides, snickering.

YOU SWAM IN THAT?

East Sandy Creek was once a sewer for the waste of the coal mining industry. They polluted it with silt when they opened the mines, then they poured the acidic water from mine dewatering into it and finished off whatever life had been there. When they burned the coal, acid rain fell on the watershed and prevented a rapid comeback. But Ma Nature has friends and they worked long and diligently and, eventually, through modern technology, some life came back to the stream in the beautiful, wooded valley. With better water quality came the fish stocking truck. But the distinctive mine-acid orange staining on the creek rocks never went away.

After stocking East Sandy Creek one warm May day, I pulled to a large hole along the creek and noticed many cars and kids. I suspected shenanigans because I was a kid once and recognized the right mixture of water, trout and kids skipping school. However, I was surprised. The bulk of the kids were sunning themselves on a big rock on the other side of the creek, like so many turtles. One young loudmouth was sitting on a stump, smoking a cigarette and playing the part of the tough guy.

"What do you want, fish cop?" he challenged.

"How did they get over there?" I responded, motioning toward to the young people across the water.

"Swam. How do you think?" he mouthed.

I saw the smirks on the faces of his fan club.

"In that water?" I said pointing and acting surprised.

"Yeah. Why? Is there something wrong with it?" He was worried now.

"Wow," I said, shaking my head. I drove away, noticing in the rearview mirror the fading smiles on the rock across the creek. I wish I had more time to sneak back and watch how many swam back, how many tiptoed through the shallow riffle, and how many walked down to the bridge a mile below.

CALL THE POSSE

"There's a pollution in Carbon County and Officer Ohlsen is on sick leave. We need you to get there fast. State Police have Interstate 80 shut down."

When the boss calls, you run. I jumped into my uniform, saddled up the Matador and hit the highway. Once I got on I-80 I reached under the seat, blew the dust off my coffee-mug-sized, plug in the cigarette lighter accessory hole, red light and stepped on the gas.

In fifteen minutes I was converging on the traffic backup. I took the berm around them and arrived at the state police road block. They waved me through. I stepped on it ... for about 100 yards, stopped and backed up.

"Why is the road blocked for a pollution?" I quizzed the trooper.

"Toxic gas truck rolled over, fish are dying in the creek."

"Do you think this uniform and badge is enough protection for me to go in there?" I further questioned. He smiled.

We waited for the moon suits to show up from the Department of Environmental Protection. I got copies of their reports in the mail, counted dead fish a few days later when the air had cleared and settled my emergency pollution case.

The moral of the story is to never be in a hurry when you are on overtime.

At right, taking water samples to test for pollution.

CHAPTER 9:
Thou Shalt Not Litter

Humans, for the most part, are closely related to pigs. Until they evolve to where they quit throwing their rubbish to the ground of their world, they stand no chance of becoming the earth's dominant life force.

CATCHIN' THE FLYIN' BOTTLE

The falls at Bear Creek were located several miles upstream from the Francis E. Walter Reservoir. Since this was just around the corner from one of my primary work locations, my deputies and I would often find time to work the falls for littering violations. Waterfalls along a road in a wild area five miles out of town are an attraction of great magnitude for party animals. They can't seem to enjoy the beauty of the place without a beer in their hand. They also like to watch the cans float over the falls.

One summer, the deputies and I decided to clean up the area through an all-out antilittering campaign. It was a very easy area to work when there was a crowd. You would just park along the road among the other cars, which oftentimes numbered nearly 50, and slither off into the beautiful rhododendrons that surrounded the falls area. With a pair of field glasses and a little patience, within an hour you would have an opportunity to watch a bottle or can pitched into the brush, a sure and solid case.

Among my crew, one officer in particular was the most patient on this assignment. Bob took it real personal that people were ignorant enough to litter. I always tried to assure him that it was just job security at its best. As you can imagine, as that summer progressed, it became harder and harder to get a case. The quarry was getting gun shy, and new techniques were needed. So we would slip into a different patch of rhododendron each time from a different parking area.

One sunny day, my ace litter man moved in behind a party of six or eight young fellows basking on the rocks like seals and sucking down the suds. The deputy took a seat some 10 or 15 feet behind them, on a stump surrounded by head-high greenery. It was only a matter of minutes until one of the young fellows put the final tilt to a brown-bottled beverage. After enjoying every last drop, he sighed, wiped his mouth on his shirt sleeve and flipped the bottle into the bushes.

Much to his amazement a hand came straight up out of the bushes and caught the bottle. There was no argument on that case.

KAYAKS AND THE WINE BOTTLE

To have been chosen and trained to operate the first and only patrol kayak in the Fish Commission was quite an honor. I reflect now and realize, as that was when I was at my paunchiest, they could have saved the cost of a spray skirt. When you added to this not-so-lovely scene a plastic helmet and a pair of blue, baggy shorts, you had on the placid waters of F.E. Walter Dam what appeared to be a lot of things, none of which was a fish warden.

With the sun shining brightly, I watched a green jug of wine take four college guys around the point for a party. I paddled near them, anonymous among dozens of other kayakers-in-training during the day. A little after three in the afternoon, I noticed the guys set the bottle on a rock. Picking up stones, they stepped back and began pelting the bottle until it broke.

I paddled in and started off with, "You guys ain't goin' to believe this. Come here. I want to show you something."

When they moved close, I reached into my kayak and fumbled a plastic bag from my baggy shorts. I untied the twist tie and produced a very shiny ID and badge. I sent them down to the state car, where I met them and proceeded to relieve them of funding that I'm sure they felt could have been better spent on more wine.

SUPERMAN

Littering has always stuck in my craw. It takes a life form lower that a possum's belly to throw trash along streams, roadways and other wild places. I am convinced that mankind would cover itself with its own garbage, given half a chance. I have felt that way since very early in my life. I used to get upset with other kids in grade school who threw candy wrappers on the ground.

It was late the first day of buck season, 1974. I was just out of training school, having graduated the week before. I hadn't even gotten to try my badge on anyone yet.

The snow in Somerset County forced my wife, Lin, and I to forego our hunt there and try to make it back to Franklin, where I was to be at work in the morning. As we traveled north, the roads got better and better. By 2:30 in the afternoon we were getting out of the truck along Rt. 8, on State Game Lands 39.

There was one car parked next to us. In it sat an adult and an older teen. They were eating their lunch. Six feet away we were suiting up to hunt the last couple of hours. Just as I went to leave, out of their car windows came their lunch wrappers and such.

I quickly jumped back into the bed of my pickup, on which I had a stand-up cap, and put on my Fish Commission uniform. I exited the rear door in complete officer regalia. I apprehended the litterbugs and they paid fines.

"You did that just like Superman," was the only comment I heard as I wrote the tickets.

ADDENDUM: This was the first case I ever wrote. It was fitting that it was a litter case; I went on to write hundreds of them in my career.

WHEN YOU'RE TIRED OF RUNNING, WE'LL WRITE THIS

After spending 16 months as a freelance warden, working out of the Northwest Region Office, I was assigned my own district. I was located in Luzerne County, in the northeast part of the state. The Deputy Chief of Law Enforcement at the time was Ed Manhart. Ed had been an instructor at our training school. He also had had this same district before he was promoted into the Harrisburg headquarters.

One sunny spring morning, Ed drove up from Harrisburg to work with me in the field for a day. It was a sort of "show the new guy around" visit. We had gotten some cases and, as the afternoon wore on, Ed decided he would show me one of his old littering hot spots. I forget the name of the little run now, but it was blessed with waterfalls in a wooded glen. Waterfalls and big rocks lent themselves to beer parties. For all its blessings, the stream also had a curse. It was right outside of Wilkes-Barre.

We drove along until we spotted several cars sitting in a cluster at one of the spots Ed knew accessed some large, streamside rocks. Sure enough, as we crept in, a party was in progress. I eased as close as I could and watched until someone pitched a beer can into the water. It happened to be a pretty young girl in shorts, halter top and a pair of platform shoes.

As I "magically" appeared from the trees, someone shouted, "Cops!" and the whole crew scattered like a flushed covey of quail. I began running behind the young lady that had thrown the can. As we ran I spoke to her: "When you get tired of running, let me know and we can sit down and write this citation."

She quickly realized that she wasn't going to outrun me and sat down and began to cry. That didn't work either. Soon her friends began to return to the scene and, seeing us sitting on the rock, joined us. They all kicked in and paid her fine.

MILLER FARM BRIDGE CASE

A young officer learns early that not all is as it seems most of the time. Generally it is worse. You are trained to think that way and it becomes a self-preservation technique.

I stood in fishing togs on Miller Farm bridge over Oil Creek, waiting with a friend for the evening mayfly hatch to begin. There were still four hours of daylight left. On the bridge were a young boy and a woman fishing to trout you could see below. It was amusing to watch the trout chase the bait as it swung past them and then reject it once they had identified it as a hoax.

On the west abutment sat a rather large, soft-looking guy with two bait containers next to him. I had him pegged as the father/husband of the two on the bridge. Five or six cars passed by and several screaming dirt bikes. I was wishing I was in uniform. The dirt bikes weren't licensed and are not allowed in the state park. They didn't even throttle down, so I made no attempt at stopping them. For a park violation, I couldn't see getting anybody hurt, especially me.

I moved and looked off the downstream side of the bridge for awhile, still watching for the flies to begin hatching. When I turned around, the big guy was walking toward the east end of the bridge with his equipment in his hand. The bait containers were on the ground along the abutment. He got in his car and started back across. I figured he was going to pick up his wife and boy and leave. He had littered. I flagged him down, badged him and instructed him to pull over. He began a vehement recitation that ended in his getting a ticket.

Clearly, in my mind he had pitched the containers, went and got the vehicle, was going to pick up his family and leave. He would not have thrown the containers down along the abutments if he was not going to leave them.

I was surprised that he elected to take a hearing. Generally on something this cut and dried, the defendant realizes that he got caught and pleads guilty and pays the fine.

At the hearing I gave the state's testimony in the beginning and listened as the defendant presented his defense. He stated he had not intended to leave at all, but was moving the car since there was all the motorbike traffic and his young daughter was sleeping in the vehicle. He hadn't wanted to be that far away from her. The containers probably blew off the abutment after he walked over to get the car.

It made sense to me. I signaled the magistrate I would like to have a recess for a few minutes. I met with her in the back room. I told her the state felt that he should be found not guilty, as there certainly had been a little girl in the car. I remembered her laughing with the young boy while I was writing the ticket. I regretted that I had not been presented with these facts in a nonvolatile manner the day of the occurrence.

The defendant was found not guilty and informed of the state's apologies. I relearned the lesson of not hurrying to write a ticket until you have calmed the situation and reviewed all the evidence.

ADDENDUM: The defendant many years later was arrested for embezzling a large sum of money from an old lady. Maybe I should rethink that relearned lesson ... but probably not.

PLAYBOY UNDER THE MATTRESS

There is a little coal-patch town in Schuylkill County that they call Mary D. I'm not sure why. But the greatest litterbug arrester of Fish Commission history was raised there, Officer Joe Kopena. Joe was driving coal trucks and being a deputy in his spare time when he got called up to "the show." Joe's first assignment as a full-time officer was Forest County.

Joe was a large, robust man. He was as loud as he was powerful and he often threw up a screen of bluster just to confuse the situation. But no matter how long it would take, Joe would wait out someone that he thought was going to litter. He prided himself on always getting his man when it came to litterbugs.

The morning was cold when I left to work with Joe, stocking Tubb's Run. I arrived at the Tionesta Hatchery, the meeting place, before Joe. I was talking to Melvin and several of the other hatchery and maintenance workers, when one of them mentioned that someone had dumped two old mattresses over the bank on the first turn in the road along Tubb's Run, just above the hatchery.

Melvin had a plan. He had borrowed a couple of Playboy magazines from Joe. They had Joe's name and address on the label. Magazine labels had been the downfall of many litterbugs when Joe got to rooting through garbage bags. The plan was for me to hurry up and place the magazines between the mattresses. The deed was done without even time for a peek at a centerfold.

The fish truck was loaded and we quickly had a procession of twenty or so cars to help us stock. One of the stocking help, knowing Joe's anti-litter campaign, mentioned the mattresses to Joe.

"I'll get the dirty bastard," Joe said.

He took littering in Forest County real personal. By the time we got up to the mattresses, Joe was worked up to a lather, foaming at the mouth. He was stomping and snorting and bellowing as only Joe could.

"I'll get 'im! I'll get 'im! I'll find out who the dirty sumbitch is, and I'll get 'im!"

He got louder and louder. He stomped down over the bank and, like the bear of a man that he was, took one of the mattresses by the corner with one hand and tossed it up toward the road.

When he did, the magazines slid down the top of the other mattress. He pounced on them like a cat on a mouse.

"Now I'll get 'im! Now I'll get the dirty bastard!" he bellowed, holding his prizes up and waving them in his hand. He literally jogged back up the bank to his car.

"Whose name's on them, Joe?" someone in the crowd called, seeing Joe study the labels.

Joe went around the car and reached in and got his reading glasses. Then he flushed red.

"Whose name?" came the cry again. Still no answer.

Finally, after looking at the labels for a moment and regrouping his thoughts, he said, "They're torn. I can't read them."

The stocking went on throughout the day, me riding with Joe. Every now and then he would look at me and say, "You knew."

"I didn't know, Joe."

"You knew," he would say and he would stare at me.

FISH BEAR ON A BIKE

When violators get caught doing something stupid, they inevitably have an excuse that makes sense to them or they try to make it your fault for catching them. You get used to it.

One lovely spring day toward the beginning of April, I got my issued patrol bicycle down off the rack and planned a patrol of recently stocked Oil Creek. The only access is along the bicycle trail at Oil Creek State Park, so it is a relatively safe bet you will not encounter any violations. However, it is absolutely necessary that you patrol it occasionally, just to keep the honest persons honest and to reinforce your conviction that nothing is going on.

Since it was so nice, I invited my wife, who had once been a deputy, to get her bike and ride along. A perk of the job, I suppose. We did the ride up along the creek to Drake Well Museum and roamed around the grounds for a short while, then sat on a bench in the upper creek access parking lot. I was in uniform and her in civvies, watching the people and stream and somewhat hidden by two bicycles.

Two young couples arrived in a car, got out and walked right by us and looked at the stream. Beside me was a garbage can. One couple was drinking beer. I doubted they were old enough, but they hadn't been driving and, without a vehicle and radio, I would be getting beyond practical law enforcement to pursue that avenue at that time. So I just watched.

After finishing off the beer, the young fellow walked to the woods edge and dropped the bottle. This amazed me, since it was a farther walk than the garbage can. I figured he had seen the badge and didn't want to risk getting close to me again with the beer, since he was underage.

As they were about to reenter the car to leave, I rode over on my bike, leaving my wife sitting on the bench. I told him I would need to see ID and, much to my amazement, he was over 21, as was the girl. However, he had littered and would have to deal with that.

He began a tirade about how he didn't have any money, and if I cited him his girlfriend would leave him, and if she left him he would probably quit his job and eventually commit suicide and it would be all my fault. I had trouble following the line of logic, so I asked him to repeat it. Seeing things were not going smoothly, Lin had pedaled to where she could be inconspicuous and listen. She jotted down some ID on the vehicle and persons, should things turn ugly. They didn't. They just got funny.

The litterbug went on and repeated the whole line of logic again for all to hear. When he finally ran out of breath, I turned to his girlfriend and asked, "If I cite him, are you going to leave him?"

She looked at him and then me and replied, "No."

"Good," I said. "I didn't want his suicide on my conscience forever." And I gave him his ticket. He paid promptly.

The return trip was filled with looking at wildflowers, talking to nice folks riding their bikes, and stopping occasionally to repeat the young fellow's "logic" and laugh.

HARVEY'S CREEK NIGHT PATROL

Nighttime. Dark is the time of smells and noises. The pleasant sound of a creek. The perfume of a lady at your side. And a place back away from it all to park the car and talk.

The 1996 trout stamp depicted a creek that is just such a place, Harvey's Creek. Every Saturday and Sunday morning, anywhere a fisherman could pull off the road along the stream would be littered with fresh beer and soda pop cans. From time to time my counterpart in northern Luzerne County would set up a raid on the many parking spots along Harvey's Creek. Generally there would be three or four district officers, some local and state police and a bunch of deputies.

The trick was to hide and when a bottle or can hit the ground, turn your lights on and come out of the bushes. If you saw anything that the police were interested in, underage drinking, drugs or the such, you would call for them. If not, you would write a littering ticket. For lack of anything better to do on weekend nights, I would round up a car full of deputies and participate in this drill.

One such rainy evening, we turned into a long, narrow parking area. When we pulled off the road, we had our high beams on and noticed a car at the far end of the pull-off. Knowing we couldn't get out and hide, I just sat, wipers going, with the high beams on. Earl was sitting in the middle and Bob was at the other door of the marked pickup truck we sat in. I figured maybe we would get lucky and someone would throw a can in front of us before they could identify the vehicle.

Since they had the music blaring in their car and the windows down, we followed suit. Something about when in Rome. Soon one of them hollered at us to turn our high beams down. I ignored them and turned up the country western music until it drowned out or at least made their hard rock hard to hear.

The next thing that I knew, their car moved towards ours and stopped about forty yards in front of us. Four high-school-age kids jumped out and one shouted to turn off that hillbilly music and turn down those high beams. The expletives he interjected in his demands indicated, to me, that he was not happy when someone infringed on his right to listen to loud music. I once again did nothing.

Finally, the mouthpiece threw his beer can to the ground and said, "That's it. Let's kick some ass!"

With that battle cry, they all puffed up like bantam roosters and began to stride for the car like miniature John Waynes. Earl, in the middle, wanted to get out and assume a battle line. I had more faith in badges and insignias and told him and Bob to just sit tight.

Finally, as the high-school hotshots closed to within a few feet of the hood, I swung open the truck door, complete with insignia, and rounded it with the flashlight in my hand shining on my badge. I stated loud and clear, "State Officers, fellows. We will need to see some IDs."

There was a lot of blubbering and "I didn't know" and "please don'ts" and all the other things that you normally hear when someone finally realizes that their aggressive posture has just reduced their state of being to so much paperwork.

When all was said and done, I would like to say that with our help these four young men had seen the light and never drank strong liquor again. I doubt it, but I do bet they found another place to drink it and they probably just leave when someone pulls in with high beams on.

CHAPTER 10:
Publicity Stunts

Media interviews are fun. In a pre-recorded interview, you can say a bad word and the cameraman knows that you made a mistake and they start over from the question. Generally they are very helpful. I always enjoyed working with the media to present the Fish Commission's viewpoint or information. Live interviews are great fun. You own your mistakes. There is no chance for a retake. The public has already heard you. You got to be on your game.

Doing presentations to clubs, assemblies and other large groups leaves no room for error, either. Even after I retired, I continued doing standup speaking engagements. I was pretty darn good but, as they say, "nobody is perfect" and "you can't win them all."

BISHOP HOBAN FLUB

George was the environmental class instructor at Bishop Hoban High School in Wilkes-Barre. For several summers, every Monday, George and his students would show up to work on stream habitat improvement on the Oley Creek in the Game Lands. Many jack dams, deflectors and mud sills were constructed by this fine group of young people.

I looked forward to working with these kids, as they moved wheelbarrows full of rock, logs and dirt to restore the beautiful, small brook trout stream to some semblance of normalcy, after the flooding of the early 1970s, coupled with the redirection caused by I-80, had adversely impacted it. Some stretches of this stream had been left relatively barren and featureless.

Their sweat and determination eventually led to the group's winning a national environmental award. Imagine the pride I felt when asked to present the award to the kids at the graduation ceremonies at the high school.

I am normally a very good public speaker. I do large crowds often and adlib well. I had so many good things to say that I didn't bother to write any of them down. I felt certain they would spontaneously jump to mind as I needed them, and I could give it a personal touch that would be better than any written presentation speech. I elected to do the presentation in our "public relations suit," a green affair with only a pocket emblem on the blazer.

I was paralyzed as I stood in front of these kids and their parents, friends and teachers. I could only read the certificate and nothing more. I couldn't even remember what it was that they had done. I had given my absolute worse performance at the biggest game in my career. I had let my friends down. I was upset with myself. I was feeling low.

As I walked to the state car, an older man approached me and flashed some credentials.

"What are you doing using a state car to attend your kid's graduation?" he quizzed.

"Get out of my way before I arrest you for interfering with an officer," I snapped, moving aggressively toward him and the car door. He stepped aside and I drove away, "in a mood." If he followed up on it, he must have found out what the deal was because I never heard another word out of him.

ADDENDUM: In January of 2020 I walked the Oley Creek and could still identify five or six of the stream improvement devices the high school kids and I put in during the summers of the early 1980s, nearly forty years ago. Our motto had been, "Big rocks last forever. More big rocks."

LIVE AT FIVE

One evening, with the rain pelting down and the wind howling, driving it sideways, I got a call.

"This is WBRE-TV in Wilkes-Barre. Tomorrow is trout season and we were wondering if we could do an interview with you at F.E. Walter Dam," the caller said.

"Sure, when?" I replied.

"In about an hour." Click.

I headed over, expecting a taped interview for the 11 o'clock news. When I got there, they were trying to set up and were in a panic.

"We can't get our signals out and only have ten minutes to live broadcast," they said.

"Follow me."

They quickly reloaded their van and I headed them up to the top of the dam. I had a gate key.

The equipment was reassembled and then I was told, "You are going to be live on the sports segment in a few minutes. This monitor here will have the sportscaster on it, this one will let you watch yourself and this one will show you what we are showing at a given time. Ready, one, two, three," and a bank of lights came on from the inside of the van.

"So tomorrow's the big day," the sportscaster started.

"Yep," I replied, holding onto my hat in the howling wind. The camera only focused on me a minute and then it was back to the studio, where the warm and dry sportscaster that knew nothing about fishing went fishing for some more questions.

"Fishing season starts?" he asked inquisitively.

"Yep."

"What time?" I thought he was shouting, but I wasn't sure.

"Eight."

Before I could regroup my thoughts, the camera would go off of me and back to the studio.

"How big is the lake?" he struggled for more to say.

"One hundred arrows," I replied.

The wind howled and I leaned into it, shivering and shaking. Every time I looked for myself on a monitor, it was the sportscaster. When it was me, I couldn't talk and watch myself. It's kind of like walking and chewing gum at the same time. My Stetson was always down over my eyes and the wind blew my tie over my shoulder.

"Thanks," the warm, dry sportscaster said and then I watched him say, "That concludes our interview with the game warden on this, the night before trout season."

All was not lost.

MY GREATEST PUBLICITY STUNT

Whether doing law enforcement or public relations, you must seize the moment. The Army Corps of Engineers had started to raise the water level in the F.E. Walter Dam. It was rising over the parking lot when we arrived. One car remained on the parking lot and the wheels were already in the water.

I grabbed my boat and ran up and found the hapless chap in his canoe, way upstream several hours later. When we got back to the ramp, his car had water up to the bumpers.

It was then I noticed a crowd had formed and deputy Don was there with his ever-present camera. He worked as a photographer for the area's newspaper. I was about to seize the moment. I quickly uncoupled the boat trailer, walked past the little yipping dog that tried to block my entry and grabbed a tow chain out of the back of my patrol truck.

I backed in as deep as I dared without flooding my vehicle's working parts, and got out into the water with only uniform boots and clothing and helped the guy hook the chain to his car. I hooked it to my trailer hitch and he reached in and popped his car out of gear. I towed it to safety with cameras clicking and a crowd watching. I made the sports page.

The stuff heroes are made of. Sometimes it doesn't take much.

ANGLER SALES, LAKE IRENA

At one time, the sale of the official agency magazine, "The Angler," was a highly stressed part of each officer's duties. I set a goal for myself each year of 50 subscriptions and worked at it through the year. It was a good little magazine that tended to sell itself if you could show someone a copy, and soon I had sold copies to all the persons that were easily swayed. Then when their renewal came in the mail, they would just fill it out and send it back and I would get no credit for the sale. I decided to do something about this problem to make it easy on myself.

Trout stockings were announced to the public at that time, so I knew there would be a crowd at Lake Irena this fine spring morning. My "Angler" sales were lacking behind my self-set goal, so I decided it was time to make a move.

I arrived at the lake an hour early and started to peddle magazines. The five or six individuals that bought a subscription that spring morning were given a receipt from an official pad, which was yellow in color.

When the truck arrived, I started at the one end of the lake and generally made two or three stops on each of the two sides I could get to easily. As I began to unload the first buckets of fish, I recognized one fellow that had bought a subscription. I asked him if he had a "yellow slip" loud enough for all to hear. He held it up and waved it.

I instructed the bucket carriers to make sure they put several buckets right in front of that guy. That is when the thought hit me. I stayed on top of the walkway on the truck and moved to the next yellow slip. I asked him good and loud to "show me your yellow slip" and he did. Again I instructed the carriers to put several buckets right in front of him. By the end of the stocking, each of the persons that had bought a subscription had received their perceived bonus and the trout were distributed the same as they always were.

Before I could leave, I had several fellows ask how they could get a yellow slip for the next week. I explained about the subscriptions and that I only sold them in the morning before the truck arrived, since I got busy with law enforcement after the stocking. I also explained to a few that said they had already subscribed that I could renew subscriptions if they carried their mailing label with them, so I could tell when it expired.

From that day on, I never had any trouble selling my quota of subscriptions to the Fish Commission's fine magazine.

THE TRUCK DIDN'T DO NOTHIN'

Sport shows are a special assignment. You either love them or hate them. One thing you don't ever do is go out and find a new one and suggest that the agency would do well to be represented there. I did.

Officer John Weaver, my neighboring counterpart, and I found ourselves at the Suffern Sport Show, in New York's Rockland County Community College, for a week because of my big ideas. I knew it was a great show when I visited previously and knew that the agency would do well. We did. But it wasn't easy. At the time, when you worked a sport show you huckstered books, patches, hats and licenses. Carried boxes of stuff in and then back out and locked it up in your car each and every day.

John and I were at the show alone, except that a couple of my deputies drove over to help on the weekends. It was a good time and we met a lot of nice people, but we had to carry all those accountable items each and every day, in and out of the show.

I finally realized that the heaviest item that we had were the "slimy critter" posters. We had 100 each of four or five different posters. They were on good, heavy paper stock and hard to carry because of weight and bulkiness. I decided they had to go.

I tried a half dozen different marketing techniques that afternoon, but nothing worked until someone, the hundredth person or thereabouts, asked me for one of our commission-logo litter bags to carry literature in. I had an inspiration and we got busy.

As fast as we could roll posters and put them in a bag, we would set the bag on the counter. The first person walking by would see the bag and ask if he could have it.

"The bags are fifty cents with a copy of our magazine, fishing regulations and a reptile and amphibian poster," we would tell them.

In several hours we were out of posters. The trip out of the show that night wasn't much better carrying all those quarters.

There are some problems that come with out-of-state travel in an official capacity that no one seems to think of until it is too late. Weaver and I were at the Suffern Sport Show for several years, on behalf of the commission. Everything went smoothly until one night when John had a chance encounter with a "client" of his from his early years as a patrolman in Lehigh County. When we got to John's car that evening, we found two of his tires flattened.

This is when you find out that no one takes the out-of-state state credit card, when you need to get tires fixed, especially at 11 o'clock at night. This is also when you find out that other officers representing other states will come to your aid and provide you with limo service until you can get them fixed.

HORSE COLLAR ANGLERS

The Pennsylvania Angler (now Angler & Boater) is the official magazine of the Pennsylvania Fish Commission (now Fish and Boat Commission). The publication's function is to promote fishing and boating recreation in this state, while providing a forum for the commission to advance the conservation of the Commonwealth's aquatic resources. It only makes sense that the more persons that read the magazine, the easier this job should be. If they understand why something is done, then they are less likely to make problems about that program. When things go smoothly, life is good.

Deputy Bob was an avid Angler subscription salesman. He would work the boat ramps, while two of us would run a patrol. He would preach the gospel about safe boating and by the end of each day, he would have sold three or four subscriptions and made a few allies for the commission.

His favorite method, however, was a little unorthodox. Uniforms at that time consisted of green Lee workpants and a tan work shirt. It was practical, but not official-looking in the least, despite the arm patches and badge. So Bob devised a quick and easy way to stand out in the crowd. He would wear one of the old-style "horse collar" life preservers in bright orange. People would stop and listen to Bob's safe boating message and listen to him talk about fishing in the lake and would buy a subscription.

At age 40, deputy Bob was bald on top and had curly black hair around the edges. It often stuck straight back on either side, like wings. He was built like most well-to-do 40-year-olds, sporting a minor spare tire. With the orange "horse collar," he was a sight to behold.

CHAPTER 11:
They Walk on the Water

After fishing, boating and hunting season comes ice fishing season. No. Maybe it comes first. I don't know; they all run together. But I am sure of one thing: If you are going to walk on water, you need good solid water.

OIL CREEK ICE-CAPADE

I had worked for a year and a half to get a special lures-and-flies-only stretch put in at Oil Creek State Park. Finally the rulemaking had passed and the special regulation area on Oil Creek would go into effect on January 1, 1990. I was jubilant. The Oil Creek Chapter of Trout Unlimited had helped push for the program, and they had offered to help post "the stretch."

The plan was to post the area during the Christmas holidays, so it would be ready for the first of the year. I couldn't wait. December 22 rolled around. It was 40 degrees and drizzly. The ice that had covered the creek had blown out of the middle the week before, leaving six and eight-foot-high walls of ice sheets along the edges. I grabbed a backpack full of posters and my staple gun, donned my hip boots and headed for the park.

I decided to do the toughest stretch of the project first, since the weather was cooperating. It was a nice afternoon to be outside. In a heavy wool shirt, I was just comfortable. I parked near the railroad bridge, crossed it and started up the steep back side of the creek, working upstream toward the park office.

The afternoon went along routinely, slapping up posters on trees every 50 or 100 yards. I didn't want anyone able to testify that they hadn't seen the posters when I caught them bait fishing. I climbed the icy banks and got out on the edge of the ice to get extra height on the posters. Eventually I worked to the mouth of Rattlesnake Run where it came out of the lower end of the wetlands below the picnic area.

Ahead of me lay an ice field a full 50 yards across and extending 100 yards up into the woods. The ice sheets had been deposited by the previous week's high water. I tried to recall the terrain from my memory of a few previous trips. I remembered a sandbar, but no underlying stream. I hesitated and reasoned I was alone and should walk around the ice field. Then I decided the ice was high and dry, and if I had to walk around it, it would be well after dark when I got back to the car. It was after three o'clock already.

I had gone about 30 yards across the ice when it gave under me. I flung the stapler and backpack I was carrying ahead of me as I went down. I tried the normal frantic exit from the ice, but to no avail. I was trapped in waist-deep water, left foot on a rock and right foot swinging free in the flow. The sheets of ice I had fallen through were higher than I could reach with arms extended above my head.

Slush ice was running out from between the sheets, filling the hole around my body. I tried frantically to escape, but was denied. I tired quickly, valuable

133

minutes passing. I tried to think, but onrushing hypothermia was making me lethargic. The light drizzle made the ice slippery. It was impossible to get a handhold on the ice. I began to get drowsy. I thought of my wife, my brother's family and my mother. Christmas, a few days away, was going to be sad for them with me lying in the funeral home instead of visiting.

I sucked it up and fought the drowsiness. I had one more chance and then the adrenalin would be gone. "Think!" I kept saying out loud. There was nobody in the park and I was back in a lost corner, away from any of the people-traffic areas. I was getting nowhere. Could I swim under the 20 yards of ice out to open water? I vetoed the idea. Hip boots weren't made for swimming, and if there was any obstruction I would drown. Once I did get out, I would have the heavy main flow to contend with in a now very weakened state.

"Think!" I was getting very drowsy now and cold. I gave up. I would die a quiet, peaceful death. I relaxed. Euphoria set in.

"Think!" I cried out. Then I got a break. One of the lower sheets in the pile shifted. Instead of pinning me, it created a 2-inch lip. I submerged my hand and grabbed the top of my hip boot and pulled and tugged while lifting my cold-stiffened leg. I eventually got it contorted to wedge it in the hole on the slight lip. At least I would be found there in the hole; my body shouldn't slip under. I had new hope, but not much time left.

I forced my cold-slowed brain to think. I had done a good bit of free-climbing of mountains the year I spent in Alaska when I was young, and now I had a foothold. Leaning my back against the broken ice sheets I cross-pressured with my arms, while beginning to apply weight to the foothold. I was "chimney climbing."

The projecting sheet must have been large. It did not give. I began to slowly rise, inch by inch, applying opposing pressure until at last my head cleared the surface of the icy tomb. Five feet ahead of me, on top of the ice, lay a log, root end toward me. The top end was tangled in a sycamore on the shore. If I could get a hold of it, I might survive.

I maintained my new-found composure and, after a small lifetime expecting a sudden cave-in, worked myself out of the hole. I lay spread-eagle on the ice, distributing my weight. I caught my breath, evaluated my position and, with what strength was left, gave a mighty lunge. My hand barely touched the root end of the old snag, but my numbed fingertips grasped it and I slowly pulled myself toward it. Once I got my arm around it, I grabbed my gear that lay nearby and used the tree and the handle of the staple gun to belly slide safely ashore.

I stood, drained the slush ice from my boots and conceded that WCOs are not the highest force that reigns on earth. Then I tried to act nonchalant by putting up the next poster, as though nothing had happened. Suddenly I was overcome with shakes. Fear and cold racked my body. I fell to the ground. I regained my footing and began staggering for the park office, over a half mile away.

I was walking and falling, when I finally reached the picnic area. Hypothermia had me big-time. A park employee, the only one working that day, was getting in her car to leave. I was able to wave her down. I explained, shivering and stammering, what had happened. She got the office open again and I went in. She called the maintenance crew and they took me to the barn, where a wood burner was roaring, while they warmed my car.

After a half hour, I drove home and ran tubs of warm water that became cold when I submerged my near-frozen legs in them. Several times I repeated this and, after about an hour, I began to thaw out. I had been very close to the point of no return. I had given up, then forced myself to live. I took my wife out to dinner to celebrate that night. I was celebrating being alive.

I still get choked up when I write this or tell this story. The local fly shop owner has a brochure naming the pools and runs throughout the "stretch," which he gives new customers. One corner just above Rattlesnake Run is named "Warden's Folly." Only the locals that have heard my story understand why.

ON THIN ICE

Ice is a marvelous natural phenomenon. At 33 degrees Fahrenheit there is none, and then at 32 there is. Waterways Conservation Officers walk on thin ice in more ways than just figuratively. We often get to feeling that we can walk on water. Once in awhile we are reminded that we are only human.

Thin-ice fisherman checks are not unusual. There is no way of really knowing if the ice will hold you without walking on it. If you do and it does, you win. If you do and it doesn't, it won. If it wins and you're lucky, you go home, get dry clothes and carry on.

At Lake Irena in the Hazle Township community park, there was a retired or constantly laid-off union carpenter. They called him Dramey, and he always smoked a stogie. Dramey had a slight speech impediment to where he always sounded funny. He was like a vaudeville act unto himself. He had a weird sense of humor to go with it all.

I looked forward to Dramey being at the lake when I went up to check it. My dad was a union carpenter and Dramey and I had a bond. When first-ice formed on the lake, Dramey, with hatchet in one hand, a 4-foot piece of plywood under his chest and a jigging rod, was always the first one on the lake. He would scoot around all over the ice, spread-eagle, catching trout. I would begin checking the lake for ice fishermen as soon as I felt ice would be forming.

As I appeared on the shoreline, in the full splendor of my uniform, a voice would cry from out on the lake: "Hey 'teiner, 'um out and check me."

I would respond, "You go to hell, Dramey. You want checked bad enough, you'll come in here."

We both would then laugh and carry on a normal conversation. I did, however, get to thinking of this conversation as a ritual that officially announced the beginning of ice fishing season.

ACROSS SIXTY FEET DEEP ON A AN INCH OF ICE

Getting to know a new lake and new people is one of the biggest delights of transferring districts. All of your old mistakes are immediately forgotten, and all your new ones are immediately in front of you. Arriving in Venango County in December meant that my first introduction to my new lakes would be on the ice.

So it was that one Saturday morning a week after new ice, I set out to patrol Justus Lake. A new snow had covered all the old tracks, as I checked the few fishermen on the edge near the beach. They had five inches of ice there and I continued on. Soon I noticed a lone fisherman down near the dam breast, a ten-minute stroll across the lightly dusted ice.

I set my stride and kept watching the fisherman for any quick, unusual moves. Anything that would tell me he had "made" me as an officer. He just kept fishing, obviously having nothing to hide. Then, when I got about 20 yards from him, he motioned me to stop. I did and then he explained.

"We only have a little over an inch of ice here and even less out there in the middle where you just walked across," he said.

We both walked to the shore, I checked his license and his bucket and then returned to my patrol car via the shoreline. I had crossed 60 feet of water on about one inch of new ice. It just wasn't my turn.

YOU'RE NOT CORTEZ, ARE YOU?

Kahle Lake lies on the border of Venango and Clarion counties. I stopped to take a stroll on the ice one day and meet some new people. I have always held ice fishermen in high regard. They are the real outdoorsmen of fishing. Nothing fancy; just hunker down and fish. I like them.

I had just checked an older fellow sitting on a bucket, found everything to be in order, and began to stroll away.

"You're not Warden Cortez, are you?" he shouted after me.

"No," I replied. "I'm Steiner. I'm assigned to Venango County. Cortez is assigned to Clarion."

"I wouldn't walk over that way if I were you," he said, pointing to the path I had begun to take. Then he continued, "That was open water there on the channel yesterday."

I don't know what the difference of opinion was that he must have had with Cortez, but to have considered leaving him walk into a cold lake, it must have been serious.

JUMPING ON FLOTSAM

Checking fishermen along the Susquehanna at West Nanticoke right after ice breakup was a spring tradition. Fishermen would be standing on sandbars and rocks, where they could climb down to them, or on the ten-foot-high flow ice stacked along the shoreline where they couldn't.

The fishermen were all bundled up and stood working jigs, obviously not happy with having to take a break from their rhythmic fishing to have their licenses checked. But they all complied. As I worked my way down the edge, a fisherman stood on a rock that was protruding from the flotsam-covered sandbar.

I was young and agile and began to jump the eight or ten feet down to the sandbar from atop the ice. As I started my motion, a fisherman spoke to me by name. I stopped.

"I wouldn't jump down right there," he said. "It's just flotsam over about 10 feet of water."

If I had been alone, I would have plunged into the icy water and been carried the 30 or 40 yards downstream and under the ice wall that still spanned the river. Being in my 20s, the finality of what could have happened didn't sink in. Now that I'm over 70, I fully understand.

MATADOR AND STAN ON ICE

Stanley, my deputy, was raising his nephew Angelo. Angie was a good kid, in his mid-teens. Angie loved to fish. At the time, Lin and I had three fishing buddies that were hard to shake. The other two were girls about the same age as Angie. When we fished, they fished. When ice fishing season rolled around, we got the three kids bundled up one afternoon and took them along. A good time was had by all and lots of panfish were caught.

The good time ended when I returned Angie to Stan's house. In no uncertain terms, Angie and I were reprimanded for ever going on the ice, and Angie was told his ice-fishing days were over. No amount of coaxing, cajoling or feeding Stan perch fillets would make him relent.

Finally in mid-January, with everywhere in the Poconos reporting two and three feet of ice, Angie was allowed to go, if he promised to wear a life preserver, the horse collar type. A chubby kid bundled in ten layers of winter clothes, wearing a horse collar PFD and walking on two feet of ice in a pond three feet deep brings a lot of comments. Most of them came from the two girls fishing with him.

Nevertheless, true to his word, the PFD stayed on Angie. I saw a mission. I had to convince Stan to let up on the kid. One bitter cold February day, after a little coaxing and promising that we were just going to look at lakes from the car, I got Stan to ride on ice patrol with me. I would do all the ice walking I assured him. He could guard the car. I had a plan.

The road into Lily Lake is almost a straight shot to the boat ramp. I came up the road at 10 or 15 miles per hour, slowed and just kept rolling. The ice held not only Stan and me, but also the Matador we were in. After his breathing returned to normal, I backed the car up the ramp. Stan never rode another ice patrol, but Angie didn't have to wear the PFD anymore on good ice.

ROTTWEILER RESCUE

Late winter means rotting, seething ice on major rivers. The ice surges and booms and cracks in anticipation of spring breakup. The ice control dam on Oil Creek was designed to hold this back and stack it up in the relatively uninhabited confines of Oil Creek State Park, before it gets to Oil City and does damage. Sometimes after a good hard rain, this rolling ice spectacle can be awesome. Ice stacks ten or twenty feet high and has six or eight feet of muddy, surging water passing under, over and through it. It attracts spectators.

I was stopped at Oil Creek Outfitters, a fly shop concession in the state park, just across from the park office. The park supervisor came down and asked me if I would go with him. A woman had reported a large dog trapped in the surging ice on the corner just above the ice control dam.

When we arrived, I immediately saw that the situation was hopeless. Only the dog's head and one paw were out of the water, and he was out at least thirty yards. The rolling mass of ice chunks and water were as high as I had ever seen. A small crowd of onlookers was forming. There was nothing to do but watch and keep other persons from trying to become heroes.

The woman returned. She couldn't believe we were "just going to stand there and do nothing." She referred to the park superintendent and me in unladylike terms. I had identified the dog by now as a Rottweiler. I took the verbal assault for a while, and then I clarified the situation for all to understand. I looked to the crowd, then to the woman.

"Let me get this straight lady. You want me to climb out on that broken, rolling ice that is jammed on top of ten feet of thundering, muddy water so I can get bitten by a Rottweiler. No, ma'am, I don't think so."

She didn't like the answer, but rather than watch the dog drown she left. We stayed until it disappeared under the ice to be sure no one would try and be stupid.

TAILWATER RESCUE

Observation and training play a major role in this job. Regularly the officer finds himself in a situation where he is relying heavily on one or the other. Training usually leads the way through the situation. For a change, observation was to make a deputy and me heroes, at least in our eyes.

We had worked into the dark on a Sunday evening at F.E. Walter Dam, as was so often the case, making sure the last beverage container there was properly disposed of. Just as we were getting ready to wrap it up for the night, an older gentleman came to us in a quandary. His wife and daughter had disappeared hours ago to take a walk and had not returned.

In an area this remote and yet so close to metropolises, many thoughts race through the officer's head, but each situation must be treated at first as it appears. I called another deputy unit and got them to calm the old man, while we did a nearby road and access road search in my vehicle. I believed all the time that this woman, who had a history of heart problems, had just walked beyond her capabilities and now was sitting patiently waiting for a ride. However, after nearly an hour without success, I called in some reinforcements and began an earnest search.

After several hours of frustration, I fell back on what I did best at the time. I went to the top of the dam and set up my spotting scope. I began to slowly glass the wooded hillsides on both sides of the rugged whitewater of the Lehigh River. After another hour and now nearly midnight, I got the break I had been waiting for. The woman with a heart condition lit up a cigarette and I spotted its bright light as she puffed.

I was able to get my vehicle near the water's edge and, with a life jacket and a length of rope, crossed the stream to where the two women sat on a rock along the river. One at a time I assisted them in crossing the turbulent, waist-deep flow. To attempt to go down to the bridge or up to the dam through the tangled laurel and rhododendron would have taken hours. How they convinced one another that they were on the wrong side of the river and had crossed away from all the access roads is to this day a befuddlement to me.

Long days "afloat in a boat" were the rule for much of the summer, patrolling for fish and boat law violations on lakes and the larger rivers in my districts. The boat pictured was a step up from my first issue boat, which I chose from fifty or so that had been impounded or abandoned on Fish Commission-owned lakes. After I selected one, my boss then extracted a six-horsepower outboard from the dusty corner of a barn that served as a storage building and issued it to me. With a little help from my mechanically minded deputies, we made that boat run ... most of the time. Notice, however, the oars. This "Tin Lizzy" wasn't brand new either, but at least it had only been worn out by one officer previously.

CHAPTER 12:
Afloat in a Boat

Boats would most correctly be patrolled by sheriff's or local police departments that have more than one-man forces. Boats have all the same problems as vehicles when being operated. One man in a county cannot hope to correct erroneous boat operating behavior.

IMP

Sunny summer days on the big lakes are days for powerboats, water skiing, and those ever-present bikinis. Even a longtime officer occasionally notices a bikini with outstanding attributes, but when you have a young officer along, the results can border on hilarity ... especially with a little setup from two veteran officers.

There was a beautiful powerboat named the Imp that played on Beltzville Lake both summers that I was assigned there. It was sleek and fast and trimmed in chrome and bikinis. I am not sure what the business of the owner of the boat was, but he always seemed to have two or three beautiful young ladies on board, just gathering rays with the skimpiest bikinis available at the time.

I had spent the winter working with a new, young Game Commission deputy by the name of Tom, and we had often discussed the relative hardships of the jobs of that agency and mine. Tom contended the toughest checks and citations were when you were out there in the wind and snow, outnumbered by orange-clad hunters, sorting out a mess of dead does and doe tags. My contention was that anyone could check and sort a bunch of hunters and get the job done, but it took a warden's warden to stare into a string bikini and tell her she was under arrest. Tom would laugh and say, "Throw me into that briar patch."

As the summer rolled along, my deputy Joe, who often worked Beltzville Lake, talked to the owner of the Imp several times. A friendship developed between Joe and the owner of the boat. Joe was soon on a first-name basis with the guy. I had a plan.

One Friday night, I made arrangements for young, single Tom, who dated very little due to his dedication to his job and its rigorous schedule, to patrol Beltzville with me. I would meet him and we would run the 330 boat, which was our chase boat. Joe would get another deputy and begin an earlier patrol with the other boat. We would hook up with them and set up some planned details for looking for drinkers (boating under the influence) and such.

When we arrived at the lake, all the state park lots were full and the gates were closed. It promised to be a busy day on the water. A little over an hour from Philadelphia, Beltzville became a circus early on weekends and stayed that way until late Sunday. It was like an 800-acre water park.

We had no sooner arrived, when a park vehicle pulled down to our boat dock and asked if we could go out and chase a rubber raft out of the water-ski zone. Since the ski zone was limited and already crowded with power boats and skiers, we hurried out, hoping to get the rafters out alive.

What we were greeted with was a young couple, lazing the day away in 100 feet of water, among the powerboats, with no life preservers. We escorted them for nearly a half hour to the shore. When they were safely on the ground, I couldn't help but notice that the young lady had removed the modesty liners from her sheer, white, wet bathing suit. She looked like a young movie star. As I stood taking grief from her, her father and her boyfriend, I wrote her a ticket. She had been the operator of the raft. Young Tom was beginning to see what I meant about this job being tougher than that of a game guy.

We fired up the patrol boat and began a slow cruise of the ski area, motoring up the southeast side of the lake. Soon the portable radio crackled. It was Joe on the other boat. He said he was busy on the northwest side, but had been watching a green boat that he suspected was overindulging, since he had seen the operator drinking from a can off and on all morning. I radioed back that we would make the stop and got directions from Joe as to the location.

Now, secretly I knew Joe had talked to his friend on the Imp and the stage was set to put one over on Tom. I prepared Tom and told him what to expect during the B.U.I. check. As I got closer and was sure the setup was on, I explained to Tom that the water was choppy from the traffic and I wouldn't be able to do an alongside inspection, so I wanted him to go onboard and check safety equipment and talk to the occupants and try to determine if alcohol was a problem. We set a signal, and if there was a problem, he would motion me and I would pick him up and we would back off and observe until the other boat was available.

As I pulled alongside the Imp, I could see mischief in the eyes of the scantily clad girls before I even hailed the operator. I gave the usual spiel about a routine inspection of safety equipment, and that I would be putting an officer on board to complete the check. The operator welcomed the check and Tom jumped on the boat. I backed off far enough to watch and listen without being obvious that this was a setup.

As Tom very professionally attempted to complete his assignment, I couldn't help but notice the bikinis making provocative moves as they reached for the required life preservers, fire extinguishers and such. The blonde girl in the black bikini whispered in Tom's ear something and giggled as the brunette with the white bikini would bend over to get a life jacket, and then the roles would change. I kept a straight face as the situation progressed.

When the check was complete and Tom signaled for pickup, he was beet red in the face and sweating beyond that required by the weather. That's when the girls asked why he was so shy and could I leave him there with them for the day and a bunch of insinuating questions. I, being the reliable backup man that I am, assured Tom that it would be no problem. Joe had two deputies on his boat and I would just get one of them to accompany me. I told Tom I could pick him up at dark and tried to be all the "help" I could.

Finally after letting Tom enjoy/suffer as much as either of us could stand, I took him aboard and we bid goodbye. Tom assured me that the only thing on board was soda-pop and the boat certainly was well equipped. He then said he was very thirsty and could use a drink. His mouth had gotten dry during the check. I told him we would head for a concession stand, where he could cool off and get something to drink. As I pulled the boat into the sand along the beach, with its 400 yards of bikinied swimmers and sunbathers, I pointed to the concession stand beyond. You can imagine the look Tom gave me.

I would like to tell you that Tom got older and overcame his fear, but it was not to be. Knowing that he couldn't handle this situation on a day-to-day basis, he became a Game Commission officer.

RED AND GREEN BOBBERS

I like patrolling at night. I know what I am looking for and they don't know I am looking. However, on one such occasion I sat and watched the red-and-green bow light of a boat, across Justus Lake, for nearly an hour. For the life of me, I couldn't make out anything else, even with field glasses, other than the bow light. Finally, as I watched, the green light was reeled into shore and recast through the air. This was my first experience with lighted bobbers.

BEWARE THE SEESAW

People have trouble staying in boats when I am around. I never could quite understand that. I think it must have something to do with being flustered at my arrival or presence, but I'm not sure.

It was a lovely fall evening, the leaves were changing color and the sun was setting on one of the few remaining warm days. As the boats glided to the launch ramp and dock at Justus Lake, I would walk down to them, make some small talk and then check their safety equipment and catch. I was encountering no problems and, with the knowledge that the busy season was winding down, I had a little extra bounce in my step.

A canoe came into the floating dock to the right of the ramp. There were two passengers. The dock is hinged at the shoreline. The first canoeist had exited the canoe by sitting on the dock and getting out, swinging his feet onto the dock and then kneeling to hold the canoe for his fishing partner.

His partner had one foot on the dock and one foot in the canoe, when 200 pounds of friendly fish warden came bouncing onto the dock, just beyond the hinge at the point of the most leverage. The results were spectacular. It was like the tumblers in the circus, where one man stands on the end of the board on the ground and the second man drops from another's shoulders, flipping the guy on the board into the air.

Only the second canoeist did not land on his feet, because as he tumbled over the canoe, he landed in water too deep to stand in. Fortunately, he could swim, because his buddy and I were laughing so hard we could not have helped him. He came ashore wet and indignant, but soon saw the levity of the moment and joined in the laughter. I did apologize, between chuckles.

DADDY, IF HE GETS WET YOU'RE IN BIG TROUBLE

It was midsummer when deputy Don and I entered one of the development lakes in the northeastern corner of Luzerne County.

Many of these lakes were natural bogs and ponds. The development of them for second homes for urbanites was the worst thing that could have happened. First, the ecological value of such a lake goes downhill rapidly with man's invasion. Secondly, the only people that could afford these places were city folks that thought they owned the world and made the laws. This was their property and you weren't going on it.

In an effort to make my patrols as painless as could be on these lakes, I sent letters to the lake associations, explaining the law and volunteering to speak at their meetings. Several lake communities had me do that. Additionally, I would notify the president or head officer of the association when I was coming to patrol, at least narrowing it to a weekend, in advance. Still it never failed; there were violations and arrogant urbanites that felt they were above the law.

This particular day was sunny and breezy. I was surprised to see only one sailboat on the lake. Don and I threw the canoe on the water and paddled out. Upon getting a good look at the boat, I could see no life preservers in use or on board. With a bullhorn I instructed them to go to their dock and then met them there.

On board were an enormous man and his teenage daughter. Somehow I managed to get myself on the end of the dock with him between me and the shore. Don, however, held the key position at the shoreline.

As I explained the violation, I could hear the rumble and rage welling in the defendant. Soon he was puffed like a 300-pound rooster, all six-foot-six of him. In swimming trunks, it was obvious this guy was muscle, not just flab. I was retreating toward the water and had to take a stand.

He edged ever closer. Around the side of him I saw Don winding up with a canoe paddle from our boat, like it was a Louisville Slugger. I was thinking this thing was going to get real ugly in a heartbeat, since only my toes remained on the end of the dock.

Then the big guy's daughter spoke, breaking the magic of the moment.

"Daddy, if he gets wet, you're going to be in really big trouble."

He de-puffed, backed up and sat quietly as I issued the ticket. It was paid in short order.

Several years passed and Don and I were working the Suffern Sport Show, in New York. A fellow walked up to get his fishing license and, as I was filling in the blanks, he recognized me. I had recognized him right away. It was "Big Daddy."

He flushed and said, "I know you guys. You patrol our lake in Luzerne County." He was obviously beginning to work himself into a frenzy again.

I extended my hand, introduced myself and assured him I didn't recognize him, but I was certain it was a pleasure to meet him and I would look forward to seeing him in the summer.

SENATOR "NEEDMORE'S" REQUEST

It was in my first summer when the boss, Walter Lazusky, got a call from a state senator that not nearly enough law enforcement was being done on Conneaut Lake. Walt sent my wife, Linda, at the time a deputy, and me up to work with a Crawford County deputy.

The day was exciting. We had a pontoon boat full of violations. The operator laughed every time I asked him for something.

"Life preservers, please."

"Ha-ha-ha, he-he-he," he responded.

"Fire extinguisher."

"Ha-ha-ha, he-he-he," he would say, and so it went.

When I issued the tickets, one of the several bikini-clad young female passengers looked at him and said, "Ha-ha-ha, he-he-he, told you so."

We kept a straight face.

Later in the day while writing up a violation, we had to duck a ski rope as a skier passed on one side of us and the boat threw water on us on the other side. All in all it was a very busy day.

Monday, after the weekend was over, the senator called back. They had had plenty of law enforcement for a while, thank you. We could let up. Always wondered just which of the 15 or so violators cited that day had been the senator's friends.

CANOE ACCIDENTS

Canoe drownings are routine investigations. You go talk to the survivors or witnesses or just look at the situation and what you have is a canoe, nobody in it. Some things make me nervous, though.

Two guys are reported pushing and shoving each other in a bar. They were arguing over money or a woman or something else trivial. A beer or two later, they jump in a canoe and start across a deep lake to their cottages. One guy is swimmer. The other isn't. In the middle of the lake on a rainy, cold day, the canoe upsets. The swimmer lives.

In another instance, a guy reported to be drunk gets in a canoe on the river, after having a fight with his friend, and starts downstream toward another friend's house. It is a dark, cold night. The canoe is found swinging in the current, anchored, the next afternoon. Nobody is around. He hadn't made it more than a few hundred yards.

I go to do the investigation and those I talk to are more interested in mowing the lawn before the rains come than answering questions about their missing relative, who is later found downstream, floating dead.

I often have heard it said that the easiest way to kill someone is to do it as though it were a hunting accident. I don't agree with that.

GAME DEPUTY'S HAT

In Venango County there are 59 miles of the Allegheny River. My assigned patrol area included that and then some. Often I was covering everything from Tionesta to East Brady, nearly 100 miles of the wild and scenic river. It was an absolutely beautiful office to go to work in.

I averaged at least sixteen and often more hours a week during the late spring to early fall period on the water. To patrol this, I had two different jet-drive outboard boats. Both required little or no water. Wet gravel would usually do the trick. I often told folks that the first law of jet-boating is, "If you see a rock and hit a rock, only then is it a rock."

Persons who see a jet traverse a riffle or ride in one the first time are simply amazed. Many were the fishermen who tried to follow me through a riffle with their prop boats, thinking I knew where the deep channel was. When, in fact, I had run through on only a few inches of water. More than one lower unit and prop have been repaired when other boaters thought they could do it if I did it.

Fresh deputies or other officers riding in a jet for the first time were certainly fun to watch. They'd cringe, hang on and go through all kind of "we're going to crash!" gyrations, while I, the experienced operator, knew there was no danger.

One sunny afternoon on the river, a Game deputy, John, was riding co-pilot with me for the day. John was a good deputy and proud do be with the Game Commission. He wore a nice, neat uniform, as usual, and a ball cap with a metal Game Commission emblem on the front. It looked sharp and he was proud of it. The emblem had cost him eight or ten dollars.

I ran a routine upstream patrol from Oil City. This would show John a section of river he was familiar with, from a different perspective. Everything went as could be expected. No big problems, a few minor violations and a pleasant boat ride.

As I started back down the river before dark, I cranked it up and took off. The water was somewhat shallow, so I had to "play" the river on the edge. You have to pay extra attention going downstream, as the current pushes you around, also.

I had noticed coming upstream that we would have to make a series of sharp turns going downstream, when we got to Peaceful Valley. The first turn would catapult us toward a large boulder, the size of a house. Then, before the boat could fully respond, I would have to begin cutting it the other way. We would slide toward the rock sideways, and the jet would grab water about five or six feet before slamming into the boulder and head us on down the river.

This may sound like a dangerous maneuver, but it is typical of running a river on low water. You have to be able to turn, slide and change directions like a waterborne hummingbird, if you are going to be good with a jet boat. It is not a sport for the faint of heart.

John was sitting on my left as we neared the Peaceful Valley turn. I yelled, "Hang on!" and cranked it hard for the boulder, and then cranked it downstream.

John panicked, thinking for sure we would smash the large boulder. When he did, he jumped toward me and right out from under his hat. It floated for a few seconds, and then the weight of the emblem pulled it down into the swirling currents. It was gone for good.

He cried about the loss of the emblem for several weeks, but got over it when all the Fish and Game deputies he ran into told him they liked his new hat, "without that tacky emblem" on it. John said he enjoyed his river tour, but never again volunteered to ride a patrol.

RUNNING ON WATER SKIS

A few things in this job gave you much satisfaction. Helping someone avoid a dangerous situation certainly was one that did.

I was running the jet boat on the Allegheny River, along Rt. 62 above Hunter's Station. I was staying on the back side of the islands, looking for a shallow spot to beach the boat and have lunch. Around the bend came a jet boat towing a skier, right at me. I reached for the blue light switch and siren, and then stopped. As they went by, I just waved and watched them go down toward deeper water under the bridge.

The young girl skiing was no more than 12 years old. Her dad had pulled her through less than a foot of water with his new jet boat. He was proud as punch of where that boat could go. He never thought of the consequences of his skier dropping off or falling in that shallow water. I had realized, in the nick of time, that had I flipped on the lights he would have throttled back and she would have gone down on the wet gravel she was skiing over. I was always thankful for having the intuition to diagnose that one ahead of time.

When I stopped the boat farther down the river in a safe spot and explained the problem to the father, he just shook. He couldn't thank me enough for calling that to his attention. He had just gotten the boat and was testing it in shallow water. He never gave the skier's falling a thought. I sure am glad I did.

OPENING DAY SUBMARINE LAUNCH

Opening day of trout season is always hectic, but back then it was hectic without sleep. You'd start Friday and often not really sleep until Sunday. Sometimes it would be nearly 48 hours without rest. Things have changed for the better over the years.

First days meant the warden had to be everywhere. The object of the game was to fly the flag as often and in as many places as you possibly could. With a good deputy crew, it was possible to have uniforms in many locations at one time. The logistics of this type of operation were taxing if you had had rest and overwhelming without it. Drop guys off for early season undercover work, then, as the season opened, get them in uniform and back on the beat to be seen. Get your boat in place for the boat crew and get your horse saddled up for the all-day ride.

The routine this particular morning was for me to drop the boat, a 14-foot "Tin Lizzy" with a 10-horsepower engine, at the dam, move the trailer to the locked compound and then ride off. A pair of my best deputies would arrive a half hour after I left the boat and would take it on patrol. I would return around noon, load and tow the boat to storage, and then we would be off on another phase of patrol.

My part that day went smoothly. I got the boat out of storage. The trailer lights worked, which gave me time to have a coffee from my Thermos. I towed it over, launched it, and set the anchor behind a shoreside rock. Then I tied it to the boat. As the sun was rising, I rode off to patrol several streams.

My morning was routine. Nothing earthshaking. I wrote a few cases. About 11:30 I returned to the dam to meet my "A" team and check on their progress. They were covered with grease and sweat and far from professional looking in their newly purchased uniforms.

"How did it go?" I queried. I received death-ray looks and snarls.

I got out of the car and listened as the story unfolded. It seems that a boat floats better when the plug is in it. When the deputies arrived at first light, they could see no boat, only an anchor. The boat had sunk at the end of a 30-foot rope in about that much water. Fortunately, the rope was stout. With the aid of several of the first-arriving 4WDs, they were able to get it high and dry. But not until they had exhausted themselves, tugging on the rope with the little tin boat covered by tons of water.

Then after borrowing a cooking pan from a traveling fisherman and bailing and drying the boat, the damn engine wouldn't start. They borrowed tools and got good and greasy before my timely arrival. Any criticism that day of their uniform appearance or the lack of productivity of their morning patrol was met with cold stares. The boat was stored in an airy, sunny place with the motor cover off for a few days. It served on until long after my departure from that district. We never even had to change the spark plug.

RUM SWIZZLE CRUISE

When I first noticed the pontoon boat, it looked like the occupants were all standing in the water. When I got them stopped, it was obvious to me that the operator was pretty well "lit," so I got him to park it. Further inspection revealed no life jackets. I counted 17 persons getting off.

This was before the days of Boating Under the Influence, so I stuck with the Fish and Boat Law violations I encountered. The fines totaled nearly $200, which the operator's middle-aged daughter went and got for him as I did the paperwork.

I can understand how one man gets drunk enough to risk the lives of 17 on a "rum swizzle cruise." I just could never understand how the other 16 got drunk enough to ride with him.

WHITEWATER CHASE SCENE

I was working the F.E. Walter Dam area and had a crew of three deputies patrolling from the Lehigh Tannery bridge for life preservers on canoes, kayaks and rafts, as was our habit on Saturday mornings in the spring. One of my deputies radioed that we had a problem and they needed help at the bridge. I saddled up my Matador and rode the ten miles to the site.

The deputies explained that they had a canoe, but no occupants. The canoe had had three men in it with fishing gear, but when the officers used the bullhorn to ask for licenses, the men pulled the canoe to the bank and jumped ship, running into the brush. Obviously, the men felt they were in violation of some kind or they wouldn't have abandoned an expensive canoe and fishing tackle.

When I arrived I sized up the situation. By now, three more deputies had responded to the backup call, bringing our numbers to seven. I decided that sooner or later commonsense would prevail, and the men would realize that the fines would not amount to a net worth equal to the abandoned gear. With that in mind, I went down over the steep bank and, being an accomplished whitewater canoeist, secured the gear, donned a life jacket and took the canoe down through a stretch of powerful water and into an eddy, where we could pull the boat up the bank and impound it.

As I got in the eddy, I spotted a one-man raft. Upon checking it verbally, I realized that the finger the young guy showed me in response did not mean that he had one life preserver. Rather, it indicated a gross disrespect for uniformed authority. I hollered to my deputies to come down over the bank. I pulled the canoe over and met the first one who got there. He jumped in and we began our downriver pursuit.

The maneuverability of a canoe is much better than that of a raft. As we closed the distance, the rafter headed for shore to make an on-foot escape. We were closing fast when the impounded canoe I was paddling ran onto a sandbar, the bow pushing over and the boat becoming high-centered. The rafter appeared to be making good his escape as we sat high and dry on the sandbar.

The way you float a boat or ship when you run aground is to discharge unnecessary ballast. I gave the order to my deputy, who was riding in the bow, to get out. He looked over the bow, then back at me. The raft was getting closer to shore and escape was within the violator's grasp. I barked the order, "Get out!" with more authority this time. The deputy was new and certainly not going to disobey a direct command. He stepped over the bow of the canoe in full uniform, going chest deep into the cold water.

Without the added weight, I was able to rapidly close and effect the arrest. The resistance I got from the violator was only verbal. He, however, was not one of the three men missing from the impounded canoe.

The deputies and I got a rope on the bow and, with all hands pulling, were able to get the canoe to the railroad grade. I drove the car in and we loaded it on the roof rack. I was sure that the escaped fishermen were watching from the wooded hillside.

Just across the bridge was a camp and sporting goods store. I parked obviously in front of it and went inside. The folks that ran it were acquaintances of the crew, so I explained the situation and left one of my cards. I told them that when the men came in looking for their canoe to have them contact me.

Several weeks had gone by without my hearing from the missing fishermen, when I answered my home phone. It was the wife of one of my deputies from that day. She, a transplant from Brooklyn, New York, had brought her heavy accent with her. Even though I knew her and often talked to her, I had to listen carefully to understand her.

She had gotten a call from a man with a heavy Southern accent, who said he was from West Virginia and had "lost" a canoe and understood I might have it.

I returned the call and talked to a man from West Virginia who sounded as though he had never been exposed to the English language. I could only imagine the conversation between him and my deputy's New Yorker wife. I explained to him that the canoe had been used in a violation and that fines would have to be paid before he could recover the boat. I told him to call me when he and his friends were prepared to settle the violations.

It was spitting snow one fall afternoon and I was preparing to go archery hunting, when the phone rang. It was the "Grits." They were in a restaurant near my home and wanted to pick up their canoe. I loaded it on top of the Matador and met them at the state police barracks on top of the hill. They were all charged with fishing without a license, paid their fines and left, heading south on I-81 in a large laundry truck, with a 17-foot aluminum canoe strapped on top.

STEPPED INTO RAFT

The spring runoff was being held in the dam. The water was just over the parking lot about a foot deep. Four deputies were working in plainclothes at the dam that morning, as it was early in fishing season. I was the uniform.

Soon a rubber raft, with seven young fellows onboard, came off the lake and into the ramp. When I asked for their life preservers, they just seemed to ignore me. They picked up their raft and started walking for their cars, some 200 yards away. They were all of college age and weren't going to be bothered on their day off from school. I spoke again, a little louder this time, alerting my deputies to the unfolding confrontation. I saw my deputies begin to make their way toward me.

My mental calculations, like that of a quarterback, told me the violators were going to be able to escape before the "cavalry" arrived. I had to think quickly. They were nearing the getaway vehicle. So I stepped into the raft.

The additional 200 pounds caused the violators to drop the raft to the ground. Then one, obviously the spokesman but not too smart, suggested and motioned for the seven of them to circle me and jump me. One noticed my gun, a snub-nosed revolver at that time, still holstered on my belt. About the same time, another heard the thundering hooves coming from several directions. It was all over except for the paperwork.

CHAPTER 13:
In Front of the Bench

Some folks believe so strongly that the law they obviously violated was not just, that they are willing to pay attorneys large sums of money to avoid paying a small fine. Oftentimes these attorneys, because they have no training in fish, game, park or pollution laws become the "witless" for the defense. Of course, sometimes, because of circumstances and officers having to make on-the-spot decisions, the cited are actually "not guilty." This is why we have a judicial system. Having worked with many district magistrates and a few judges and juries, I sincerely feel we have a wonderful, fair system.

BACKHANDER
The law dictates that children be dealt with differently than adults. That is good. Hardened kids when put in with hardened criminals will become hardened criminals faster than if left to harden on their own. I understand the philosophy.

I had a magistrate that dealt with children differently, as well. This "child" was in his late teens or early 20s. His father was a deer poacher. Nolfie, the Game Commission officer, his deputies and I had caught the father several times over the years with illegal deer. His favorite game was to walk from the house and shoot with a flashlight. Our favorite game was to park at the cemetery and walk up behind his house and wait for him. We were ahead in the game.

Nolfie and I had just served a warrant on our poacher and taken him to the magistrate's office. She explained to the violator that he was at the point where he either paid or went to the "big house" for a spell. He called home to get the money. His son brought it down to the magistrate and they left.

While this action was taking place, we were out trying to serve another warrant. When we returned with our second customer of the day, we were told the story by the secretary. It seems that when the kid came in, he took a seat in front of the magistrate, next to his father. As the kid counted out the money to pay the fine, he got irritated. Finally his mouth overloaded his brain and the steam valve let go.

"If those bastards, Nolfie and Steiner, ever come for me, I'll kill them."

In a heartbeat, with a pounce like a grandmother accustomed to correcting unruly children, the female magistrate, a large formidable woman, jumped up and slapped him with the back of her hand across the mouth, nearly knocking him from his chair.

"If anything ever happens to either of those officers," she said to him, affixing him with a cold stare from pointblank, "I assure you, you will be the first person the state police will talk to. Now get out of here."

That was about the end of the violating for them. All the fines and legal games had never meant anything to them. But when she showed that the side of justice can be tough and not bluffed, the games came to an end.

WHEN YOU WHIZ IN THE WOODS

Beer makes me pee. It makes most people pee, especially if they are drinking lots of it. The brand doesn't seem to matter. You just get saturated to capacity and natural systems go into effect.

On Nescopeck Creek, behind the old slaughterhouse there was a hole with an abandoned bridge abutment. Like most such places, it attracted the local "hoodlums" for beer parties and swims when the sun first warms the earth in late May.

My deputy and I were methodically patrolling the creek and checking activity along it for violations. We were leaving no stone unturned. As we approached on the road, we could see vehicles in the parking lot along the creek behind the slaughterhouse. We pulled off and parked to observe with the spotting scope.

There were boys and girls and beer in clear-glass bottles. The labels were distinctive, and we soon locked onto several participants each. We began noting when they drank from the bottles and when they set them down, etc. This is an exercise I found makes good testimony in a court case.

One nice-looking, dark-haired girl, dressed in a black bathing suit with a pair of blue jean shorts overtop, walked into the woods, carrying a beer bottle that was nearly empty. Another girl accompanied her, so I assumed they were either taking a walk or going to relieve themselves.

Since the spring greenery was nearly at full leaf, we were unable to see which it was. However, we did know that black bathing suit had a bottle when she entered the woods. In a few minutes she returned without the bottle. Since littering is a violation of the Fish Law and really the only reason we had camped on this group, we swung into action.

Over the years I have learned that a lesson taught to one is taught to the group, and it is easier to cite one and control the rest than to try and cite them all. These factors considered, we cited the girl that had discarded her beer bottle in the bushes.

I was surprised that a hearing was scheduled. Her father, a prominent businessman, was not known for his respect of the law and it must have been genetic. When hearing day rolled around, I was expecting a cakewalk. A couple of shouting people that the good magistrate would listen to for a little while, then find her guilty. After all, she had left the bottle and there were no trashcans in the woods. In fact, I had recovered the bottle next to the toilet paper.

I was surprised when I walked into the courtroom to see she had an attorney. As the hearing began, his first move was to have me prosecuted as a Peeping Tom. The magistrate nodded, then listened to my deputy and me testify. The attorney then put his client on the stand and she began.

"I went into the woods to piss. He watched me with binoculars, then, cited me for leaving the bottle."

The magistrate was an old veteran. He let the process run to the end, then, it was his turn to make a speech. It went something like this.

"Attorney Parrazza, I will not accept your complaint against the officer, for he is in the employ of the Commonwealth and was, on the day in question, doing exactly what he is paid and sworn to do. Littering is not a heinous crime and only a summary violation. Littering is, however, offensive to the good members of our citizenry. I therefore find you, Miss Carisi, guilty as charged. And furthermore, just so you know, if you must 'piss' in the woods, you always take the chance someone will be watching."

Justice may be blind, but officers are not required to be.

SIX CASES ON ONE BOAT RENTAL

People will always find a way around the law. Back then the law required that if you rented boats, you had certain safety obligations to the renters. Additionally, if you charged to fish, you needed a regulated fishing lake license, which authorized the activity and required certain recordkeeping.

I had a "slum lord" of a boat renter. He owned a small pond that reportedly had very good fishing in it. You had to drive down his lane to a locked gate to enter. He would rent you a key to the gate. Then you could take a boat out and fish the lake. He was charging a fee to fish the lake and rent a boat. He provided no receipts or safety equipment. I also doubt he paid any taxes on his ill-found gains. He was pond slime at its finest. Without an undercover "sting," it would be impossible to convict him ... or so I thought.

Then he ran against the incumbent magistrate and lost. The time was right. Early the next summer, I sauntered down the lane, climbed the fence and cited the first three boats I could get to for no onboard safety equipment. He ranted and raved, but claimed no responsibility when I asked him if he wished to pay their fines. The renters, victims of an unfortunate circumstance but violators nonetheless, also ranted and raved.

I knew this would be a fun court case. The hearings were scheduled by the magistrate, after consultation with me, for all at one time. I was hoping to convict the owner of the boats and had figured the other three charges would be a tradeoff. I had filed six charges in all.

The hearing, as many did in those days, got wild and woolly. The old justice of the peace system had just faded away, and rules of criminal court procedures were still in their infancy. Through all the shouting and screaming by the owner and the boat renters, the female magistrate would try to get a word in. Eventually, with a lot of gavel pounding, she would regain order for a little while and then all hell would break loose again.

After about an hour, she declared she had heard enough to rule on the case. My testimony had only taken a minute or two in all, and I thought I had been forgotten in the proceedings.

"I have determined that you, Mr. Larsenczyk, are guilty on all three charges. You endanger someone's life every time you rent one of your wooden boats. And you three," she said, pointing to the other defendants who had acted badly in her courtroom, "are also guilty. You should have known better, and in your arguing with Mr. Larsenczyk have proved that to me."

So, instead of three wins and three losses as I had originally planned, I strolled out of her office with six convictions in my hand. Timing, in law enforcement, is everything.

NINE IN A ROW

Magistrates' courts are often fun. You prepare your case for days in your head. You spend countless hours reviewing your evidence and trying to be ready for any contingency. You then get blindsided by a sharp attorney or a fisherman with the right answer.

Older ladies have been my favorite magistrates over the years. The best ones are stout and remind you of your grandmother. I have had the pleasure of working with two such women. I will always remember their honesty with me and some of their decisions and comments.

One such woman presided over the district court in my first district. After the hearing, she would always give you a reason when she found for the defendant. One time, though, she even caught me off guard.

A deputy had observed nine cars parked on the grass at the Fish Commission access area at Lily Lake. It was after dark and in the fall. The parking lot was vacant and yet they had parked on the grass, rutting it somewhat in the rainy weather. A dance was being held at the hotel, which sat right next to the lot. Apparently these nine persons had come late and, finding no parking at the hotel lot, had improvised.

The deputy took license plate numbers and gave them to me. I ran the plates, established the vehicle owners, and sent them all citations. I took copies to the lady magistrate to be filed. I laid them down in the order in which they were parked and explained the situation to her and why I felt we needed to make an example of these scofflaws.

She looked at each citation in the neat row of nine before her and then, after some hesitation, looked up at me and said, "Eight of them are guilty and one is not guilty."

"I'll take eight out of nine anytime, ma'am," I responded. "But, my curiosity is killing me. Which one is not guilty?"

She placed her finger on the one in the middle and said, "He is the one that is not guilty." Then after a little hesitation, she added, "He's my uncle."

"When will we have the hearings?" I questioned.

"We just did," she responded.

I thanked her for her honesty with me and left. Seven of the violators pled guilty and paid their fine. A hearing was scheduled for the owner of one of the eight cars at a later date. The hearing went as expected, though the defendant submitted proof that he was away on a business trip at the time of the violation. He continued to argue, even after the verdict had been given.

She looked him right in the eye and told him, "You know your wife is running around on you when you are out of town, and I know for a fact she was at the hotel that night. My uncle told me."

THE BROKEN OAR

Deputy Sally and I had talked the case over on the way to the court. Sal had cited the man for running a boat after dark on Lily Lake, without lights. We were in a magistrate's court where one of the grandmother figures presided. The defendant had told Sally he had fished until after dark and, in order not to break the law, had begun to row back to the ramp. Halfway in he had snapped the old oar and had to start the engine to get in.

Sally told me she had not seen a broken oar until he had gone to his car. I told her it sounded like a defense that the magistrate would buy and there was a good chance we would lose this one. However, I told her to give it her best shot. I had talked to the magistrate, and she had said the defendant had told the broken oar story when he scheduled the hearing. She was not convinced he should be cited, but would see how the hearing went.

The defendant showed up and carried a broken oar into the courtroom. I figured that the stage was set for a loss. The hearing progressed by the book, but neither the defendant nor his attorney mentioned the broken oar during the process. He fought the charges on a lot of fronts, but never the broken oar. He was found guilty.

After the hearing, we hung around while the man left with his broken oar and his attorney. Then I spoke up. "I thought he was going to use a broken oar defense."

"So did I," said the magistrate. "If he would have, I had decided it was a good one and he would have been found not guilty."

I often wondered if in the heat of the courtroom battle he and his attorney had just forgotten, or whether he had decided at the last minute not to perjure himself for the sake of a $25 fine.

THE WRONG DEFENSE

Attorneys can be an officer's best friend. I was prosecuting several fellows for violations of the daily limit of trout. They had an attorney that was obviously a friend of their father or grandfather. He was well-aged and must have practiced corporate law for years. He had been called on to defend a violation of the Fish Law, a law he was unfamiliar with.

As the hearing progressed, it became evident that he was not even defending the correct section of the law. Two totally different law sections were being talked about when he and I spoke. It was frustrating for me, Sally, my deputy, and the magistrate.

Finally I couldn't take it anymore. I signaled for a "timeout." Just like on the football field. The magistrate, a grand old lady, recognized the signal and asked that the defense attorney and I approach the bench. I approached, carrying my law book and speaking softly so the defendants couldn't hear me explain to the attorney, with the magistrate listening, that he was on the "wrong page." He thanked me. I suggested we take a 15-minute recess so that I might use the restroom. The magistrate concurred and called the recess. I did not need the restroom.

After the defense attorney had time to re-prepare, the court reconvened. Now the case went along more traditional lines. After some deliberation, the magistrate found the defendants guilty as charged. The attorney turned and exited with his clients. They were convinced he had done a good job. The magistrate called Sally and me into her office and said she had never seen a move like that and laughed. I explained to her that I had been raised to never take unfair advantage in a fight. It does amaze me, though, that with only a high school education I have been able to win 90 percent of my cases against college-educated attorneys.

BLUE, BLUE, MY JEANS ARE BLUE

The defendant, Irving's business was washing blue jeans to give them the pre-washed look that was the craze in the late '70s. When I arrived at the scene of the complaint, a little tributary stream was running blue-jean blue from a pipe coming from his plant and then entering a crystal-clear meadow stream. I took photos and samples.

The hearing was originally set for the correct jurisdiction, but much political pressure came to bear on the magistrate from local business groups. He had been told that if found guilty of the pollution, Irving would have to fire people. The fine was only $100 at the time.

At the hearing, before anything could get started, the magistrate stated that the case had been rescheduled in a neutral jurisdiction because of the pressure, and that the county judge had sanctioned the change of venue. This was bigger than I thought.

A month later, slide projector, sample analysis and my assistant supervisor, Bob Perry, in tow, I entered another magistrate's court. A court I had never been in. I didn't know what to expect. The defendant and his attorney were present and ready to get started, as I set up my slide paraphernalia.

The hearing progressed and I entered the slide presentation into evidence. One picture showed the crystal-clear stream being met by the blue-jean dye runoff turning it a striking shade of blue. I testified as to the source and pointed to the blue-tinged water.

"I can't see any blue water," the defendant jumped up and interrupted. His attorney then walked to the screen with me and, pointing to the blue water coming in, said, "Oh yeah, Irving, you can see it real clear right here." Supervisor Perry stifled a snicker, as did the magistrate and me. The defendant was found guilty. Whatever he paid his attorney, that day, was too much.

I DON'T EITHER; GUILTY

The field acknowledgement of guilt was a wonderful tool for the conservation officer. Legal procedure dictated that it was not admissible as state's evidence ... unless you could get away with it. After all, a signed confession in hand is hard to ignore.

The case dealt with a fish out of season and the defendant had pled guilty via the field acknowledgement of guilt, but then failed to pay in the time required. A citation was filed with the lady who was the magistrate in my district at the time. At the hearing, testimony by the state showed that the fish was in fact a bass and that bass season was in fact closed. I then submitted the field acknowledgement as evidence that the defendant knew he had violated and then, for whatever reason, had decided he wasn't guilty and had requested the hearing.

As the magistrate read the field acknowledgement, the defense attorney jumped up and objected, "If you are going to accept that, I don't know why we are even having a hearing."

The magistrate looked up over her glasses and responded, "I don't either. Guilty."

She then rose and left the courtroom.

ERNIE, I DESPISE YOU

Every district has a person that is a known violator that just hasn't been caught red-handed. He is usually one of those guys that skips from job to job, because they know he is either thieving or not producing, but it is easier to give him the oust and a good recommendation rather than document his ineptitude or criminal tendencies.

These guys always want to be the officer's buddy. They are constantly "sucking up," hoping you will fall for the ruse.

"Can I see the officers and the counsel in my chambers?" the magistrate, Monte, requested.

For a half hour, the counselor and I jockeyed for position. I never played my ace. "You've got to know when to hold them, know when to fold them." The words of the song kept ringing in my ears. Eventually, despite the whining and pleading by the magistrate, it was decided by the counselor and me that this one had to be fought out on the playing field.

As the case progressed, I could see that my evidence was crumbling under the pressure applied by the opposition. It was all headed for the tubes. I waited too late and when I played my ace, the case was already gone. I had detained the defendant, his star witness, Ernie, and the counselor for nearly two hours. I felt some consolation in that fact and in the fact that I had presented proof that Ernie had snagged steelhead in Erie, 250 miles away. He had pled guilty and paid the fine. I had exposed him. He was a hostile witness with an ax to grind. I had, nonetheless, taken a beating.

The deputy and I headed for the car, when Ernie called to me.

"Stein, I want you to understand that I didn't do the snagging thing. I was a victim of circumstances up there," he mumbled on.

I stopped as he approached. I put my arm around his shoulder and whispered in his ear. "I want you to understand, Ernie. I despise you."

He pulled out from under my arm and never talked to me again while I was stationed there. I can't believe I hadn't done that before.

PICNIC TABLE CHECK

"He is the best outlaw around," they said of Brent Largely when I got into Venango County. I knew it was only a matter of time until I ran into this phantom of the woods. It turned out he was a client before the first quarter of my first year had passed. We had a nose-to-nose confrontation. My nose was larger and he backed down. When the posturing, screaming and threatening were all over, he cracked the window of his truck an inch to accept his citations. He didn't want to get out of the truck out of fear.

Minutes before, I had torn after him and chased his old, gnarled hide back into the truck when he stepped out to threaten. When he died a few years later, we had had a history. I don't think he was as good an outlaw as everyone said, since he was always getting caught. The best outlaws, nobody knows. With his passing, though, I mourned. He was a good, reliable source of overtime.

When a tipster called the office and complained and used Largely's name, I was sent on the run. He was notorious. Over the years I had owned him to the point that I even sat in his house and had a coffee among the dirt and decay, while he paid not only his fine but also his friend's one night. To win the respect of these hombres, I have found that a random appearance at odd times is the best method.

Brent had a passion for catfishing. You would find him during the nights of the summer anywhere they were hitting. I liked working nights. One of Largely's favorite places to fish was below the fishing pier at the county park lake. The bullheads would move up under darkness and feed in the shallow water. I would drive by on the road several hundred yards away, see a lantern glowing and know who it was. I would drive on and eventually park around the corner, a quarter mile away. Then I would slither through the dark woods without a light, until I was but 50 yards behind him.

Sooner or later he would walk down to the edge of the lake to check his two rods. He would reel them in, check his bait and recast. While he was doing this, I would move silently and sit down next to the lantern that he left on the picnic table where he sat. When he turned around to come back to the table, I would be sitting there. I would make some small talk about the fishing, then walk off into the darkness, often right into the woods along the lake, and disappear in a direction totally opposite of the car. Once out of sight I would circle to the car and leave, knowing that he would wonder for days how I had gotten there and where I had come from. You have to keep them guessing.

PARKER PECKINPAUGH

Parker Peckinpaugh is a parrot. He rides on a tall, well-muscled man's shoulders in a motorized kayak of grand proportions and uses the man's tee-shirt for a latrine. Parker is strange.

I was training a cadet, Erin, on jet-boat skills and enjoying a nice boat ride. The Allegheny River was up and there were few obstacles. The sky had white, puffy clouds that all looked like slain dinosaurs lying with their feet up in the air. We had gone nearly 30 miles and seen one boat and four fishermen.

At the office that morning, the boss had mentioned that Officer Carter had cited a man with a parrot on his shoulder, on the Allegheny at Tidioute, on Saturday. We just laughed. Now as we rounded the bend in the river, a long kayak with a motor cruised ahead of us. We immediately noted that it had no registration visible. The operator, pony-tailed and with a hat to protect the bald top of his head, had a parrot on his shoulder.

"This should be rare," I said to Erin, wishing I had heard the whole story earlier.

The fine for a second and subsequent offense is a triple fine and would amount to nearly $200. I knew nothing about what the fellow had been cited for the first time, yet. I asked him to shore and sicked Erin on him. She bounded from the boat, all 5-foot of her, and began to quiz the man in the kayak. He quickly produced a copy of a field acknowledgement from Carter and explained he had been told that this copy would exempt him from any further legal action.

If I knew that was what Carter had said, I would have certainly respected it, but somehow doubted it. The kayaker had no boat registration and, when Erin explained the triple fine and the fact that nonresidents are bound by the pay-or-stay law, he asked to talk to a judge.

I told him to pull in at Emlenton, a short ways down the river, where he would see our boat. When we got there ahead of him, I sent Erin to call the office to verify, if possible, what Carter had said. Marlene, our secretary, said Carter had told him not to use the motor. I had Erin explain to Parker's pal the procedures again and that we could not let him continue without a registration. He said he would certainly get one. Parker said, "Rawk," or whatever parrots say to sound like words.

Erin had checked on our arrival at Emlenton, but the one boat shop that was an issuing agent was not open. We secured the two boats and Erin and me and the defendant and Parker strode through town and into the magistrate's office.

After a short conference with the magistrate, to brief him on the situation, and another unsuccessful attempt to establish what Carter had actually said, it was decided that I should issue Parker's pal a citation. The magistrate would have an immediate hearing, and then we could get this over with. This done, we were soon in the courtroom, Erin and me on one side, and Parker and his pal on the other.

The judge read the charges and Parker's pal entered a plea. Erin did a good job of presenting the state's case, and Parker's pal cross-examined and then gave his side of the story. He felt it unreasonable to expect him to know the river well enough to know where to get his boat registered. I explained that the state felt that he should have registered before embarking, but could sympathize with his plight. Parker said, "Rawk."

The judge listened intently and made a just ruling that the man was not guilty, since he had no reasonable opportunity to comply. I certainly concurred; not that my concurrence was necessary.

Parker said, "Rawk."

Erin took a loss for her first trip to the magistrate's court, but the judge added that the boat would have to be registered before it could move on. I got the county treasurer to fax the forms. The defendant filled them out and registered his 22-foot kayak, paying the fees in cash to the judge. I took the cash money, made change and wrote a check to the county treasurer.

Parker and his pal were on their way on a journey to retrace the steps of some famous explorers, for a TV camera crew. We walked them to their boat and we parted company congenially. I haven't talked to the magistrate since then, but don't imagine he was too happy about Parker's random toileting and preening feathers all over his office.

My first official patrol uniform when I still fit in it. That is Sugar Creek back in the winter of 1974-1975. Notice the near total lack of law enforcement hardware. We carried an optional ".38 Snubby" back then. Attitude, smoke and mirrors got you through the tough spots.

CHAPTER 14:
Snakes and Turtles and Frogs, Aha!

Some agency had to be responsible for the well-being of herps. The game folks got the tweety birds and the small and fuzzies, as well as the game species. The Department of Conservation and Natural Resources got trees and bushes and butterflies and such. We got the slimy herps. Can someone explain to me why fishermen are paying for the well-being of these things? Shouldn't the taxpayer pick up the bill on herps and all the non-game species the Game Commission is assigned? DCNR should have all but game animals and game fish. DCNR is funded with taxpayer money. Why are hunters and fishermen paying for all these other creatures?

SHERLOCK AND THE FROG
By the nature of the Fish Law, the only time we should get directly involved with guns is dealing with frog hunters. Guns never scared me. I've been around them all my life. But when guns and frogs get mentioned in the same sentence anymore, the hair stands up on the back of my neck.

It all started in the early 1970s. I had received a note from my Assistant Supervisor, Bob Perry, listing a person's name and address, which was incidentally located in a ghetto-like area of a Luzerne County "coal patch" town. The note read that the actor was accused by an anonymous neighbor of shooting frogs out of season with a BB gun. He was reported to shoot the frogs between the eyes, knocking them out, capture them and then confine them in a pond in his yard.

The note closed with, "Please Sherlock this." This was not an uncommon closing from Bob, a fan of the fictional British detective of much renown.

After investigating, I wrote the following response:
"Subject: The Great Frog Caper
To: Doctor Watson
From: Sherlock Holmes

Never one to postpone the administration of justice, I set aside all other callings and, being most intrigued with your note, called for my trap, donned my deerstalker cap, lit a bowl of fine Turkish tobacco extracted from a Persian slipper, and headed across the moor to my destination.

While the information in your note was only somewhat correct, I was soon to meet the huge (nearly seven-feet-tall) Mr. Walter Patuskin, of house 666 East Main Street, Glen Leigh. He answered the door only after much knocking, which aroused a rather large, nondescript black dog that was tied by a very short chain in the corner of the lot, in mounds of its own dung, near larger mounds of Stegmeier beer cans. He (Patuskin) was sparsely attired in a pair of green-and-white boxer shorts, a white-turning-gray tee-shirt and an open smoking jacket. His hair was matted and unkempt.

I was ushered into the dining chamber, where eight or nine assorted cats dined on the table. Being one of constant scrutiny, I immediately noted a Daisy BB gun leaning in the corner, behind the coal furnace. Ballistics research I performed as a younger man in the fields of western Pennsylvania were immediately recalled, and I recognized that the weapon, a Red Rider type, was fully capable of bushel-basket accuracy at ranges as great as 15 feet, even in the hands of the 35-year-old Mr. Patuskin. He surely was the right suspect.

Further noting that he seemed somewhat incoherent, I deemed the time proper to broach the evidence and questions pursuant to the crime that I was investigating. He readily admitted to being a student of frog husbandry and had at one time kept frogs (bulls) at stud, in hopes of raising the sometime-national champion. To Mr. Patuskin, the Kentucky Derby has nothing over the festivities in Calaveras County, documented by my good friend Samuel Langhorne Clemens some time ago.

He then took me for a tour of his "stable," where his prime jumpers and croakers had been kept. The "frog stable" was a unique structure, unlike any I had previously seen, even though I am a student of these things. It consisted of a two-by-three-foot structure dug to resemble a mud puddle, but lined neatly, first with black plastic and then with red bricks. Around all was screening on stakes. There were no frogs evident, and I was informed that all the frogs in his "lake" had died earlier. Chunks of smelly green slime in one corner confirmed his testimony.

I explained to Mr. Patuskin that I could understand that his frogs had all died, but that I did not feel that the cold weather affected them nearly as badly as burrowing into the bottom red bricks must have as they tried to escape the first wintry blasts.

At this point in the investigation, I decided it was time to close the case for several reasons, not the least of which was the fact that, besides being a student of frog husbandry, the prime suspect was obviously not the criminal element for which I had begun my search. He was a true lover of frogs and not necessarily mentally competent, in my estimation. I therefore advised him of the need for a fishing license and the necessity of waiting for the proper season and assured him he would hear no more of this nor would his employer, Ghost Town Park.

With that, I remounted my trap and headed it for the sweet solitude of the Sugarloaf, glorying in the satisfaction of another investigation completed and knowing fully that my administration of justice had been fair and true. I relit my smoke and pondered the sense of it all.

Stein"

This, one of my first frog-and-gun events, should have prepared me for what was to come.

SHOT FOR A FROG

The sun had set an hour ago, when deputy Bob and I approached the mud ponds at Slocum Corners. These two ponds were interconnected, hooked together by a narrow channel among some cattails and lily pads. You could slowly push a boat through by poling it, but generally it was a once-a-year patrol, since the labor involved usually was rewarded with only one or two fishermen on the back pond.

An old, cantankerous fisherman was pulling his johnboat from the water and loading it on a roof rack. Bob helped him load it, and then the man began complaining about the guys shooting frogs out of season in the back pond, at night with a light.

"When?" I countered, somewhat defensively.

"Right now," he retorted.

"Can we borrow your boat?" I quizzed, as a .22 shoot rang from the upper pond.

"Hell no. Get your own boat," he responded.

"I don't care if they shoot all the frogs back there, then," I answered. "Let's go Bob, before someone else wants us to go protect some silly damn frogs."

Bob knew something was up and, after looking at me somewhat disconcerted, jumped in the car. We drove up the road and out of sight, turned around, and I sat watching until the old duffer left. He had annoyed me and I didn't want to give him the satisfaction of thinking he had won. Now that he was gone, I pulled the state car to the nearest point of the front pond and set our strategy.

There was a bog along both sides of the front pond. One corner was passable by walking through the woods or by 4WD on an old, badly debilitated tram road. We hid the state iron and headed in the well-rutted tram road on foot past the front pond. There were always a few boats tied to the trees back there by panfishermen, and tonight was no different. One old Jeep was parked and we felt sure, since there were no other noises on the back pond, that we had the exit vehicle covered. However, a touch of the engine cover revealed it hadn't run for some time. We may be dealing with pros here that walked in.

Bob was left to cover the obvious exit. I, now muddy to my knees anyhow, would try to shadow the boat along the shore from just inside the woods. I'd be ready to intercept it if another exit was used. The night was muggy for late May and the mosquitoes were unruly, sucking pints of blood a minute. After an hour or so of observation, interspersed periodically with a rifle shot, the rowboat approached a seldom-used tram road hundreds of yards from where I had left Bob guarding the Jeep.

I hunkered behind a blueberry bush along the road, next to the shoreline. My object was to be in position to grab the catch before any effort could be made to ditch the frogs. The bugs ate my arms, head and legs incessantly. Thank God I couldn't see them. I would probably have screamed.

Two men were in the boat, the one in the bow was working the light. The other was the shooter. He would slowly row the boat and then shoot when the light man spotted a frog. All I could see was the light in the front of the boat being shined toward the shore. Soon they were slowly rowing for the old road that I stood watch on.

"There it is!" the light man said.

They were not 20 feet away and closing. The pond bottom looked muddy in the light as I peered around the bush, analyzing the footing for my initial rush toward the violators. The muscles in my legs summoned my remaining blood, mixing it with adrenaline for the charge. I was convinced they were landing within feet of me. With every sense on red alert, I tensed.

What happened next will be forever etched in my mind. The gun cracked and the bullet ricocheted off the water, slapping into a stump not a foot from my head, at eye level. Instinct took over. I flattened behind the stump, taking cover.

"You missed," said the light man, and they rowed away.

Slowly it sunk in. They had never seen me. The shot had been at a frog that was sitting on the edge, quietly eating mosquitoes in front of me. They didn't know the tram road was even there. Once they were back out in the lake, I retreated to higher ground, now pretty well mud covered. I went up to Bob. We sat on a boulder and I whispered to him what had happened.

An hour later the two guys rowed in with their illegal take. One was a juvenile and the other was of age. They paid fines and the juvenile was returned to his parents, with the gun, at about 1 a.m. The mother inflicted punishment beyond the fine, when told the whole story. We took our leave.

As we rode away in the Matador, Bob looked at me and laughed, then caught himself and said, "I can see the headline now: 'Local Warden Shot in Mistake for Frog.'"

STABBING FROGS

Memorial Day was uneventful, as one of the heaviest rains of the season pelted the northwest region. Patrols were not much more than a ride around the soaked countryside. An early quit was in order. I sat at home with friends visiting from Hazleton.

It was nearly midnight and still pouring, when my supervisor called and said that he had received a call. Someone was taking frogs illegally at Justus Lake. He was rolling, but it would take him a while to get there. I saddled up and headed out, since I lived closer.

When I rounded the bend, looking down I saw a light by the fishing pier on the edge of the lake. It appeared to be working the shoreline slowly, like a blue heron. I drove into the parking lot with my portable red light flashing and headlights on and then realized I hadn't been seen. I extinguished all lights and parked back away from the opening. These guys were engrossed in their shenanigans.

I grabbed a flashlight, but left it turned off. Their light allowed me to see their actions and, in a few minutes, I saw they had a lantern, a landing net and a knife. They would spot the frog, net it, then stab it and put it in the bucket. They were good at it, killing several in the few minutes I watched. I moved toward them through the rain.

When I was but a step away, I snatched the bucket from the one man's hand, lit my flashlight and roared, "State Officer! Freeze and drop the knife!"

Startled by my previously unknown presence, they immediately complied. When my supervisor arrived, I was already writing. The fines amounted to almost $200 apiece when the frogs were counted.

That summer was quiet at the lake. They seemed to have gotten about every frog there. You had to wonder if this was the first night they had operated. Rain and darkness are good cover for violating the law, but it is better cover for a warden with a tip.

STABBING SNAKES

Laws are for interpreting. If they weren't, we wouldn't need so many attorneys. A "fish" by definition in the Fish Law includes reptiles and amphibians. Therefore, if you need a license to possess any fish taken from Commonwealth waters, you need a license to take snakes and such.

I was driving down along Lake Creek in the heat of summer, when I saw someone moving in the stream in the alder bushes. I pulled across a bridge, got out and walked to where I could see what was going on.

Two 20-year-old men were in the creek with homemade spears, plastic-handled hunting knives wired to the front of sticks. I figured I would watch a while. Soon they took off splashing and hollering for a short distance, and then stood still, letting the mud clear. I watched this act several times and still could not see what they were after. Rather than miss my next appointment, I made my approach.

"What's happening guys?" I asked.

"Stabbing snakes," was the reply.

"Any particular reason you're stabbing snakes?"

"Fun. Why? Aren't we allowed to?" they answered.

"If you got a fishing license you can," I responded.

"Mine's up the house, I'll go get it," the shorter of the two said.

"I don't have one," the tall guy said.

Thus I became one of the first wardens to ever write a "stabbing snakes without a license" case.

SALAMANDER SALESMEN

Newts, the pretty red ones, not the political ones that cause governing warts, seemed to be the object of a search that was leaving no log unturned in Hickory Run State Park. I watched with my binoculars as a man and woman relentlessly searched through the picnic grove, each with a pail in hand. When I asked what they were doing, they volunteered that they were collecting newts.

"Making soup?" I asked.

"No, we own a pet shop in New York City. Do they make good soup?" he said.

"Do you know that commercialization of wildlife is a violation of the federal Lacey Act when a state line is crossed?" I answered, still trying to imagine newt soup.

"Are we under arrest?" the pretty girl chimed in.

"Do you have the fishing license required for recreational newt gathering?" I quizzed.

They looked surprised. I thought everyone knew you needed a newt-gathering license. I was just fishing for information before I made my decision. I was leaning toward returning the newts and a warning, when the girl helped me along to another, more equitable ending to the case.

"We do this every summer. We get ten dollars apiece for them. Are we going to have to let them go?"

They settled the fine for fishing without a non-resident fishing license, were made aware of state and federal laws and the newts were returned.

I used to think that campground kids were the biggest threat to the world's population of newts. Now I know it is New Yorkers.

TWO-YEAR-OLD WARNING

The Fish Law at the time was in dire need of rewriting and had some archaic clauses. One of these required a person of any age taking frogs or tadpoles to have a fishing license. We had begun to write written warnings on every warning situation.

One day as I pulled into the driveway of one of my most active deputies, I noticed his two-year-old daughter chasing tadpoles with a paper cup in a rain puddle. She and I were buddies. I got out my written warning report form and proceeded to write the warning for the violation taking place. I mailed it to the office and never heard a word about it.

When rewritten a few years later, the Fish Law no longer had that "persons of any age" frog or tadpole-taking licensing requirement in it.

Young Fish Law violators were easier to apprehend. This youngster admitted to wanting to catch tadpoles without a license and was sentenced to a lifetime of being my niece.

CHAPTER 15:
Game Calls

Game wardens are people, too. We have to give them some slack. Their job is even more boredom between things happening than most police-type officer's. Then, when it happens, it happens. Usually it all starts with a gunshot. I worked diligently in Luzerne County with Game Protector Bob Nolf and his deputies. By the time I got to Venango County, I had earned leave that had to be used, so I used it bowhunting and let the game guys do their thing. I have been involved in about 50 game cases and have ridden a hundred or more night patrols. I never passed by a game law violation without taking action during my whole career, and actually for some time after. Game violators make me mad.

THIRTEEN-YEAR-OLD MELANIE
It was the first day of a snowy doe season. We were on the Venango/Warren/Forest county corner. I was hunting with my walking stick, having plum run out of tags in archery season. I would roam around and push the deer and hope that they would run to one of my friends or family that was hunting in the area.

Around lunchtime, I cut a track and started to follow it. In less than a half mile I had caught up to it. Actually, there were two, with three riders. I signaled the ATVs to stop and they did, having no reason to suspect I was a warden.

I produced a badge, then checked their licenses and determined that they had loaded guns on the vehicles. I collected shells, guns and personal information and matched them to the ATV information I had written down. I began to look at the names on the hunting licenses I had placed in my pocket.

"Which of you guys is Melanie?" I asked.

"I am," a six-foot-plus hombre with a full beard answered. "It's my daughter's license."

"I would have never guessed," I replied.

Everything in the woods went as scripted, and I departed with enough information to present a strong case for the Game Commission, if I needed to. I dislike people that are too lazy to walk when they still can and just think of does as target practice. I took some personal satisfaction in this case.

Since the defendants had indicated their willingness to pay their fines at the time, I returned to my car thinking they were "camp people" that would soon be heading for Pittsburgh and their wives after the hunt. I drove to a pay phone, contacted the Game Commission office in Franklin and explained who I was and what I was doing up in that area.

I asked would they have the Game Protector responsible for that area meet me as soon as possible, since I was going home that evening and didn't want either of us to have to travel far if we didn't have to. I would be waiting for him by my maroon van, my personal vehicle, along the township road.

It was about 40 minutes later when the Waterways Patrolman for Warren County, Jonesy, came flying up to the intersection where I was parked. I was eating a candy bar and drinking coffee. As he slid to a stop, I noticed the blood all over the side of his white state Jeep. He jumped out.

"Where are they?" he asked.

"Who?" I countered.

"The guys you have at gunpoint," he responded.

"I don't have anybody at gunpoint. I don't even have a gun," I told him.

"My reception on the radio was broken, but thought you had someone at gunpoint."

I laughed and explained the case and turned the evidence over to him to present to the Game Protector, as the violation had taken place in his district.

"How did you get that blood all over your car, Jones?" I quizzed.

He turned around and looked at it and rolled his eyes back in his head.

"Right up the road here I rounded the bend and an old guy was dragging a deer on the road. I thought you had these guys at gunpoint, so I was really hauling. The road was icy. Well, the guy had time to jump out of the way, but I hit his deer."

By now I was crying from laughing. I could just see this guy explaining to his buddies at camp that the deer wasn't a road-kill, that he had killed it first and then it got hit by a car.

"I think I'll go home the long way," George said, pointing the opposite way he had come from. "That guy may be waiting for me to come back, and I don't think he had time to read my license plate after he got up out of the snow he dived into."

ATV CHASING DOES

I used to believe that television would lead to the eternal damnation of mankind. I know now that that is not true. It will be ATVs. Not too long ago, hunting required only a gun, some shells and a license and the desire to spend time in the solitude of the woods. With the ATV, it has become a contest of technology versus the prey.

ATVs afford the fat and weak of heart the same privileges of being on top of the mountain as those that earn the top through sweat and determination. Additionally, they are the cause of more posted land than all the real fishermen and hunters ever were. Their trails and "must conquer the wilds" attitude causes more and more woodland owners to post each and every year.

I was enjoying a second week of buck season hunt with my father at Two Mile Run County Park, in a heavy snowfall. The world was hushed and we were moving a few deer. I was carrying a walking stick and he was carrying his venerable .280 Remington.

I had just completed a little drive, when he dropped to one knee and started to swing the rifle, whispering, "Here comes two deer," and after a short hesitation, "Both does." Then as he rose up, he said, "There's an ATV chasing them."

I took off on an intercept line, running hard, and lost sight of the does. Then they came barreling out of the weeds so close and low to the ground that I had to do a stutter-step to keep from running into them. Soon the ATV followed, right into my path.

I motioned the guy to stop and when he did, I nonchalantly immobilized his machine by sliding my walking stick between some of the working parts. I then badged him and found him to be hunting with a loaded gun on the machine, in addition to chasing deer with a motorized vehicle.

Since it was a violation of park ordinances as well as Game Law, both agencies received the information and hefty fines were paid.

SHIVERING, WIFE'S TAG

It was a particularly nasty opening day of buck season. I had friends and relatives and friends of relatives hunting with us that year. We decided to give the Catawissa area of Columbia County a try.

The morning started as heavy rain and turned to ice and then snow, all within the first hour. It was hunting at its best. After a 10 o'clock break to get dry clothes from the van, I decided to make a little circle and try to get the deer stirring since I was tag-less, due to a successful archery season.

In front of me in the laurel I heard the shot and soon came on a steaming spike buck. The hunter was in an illegal permanent stand, built on the edge of a game lands food plot.

"He's down here!" I hollered.

"I know," the hunter said, without moving.

"Well, come down and get him," I instructed.

"I'm too cold to move," he responded.

I then looked and noticed he was in a lightweight jacket and cotton blue jeans and both were soaked. He shivered badly. I talked him through getting down. We went to the deer and he began cleaning it. He shook several times uncontrollably. Finally he asked me to go get his wife at a certain car.

"Why?" I asked.

"She's going to tag this one. It's too cold for her to hunt," he replied as he shook.

"I think you should tag it since you shot it," I replied.

"She always tags the first one," he came back.

"Not this year. Use your tag," I stated.

Now I wasn't armed, except for my walking stick, but I was bigger than him and wasn't debilitated by the weather, like him. He looked at me for a second and then asked me to get his tag from his back. I did and watched as he filled out the tag, then I left as he began dragging.

He had come seriously close to not hunting at all the next year and being short on Christmas money.

QUICK-GROWING SPIKES

It was the first Friday of buck season when game deputy Del and I strayed into the neighboring district near F. E. Walter Reservoir. Actually it was my district, but a different game protector was assigned there, not Nolfie, Del's boss.

We were traveling toward the dam from White Haven and going past a private lake, when three deer ran toward us between the lake and the road. I stopped the car and, with the binoculars, at 30 yards proclaimed that they were all does and drove on. The roads were snow-covered and the woods held nearly a foot of the white stuff.

We had gotten out of sight around a bend, when the crack of a rifle echoed from where we had just seen the does. I wheeled the Matador around and started back down toward White Haven.

Standing on the edge of the road with a rifle in his hand was a sergeant in one of the local police contingencies. Several empty shells lay on the road and his car door was still open. I was on him like a hound dog on a rabbit. I told him he not only was in trouble for road hunting and using a vehicle to hunt, but he had shot at and, by the blood trail, hit a doe. I was going to find her and charge him with that as well.

I told Del to take the car and off I went after the doe. She was bleeding a little, but not real good. After several hundred yards, I looked and behind me came Del and the cop. The cop had his rifle and Del looked worried. When they caught up, I was quickly told that the cop really believed it was a buck and wanted to see for himself.

We hadn't gone much farther when I spotted the deer lying under some brush ahead of us, still breathing. Not only did it have horns, it had six or seven-inch horns. I pointed it out to the cop and told him to shoot it again.

"Are you sure?" he asked now.

"I'm sure."

"Are you absolutely sure?"

"Shoot the darn thing, it's suffering!" I exclaimed.

The caper was over. Del was helping him dress it, when a shot rang out right ahead of us.

"Now, that is a doe," I said to Del and took off.

In short order I came on an old man standing over a deer and shaking his head from side to side.

"What's the matter, pop?" I opened, fully expecting a confession of his having shot a doe. It didn't happen.

"I have hunted deer for 39 years and never shot one. Always felt bad 'cause all the other guys had the luck. Now I shoot one and feel so bad I don't think I will ever shoot one again."

By now I had maneuvered around and, by gosh, it had four-inch antlers. The tracks said they had to be two of the three deer I had declared as does along the road. I helped the old guy clean the deer and tag it and dragged it down to Del and the cop. We dragged both deer out of the woods together.

I'll bet the third one was a buck, too.

STASHED GUN

I was working with Del in the Honey Hole section of the game lands along Nescopeck Creek. It was doe day, and I had backed the Matador up on a power line where I could see with the spotting scope what was going on below.

The deer drive we were watching was over, so we decided to move down and check their licenses. While we were still several hundred yards away, an old guy walked his rifle into the woods. He came back without it. They obviously had seen us.

We checked their licenses and everything looked good, but the old guy was missing a doe tag. When asked if he had any luck he responded, "Got a doe this morning. Just driving now, not hunting."

"Where's the doe?" Del asked.

"Out there in my car." He pointed toward the road a short distance away.

"Well, let's go have a look at it," Del suggested.

"I need to drain my bladder," I offered and headed into the woods where I had seen the gun disappear earlier.

As Del and the three guys walked out toward the car, I could see them looking back to watch me. They were soon where I couldn't be seen. I easily found the .308 stashed alongside a log.

I had to walk out to the car to them, since there was a culvert missing that even the Matador couldn't jump. I got to their car when the trunk was open and a nice, big, fat doe was in view. I stood with the rifle slung on my shoulder and said nothing. Del looked at me quizzically, knowing I was up to something, but saying nothing.

"Nice deer," I offered. I closed the trunk and motioned Del to come with me, we were leaving. Before I had gone but a few steps, I said to Del, so all could hear, "I was standing there, draining my bladder, when my eyes focused on this rifle. Someone must have left it in buck season and forgotten it. Looks like I found myself a new rifle. Nice scope."

"Hey, warden, that's my gun," came the call from the old guy.

"You told us you weren't hunting, just driving," I reminded him.

"I know. I lied. It's my gun."

"You got any proof?" I asked.

"C'mon, I was hunting and when I saw you coming, I knew I would get arrested for trying to take a second deer, so I stashed it behind a log. I can show you the log."

"That's OK, I believe you," I answered.

Del grinned.

STONECRUSHER BAITING

Nolfie always did his homework. Sometimes I felt he overdid it. But this opening morning of buck season, we were all primed and heading into a section of steep woodland near Wapwallopen.

I was part of a group of nearly 15 fish and game officers and deputies. Bob had located an area that was heavily baited, dump-truck loads, and had spent many dark nights wandering around the posted acreage and mapping it all out for today.

Three or four of us had joined him and knew our way around. We all had several other officers assigned to help. As we moved in, officers would drop off. If it didn't pan out, we would withdraw past a given point at 10 o'clock. Then we would know everybody was out. It was a master plan.

Shortly after daylight, a high-powered rifle barked, not 10 feet below me, from a blind built against the base of the ledge that I lay atop. A fine, wide seven-point buck fell nose-first into a pile of apples and potatoes that was as high as I am tall.

I arrived at the downed deer the same time as the shooter. He recognized me from shooting bow with me and quickly asked, "What are you doing here?"

As I removed his license from his back and relieved him of his rifle and shells, I explained. I encouraged him to clean the buck and drag it to his friend's stand where the party was being held. Before it was over, there were several illegally killed bucks and a bunch of tickets for hunting over bait. It was a solid case, and it went smoothly.

However, much to our surprise, the next day a local outdoor writer took us to task for the case. "It was all based on circumstantial evidence," was the report. I quickly called the writer, whom I knew through an organization of writers I belonged to, and explained that he had handled it unfairly and he should attend the hearing when it came up. In the meantime, he should talk to our common friend, the one that I had arrested, and then I would expect a retraction to be printed. To my surprise, it was.

SPLISH SPLASH

Every fisherman has done it. You walk up on your buddy and he is intent on fishing. You pick up a small rock and pitch it in the water in front of him. The splash startles him. He curses you and then laughs once his initial reaction passes. It is meant in good fun and nobody gets hurt.

It was just after daylight when I noticed John and Terry's cars parked along Sugar Creek. I slowly moved in and spotted them fishing, with Terry's dad, on the other side of the creek. I couldn't resist it. Two Game Commission deputies fishing and I was going to get to startle them. I worked with these guys regularly, and all I had in mind was good, clean fun.

I picked up a rock a little bigger than a fist and carefully tossed it, making sure it would fall short of them and maybe, if I was lucky, even splash them.

I hadn't seen Wyatt, another old timer, standing on the near side along the brush. The rock whizzed past his ear by inches and he was up over the bank chewing my butt in a heartbeat. I stood there and let him chew. I had it coming. I was just thankful I had missed.

STANDING BEAR

The Stonecrusher Mountain is a landmark in the Wapwallopen area of Luzerne County. Many years ago, I worked it with a game deputy now deceased, Vince. We would back the Matador as high up the power line at the PP&L fields as we could and sit drinking coffee and eating big bags of cookies that his wife would send. It was always a good time, but I don't remember getting even one case at the location. One night, however, I do remember getting the "bejeezus" scared out of us.

We had backed up nearly halfway to the top. I was pretty good at making the Matador climb mountains in forward or reverse. I set the brake. We turned off the lights and put a cloth over the radio lights.

We sat watching the snow fall and melt on the hood. Nearly half a bag of cookies later, the snow stopped and the moon came out. It was getting very cold and windy. We couldn't run the engine for fear of being noticed, so we sat and shivered and drank coffee and ate cookies.

About 50 yards in front of us down the hill, something walked across the power line in the moonlight, upright like a man. As sitting ducks for a rifleman and not believing there were any Sasquatches in the area, I took that Matador down the power line like a bolt from the blue.

The next morning in the daylight, I walked back up to see what was going on, but the tracks were all blown out. I'll never know if it was a man moonlight hunting that didn't see us at first or a bear that was upright and walking that had winded something and was intent on doing us or our cookie bag harm. I do know it was a long time until I sat in that spot again.

CATCH A FALLING PHEASANT

Hunting wild pheasants is about as much fun as a guy should be allowed to have. Shooting "stockers," however, is another story. What you generally accomplish is shooting a small, chicken-like critter that is full of BBs and not very good eating. However, wherever there are plenty of stocked pheasants, there will be hogs to reap the bounty.

Luzerne County got more pheasants stocked than imaginable in those days. Every field seemed to get crates full. It was a big job stocking them, and the Game Commission trucks developed a large following, quickly, if they were sighted. Some guys shunned the exercise associated with hunting and preferred to ride around in their cars and just shoot the ringnecks from the road, often through open windows. These were the guys we were looking for that day as we drove toward Scotch Valley. We had several folks in particular in mind.

It was snowing heavily and the pheasants we had stocked just hours before were sitting tight in the ditches. As darkness approached, some of the birds began to fly up into low shrubs and trees and onto telephone poles to roost.

As we rounded a bend and came to a little roller-coaster hill ahead of us, Nolfie spotted the car of one such reputed person. We began to follow. The car would go down into a dip and we would come up. We would go down and the other would come up. Suddenly the car ahead stopped. The door swung open on the passenger side and two shots were fired.

We closed fast behind him, and I watched a pheasant hit the snow just off the road. I ran and picked it up. Bob was stopping the defendant's car and getting the two persons out of it, when I heard flopping in a tall crabapple tree and looked up just in time to see a second bird as it began to fall. I dropped the bird I had in hand, knowing it was dead, and made a diving catch of the second, before it hit the ground. It also had died of "lead poisoning."

The smoking shot shell hulls lay alongside the road. I had two pheasants in hand that we had watched the man shoot as he stepped from the car.

"What did I do wrong?" he demanded.

Not only did Nolfie tell him and his wife, the driver, what they had done wrong, he wrote it down on a ticket and gave them a copy. They paid the fines and I became one of the few officers in the Commonwealth that can actually claim to have caught an illegally shot pheasant before it hit the ground.

SERIOUS, BUT NOT THAT SERIOUS

I was sitting in a barn in a Jeep with game deputy Big Jim, when the call first came over the radio: "We have shooting, dead deer, a vehicle and armed men on foot at the water company reservoir. We need a backup."

We sat in the silence of the barn. It was after one in the morning and it was drizzling. We were just outside of White Haven, and the call location was nearly an hour away. We listened to see if anyone closer responded.

Again the call came. "We need a backup." We listened for the game warden in that area to respond, but no answer came. Soon Dallas crackled on the radio.

"We have a unit requesting assistance at the water company reservoir in Carbon County, is anyone in that area?" It was still silent.

We switched channels and called the game warden, Bob Nolf, knowing he was out. "Bob, looks like we are it on that call," we said.

"Head down, I'm a half hour behind you," he answered.

"Dallas, this is 526 C, we're rolling on that call. E.T.A. approximately forty-five minutes."

"Unit calling for backup, 526C is rolling. E.T.A. forty-five minutes."

"We'll cover the truck with the gun in it until they arrive, Dallas."

"Suggest you find cover outside your vehicle if you have armed men on foot, unit."

"Ten-four."

I could never understand what makes young men hurry to get into danger, but Jim and I were hurrying. Going as fast as his Jeep CJ5 could go. The ride was exciting enough. When we got out of the car at the scene, the two officers moved to us from out of the cover of some dark hemlock, where they had stood.

"Our game warden's on vacation," one explained.

I did some quick introductions and asked what we had.

"We heard shots and started moving on them. Eventually we got to the reservoir and saw a light on the face of it and heard another shot. I have a key to the gate, so we opened the gate and eased in, without lights. We soon found the vehicle with three guys in it. When we flipped on the red light, they jumped from the truck and ran. They left it just like that," said the deputy, pointing.

"Jim, you and the young deputy go look for deer and the culprits. Stay close together and be careful. Don't use your light any more than you have to. We'll stay near the truck and look for evidence," I told them.

We soon located a couple of .222 empties and live rounds alongside the open door of the truck. A .222 rifle was on the seat with a spent cartridge still in it. Nolfie arrived and we intensified the search and came up with a pair of that year's fawns, neatly shot in the head. Big Jim roamed around with both deer slung over his shoulder like sacks of potatoes. After an hour or so, we gave up. After identifying the vehicle, we headed for a coffee.

We got our thoughts organized and sent Jim home in his Jeep. I would stay with Nolfie until we contacted the owner of the car. Since all the deputies had real jobs and were due at work, Bob and I would take it from here.

After checking at the car owner's home, without any luck, we determined from neighbors that he worked at the water company. So back over we went. We talked to the boss, who told us that the crew had a reloading outfit set up and often reloaded shells on their breaks. He thought that one fellow had a .222. He called on the radio for the man to come to the office.

After the routine denial -- he wasn't there, he didn't do it, sort of thing -- Nolfie pulled the empties from his pocket and told him we had the gun. The State Police lab is always most willing to assist our efforts, and it would be a simple manner to match fingerprints on the gun to him and bullets from the two deer to the gun. He confessed and implicated his brother and one friend.

We left for home at nine or ten in the morning, with a pretty pat case, or so we thought. I had just left Nolf and gotten home and was crawling into bed for some much-needed sleep, when the phone rang. It was Nolfie.

"He committed suicide," he said.

"Who?"

"The defendant from last night," he replied. "Our witness against everybody else in this case," he reminded me.

"Let's sleep and regroup tomorrow," I suggested. And we did.

After much thought, we devised a plan. Bob found out when the funeral was and waited until the evening after. He then called the brother that had been implicated.

"This is Bob Nolf of the Pennsylvania Game Commission. I am the officer handling the spotlighting case involving you and your brother. Sorry to hear of your tragedy. Look, if you guys want to get this over and in the past, as I do, just meet me at the State Police barracks in West Hazleton, Friday night at seven."

The brother indicated he would be there.

When we arrived at the barracks, we were surprised to find three men waiting for us in the foyer. We ushered the brother back to the room we had been assigned and he told his story and paid the fine. One by one the other two did the same. It was striking us as unusual, since only two had been implicated. The third fellow had obviously figured he better come clean or he would get caught at a later date. When all the cases were settled, Nolf and I left and had a coffee on the way home.

"I feel bad," he said. "Almost like I'm responsible for him killing himself."

"There's more to it, I'm sure," I consoled.

Despite his tough exterior, Nolfie did feel for the people he dealt with, and this guy stayed on his mind for nearly a month. Then, when the other officer returned from vacation, we went to meet him and brief him on the events. He told us that the deceased was due in court for a D.U.I. hearing the day he shot himself and the deer thing had just been one of many such escapades over a long, rough career for this guy. It really didn't surprise me.

DEER HAIR COAT

This particular year there were two regular days of doe season. It was in the mid 1970s. The weather had been rainy, and it was expected that the Game Commission was going to extend the season on Saturday. On Wednesday I took a ride down along French Creek, just to see the sights but ever on alert for the out of place. As I neared Niles Road, I noticed a hunting jacket lying along a parking area, so I stopped to investigate.

There was a hunting license on it with the deer tag still in place and some deer hair on the coat. Obviously someone had laid the coat on their vehicle and it blew off when they left. Since the owner's name was on the coat, I was able to give him a call.

An older woman answered the phone and I asked for Johnny.

"He's still at school," was her reply.

"Well, I found his hunting coat out along the road and would like to return it," I said.

"Oh, he missed it this morning and was wondering where he had left it," she said.

"Must have blown off the car or truck," I offered. "Did he get a deer?"

"Yes he did, a nice big doe," she responded.

"I'll meet him at the Giant Eagle supermarket parking lot at seven tonight," I said. "I'll be in a red pick-up truck."

"Thank you, and good bye," she finished, and then the phone clicked.

I hurried to a phone and called Leo Yahner, the game warden. I had an unused doe tag and a coat covered with deer hair and a confession from the kid's grandmother. Did he want to run with it?

Leo came to my house and we rode to the store in my personal truck. I was in civilian clothes and stood outside with the coat. Leo waited inside the cap on the back. When the kid arrived, I handed him his coat and asked him if he had gotten a deer and he assured me he had.

Before he could walk away, Leo appeared from the cap of the truck and took the questioning from there. After a few questions, the kid admitted to putting his mother's tag on the deer and gave us the names of the other members of his hunting party.

Before the case closed, we dealt with people who could not afford to get mixed up in this sort of deal for fear of losing their jobs. We collected $800 in fines. All because of a few deer hairs on a hunting coat lying alongside the road.

VALET PARKING AT THE POACHER'S

For several years, the game warden, Bob Nolf, his deputies and I had been working on jack-lighting cases around the Mountain Top and Wapwallopen areas. We could never seem to get lucky. The night shooters would shoot a deer and then they would not appear while we were out there hiding. As soon as we would take a night off, they would strike again.

Deputy Del and I worked together in the Mountain Top area on this case, while other teams worked other parts of the district. It became frustrating. It was like they were reading our minds.

Del and I had a good hiding spot on a driveway near the interstate. Only the folks that lived up the drive could possibly know we were there, and they had given us permission.

It was nearly dark one evening when I got a call at home from game deputy Tom.

"Stein, Nolf's out of town and we solved the Mountain Top jacklighter riddle. Can you get search warrants for us?"

"Sure," I offered, already getting suited up as I talked. "But it's Saturday. It will take a while."

"That's okay. Del is camped on them and prepared to stay the night until the cavalry rides in."

I got on the phone, got some help to Del to maintain the vigil, and I started rounding up state troopers and game wardens and search warrants. Somewhere during the preparation, Bob Nolf returned home and he took over. I was glad. He would be thorough.

The whole time I kept thinking I certainly should recognize the buildings that were being described in the warrants. I couldn't quite place why I knew them. While Bob did business at the magistrate's office, the posse was forming outside.

As we sat waiting, I asked Tom, "Why does this place sound familiar to me?"

He smiled and replied, "Del made me swear to secrecy. You'll see soon enough."

Now I was really baffled. When all were gathered, Nolf briefed everyone on their job and position and reminded us that Del and another deputy would be walking in from the woods when the lights started pulling into the area.

We traveled down the road, under the interstate, and right up the driveway that had been Del's and my hiding spot for nearly two years. I now knew why we hadn'' gotten lucky. If we were sitting there, the poachers didn't go out shooting. No wonder they were glad to have us.

Del had figured this out quicker than me and had taken his rabbit dogs hunting that afternoon. They had uncovered a pile of deer hides under some brush behind a barn on the property. That had started the process that was culminating with the serving of the search warrants. In the end there were thousands of dollars in fines collected and the case ended up involving over a half dozen people. We didn't get done serving search warrants until daylight.

STRING TRACKER

There must be a hundred easy ways to poach a deer and not get caught. In fact, I thought I might someday write that book. It could be a training guide for both sides, poachers and game wardens. I would have to try them all out, though, and I would not want to since, personally, I couldn't imagine hunting if I had to be looking over my shoulder all the time. Some poachers must try as hard to figure out ways to get caught, as others do not to.

On the other hand, some poachers don't even begin to think things through. Such was the case one evening at F. E. Walter Reservoir. I had been bowhunting with my wife and a friend down the gated road toward the river gauging station. We hadn't had any action.

Since I was the farthest down the road, I was the last getting to our van. I was carrying my portable tree stand, when Linda came running toward me.

"There's a guy with a bow up there trying to shoot that big buck we've been hunting, in the headlights of his car!" she blurted.

"Get my stuff," I said, dropping my bow and tree stand. I took off running the several hundred remaining yards to the gate.

When I arrived, a car was slowly cruising out of the parking area. I jumped in my van with our friend and took off down the road after the guy. At the stop sign I flashed the lights of my car. I pulled in behind him and he stopped and got out. I met him with my badge in hand and asked to see his bow. He showed it to me. I took it and laid it in my van.

"You were shooting after hours," I told him.

"It was still plenty light," he responded.

"Why did you need to use your headlights then?" I queried.

"It lights up the night scope," he responded.

I looked and the bow was equipped with a large yellow-lensed scope designed for shooting under bad light. I then noticed it also had a string-tracking unit. I gathered up identification and his hunting license and proceeded to explain the violations. He began to object.

"You have no proof I even shot," he said.

"I have two witnesses," I told him.

"My word against theirs," he countered.

"I'm also going back to find your arrows and whether you hit anything," I returned, knowing that finding lost arrows is a tough proposition in the daylight, yet alone at night.

When I got back to the van, Linda suggested we look for his arrows a short while with a flashlight before leaving.

"Shouldn't be a problem finding them," she offered.

"Why's that?" I questioned.

"He kept retying his string tracker when he missed. The arrows all ought to have a 30 to 40-foot-long piece of line attached."

They did.

DRUG STORE CASE

It was the second day of doe season and snowing heavily, those big wet flakes. We hadn't seen anything going on as we patrolled the Forest/Venango County line areas. Officer Kopena was driving his white pickup truck and I was riding shotgun. We eased up behind a stopped white van on the steep part of Poland Hill.

"Joe, there's a gun out the window," I said.

"They don't see us and are going to shoot," he responded.

"I doubt it," I came back.

KER-BLAM! rocked the quiet countryside.

We were out in an instant, one of us going up along each side of the van. Out came a father and son team that was all mouth. They weren't doing anything wrong, you're not arresting us. On and on it went. The older man faked a heart attack, until I got ready to call an ambulance, then it went away. The young boy was 17 and a lot of mouth, too. Later, after we had gathered shells, empties, gun serial numbers and personal information, we sent them on their way.

We had been heading for a pollution call at the time we ran into them, so we continued on it. After dealing with the pollution call, we returned to the scene of the shot and I went up on the hillside and found a dead deer.

The hearing was just as raucous and noisy as the first incident and eventually the defendants were found guilty on all accounts and fined $1,700 and some-odd dollars. Naturally they didn't pay and had to be dragged out of bed one morning on a warrant. You'd have thought they would have learned, but it wasn't to be. A year or two later, the Game Commission took them to the dance again for just about the same problems.

Several years after the first incident, I stopped in a drugstore one Sunday morning on my way to patrol, for some Rolaids. As I looked at the counter for the antacids, I heard a profusion of extremely foul language. Then it dawned on me it was aimed at me. I rounded the counter and on the other side were the two hombres. I was in their faces and barked at them as they turned tail and exited the store. Fortunately, most everyone in the store had seen the whole affair and had heard their verbal comments. More importantly, some good friends of mine were there that I could call on to testify on my behalf, if I needed it. Thankfully, I didn't.

SPINRAVAGE AND THE GUTTER

The call came the last Friday of buck season that sometime during the previous afternoon the occupants of a blue Jeep had shot a doe right out of the car in front of the entire secretarial pool of a large business in the Humboldt Industrial Park. We had 50 or more witnesses. The night watchman had watched all night, but no one had returned for the deer. At daylight, the Jeep came back and a guy got out and killed the still struggling deer with a tire iron, but left it lay.

I arrived at game warden Nolf's in the morning and got the details. We were going to take his old clunker of a car and sit in the parking lot and wait for the return of the blue Jeep. It was raining, so it would be easy to disappear in the large parking lot.

We had just gotten into position with Nolfie's car and put our raingear on in case we had to get out, when I looked up and saw a blue Jeep arriving. It matched the description we had been given. It drove by slowly and then began to back in along a row of trees across the ditch from the road. There was obviously an access road there of some kind. When they got to where the deer lay, I wanted to go get them. Nolfie kept holding me back.

"Wait until they've taken hold of the deer and dragged it a little ways," he cautioned.

The passenger got out and did just that. Nolfie hollered for me to go. I took off at a run and never saw the car that came rounding the bend to the left. I ran smack into its side and rolled over the hood. Fortunately, the driver had seen me coming at a run and was nearly stopped when I ran into him. I bellowed, "State Officer! Halt!" as I hit the ground again, running.

This naturally set the ball in play. The fellow that had gotten out of the Jeep and begun to drag the deer dropped it and took off, getting in the vehicle just ahead of my grasp. The Jeep started slowly pulling away. Nolfie appeared, blocked the exit with his car and got out and faced the oncoming Jeep with both hands in the air and a badge on his raincoat. The Jeep pulled tight against him and began to back him up, toward being pinned between the cars.

By now I was within feet of the back window of the car and was starting to clear leather with my sidearm when the driver stopped. I was around to his side and helped him out of the car, knocking a plastic-handled hunting knife from his hand as he fumbled with it trying to hide it, I hope.

The driver, obviously drunk, was a lot of mouth and promised that if we ever were sent to the state hospital in Hazleton, we would be dead. He was an orderly there. Tickets were written and filed. Later Nolf and I met with the hospital administration and they decided that this incident was the last straw. The driver's employment was discontinued.

After being fired, he began to hang out at one of the toughest bars in Hazleton, the "El Rauncho Pub." The regular clientele were the local tough guys. One was a very big man in his early 20s that had befriended me and the fish truck. He loved to stock fish. His nickname was The Gutter.

The tale is told that as The Gutter sat in the "El Rauncho Pub" one afternoon, the Jeep driver was sitting there making death threats on me and Nolfie. The Gutter never said a word. He just walked over, spun the guy around and dropped him with a powerful right hand. He then looked at the barkeep and said, "When he gets up, tell him I'm a friend of Steiner's."

That's the kind of friends to have!

CHAPTER 16:
Out of My League

Some officers like to pretend they can do it all. I knew when to turn an investigation over to a better trained authority. This one, simple, attribute probably saved my life a few times.

STEALING CORN

I was a cadet on field assignment with Officer Roberts, in Susquehanna County, in the fall. We were doing a uniform patrol in the middle of the day, when we saw a truck slow down and a passenger get out along a cornfield and the truck keep going.

I was dropped off to ease into the cornfield, and Dick would wait for the car. Since shooting had been reported in that area the night before, we figured we were onto an illegal venison pickup.

I crept ever closer to the rustling in the cornfield. Before I got to the culprit, a car horn honked and he ran. Next I heard Dick shout, "Halt!" and I came out running in the direction of the action.

When I got there, I was greeted with an old man and a young man, aged about like Dick and me. Dick had the car trunk open and was getting them to empty the burlap bag they had thrown into the trunk. I returned to the "in-the-corn" scene and discovered no evidence of deer or other dead critters.

After a thorough search of the vehicle for guns, bullets, cartridge empties, etc., they were sent on their way with a burlap sack with no deer. As we rode on down the road, it dawned on me and Dick about the same time.

"Corn," I said. "They're stealing corn."

Dick grinned and whipped the car around. We hadn't gotten any identification and had failed to write a description of the auto. Like any two persons, we disagreed on color, make, model, etc.

A diligent search revealed only that we weren't as quick as we thought we were.

MOTORCYCLE CASE

I was working as a rookie out of the office and Cloyd was the supervisor. Cloyd did not care for trail bikes and their incessant noise any more than I do for ATVs now. We had gone home for lunch; I rented an apartment over his garage. We were just starting back to the office one hot, sunny August afternoon, when a trail bike came screaming up the hard road in front of his place.

"No license, no helmet," Cloyd said and tore out after him.

The trail bike turned and went up over Buttermilk Hill, with us in hot pursuit. I was fumbling for my safety belt, as the race reached speeds well over 80 miles an hour. The bike turned down a farm lane, with us hot on his bumper. Somewhere along the lane, the potholes and loose gravel sent the bike spinning and flopping out through a hayfield.

The kid, badly shaken but with no noticeable injuries, suffered a good butt-chewing at the hands of Cloyd and was warned against ever riding that unlicensed bike through Sugar Creek Borough again.

This experience, more than any other, served to keep me from engaging in high-speed chases throughout my career.

DEER SKINNING

Ed was the game warden for Columbia County at the time and Nolfie was the game guy serving in my assigned area in Luzerne County. Nolfie had the reputation of being a shrewd and indefatigable investigator. Like a TV detective, nothing escaped his notice.

Ed called early one morning and asked Nolfie to come over and investigate a place where someone had butchered a deer. See if he could find any evidence that would help in the case. We were off.

We met Ed and followed him to a little out-of-the-way brick building, with an old apple tree growing nearby. There on the tree was a short length of rope hanging from a stout limb. The rope was blood-stained and under the tree there was a good bit of blood on the frozen ground. Because the ground was frozen so hard, it was tough to discern any individual tracks, but the area showed much in the way of people action.

After an hour or so of snooping around, Nolfie straightened up and out of the clear blue, after a long silence, stated, "Not a deer."

It turned out he was right. It was disclosed a few days later that the police had arrested a few local druggies for murder, and they led the cops to our apple tree. One night, a few days earlier, they had skinned a defector there and then disposed of his body in a strip mine pit.

CHAPTER 17:
Tricks of the Trade

There are a lot of little things an officer can do to make him effective in his law enforcement effort. Some you learn from other officers, some you learn with time. Due to the luck of the draw in my first couple of years, I worked with about 30 different officers each for a day or two. Prior to that I was exposed to all their antics as they worked "salmon season" in Erie and headquartered out of Walnut Creek, where I was raising fish.

BLACK BAG

Camouflage is an art form, especially for a warden. To be able to slip in on unsuspecting violators and observe their shenanigans unnoticed takes practice and originality. Over the years I have donned camo coveralls and face paint to conceal myself in forest settings to do observation work. On the other end of the spectrum, I have dressed in a suit and dress shoes and acted like a tourist to see what was happening..

However, the best case of adapting to your surroundings was demonstrated to me by a young deputy one rainy May afternoon. I would be stocking several thousand brook trout in Lake Irena in West Hazleton in an hour or two. I instructed my new deputy, Bob, to get to the lake early and "blend into the surroundings," to get into position to watch for "fish hogs," those unspeakable characters that don't get enough slime on their hands with one limit and must take more.

In completing the setup, I told Bob that I would arrive, stock the fish, ignore him and leave. I would return in an hour after that to settle any cases that he might have. On parting, I instructed, "Don't give up your identity until I signal you when I return."

The rain continued down and the plan worked beautifully, except that when I came back, I could not locate Bob among the throngs of remaining fishermen. I figured he would be there fishing incognito, but as I checked each fisherman, none of them was Bob. Finally, I walked to a little high point of ground with a great view of the lake and leaned against a tree. Here there were nearly a hundred black leaf bags in a bunch from last fall's raking of the park at this location.

As I stood and surveyed the area for any hint of Bob, a leaf bag in the middle of the group spoke. "Looking for someone?" it said.

Wearing a black garbage bag, he had slithered into the center of the other bags and had remained undetected for hours, even though fishermen ... and wardens ... had walked right past him.

FLY-FISHING GOOBER

Linda and I were on a busman's holiday, fly-fishing in Lycoming County on Little Pine Creek. We had taken a break at the day-use area below the dam, when, of all things, a fish truck pulled in. I sat back across the creek, eating hard-boiled eggs and swilling down a cola, relaxing as Officer Lauer and his crew of helpers dumped trout.

After the stockers left, four persons remained to fish. One, a young guy in his late teens, was "knocking the slop out of them" on a fly rod. Before anyone else had three, he had seven and kept them. Soon I saw him call a conference of his three friends, and they loaded into an old CJ-5 hardtop Jeep and motored up the road. My curiosity was aroused.

We got packed up and headed up along the creek until we were just below English Center and found the Jeep. As I walked by, I noticed through the open window a plastic bag lying under the front passenger seat.

I rigged up my fly rod, but not in the normal fashion. I tied a big streamer made of deer hair dyed bright orange, attached a 1/4-ounce sinker above it and a bobber about a foot above that. I proceeded to go find the fly fisherman and watch him catch several more trout. When I figured he had ten, I thought it would be sufficient to teach him his lesson.

I walked over and said, "I've been watching you catch fish here and before, below the dam, and you caught them with ease, at least ten, on your fly rod. I fished down there where you left, and now I've been fishing right behind you up here with my fly rod, and I can't get a hit. Could you tell me what I'm doing wrong?"

He was very helpful. I could see him hiding the chuckles as he told me to take the bobber off and the sinker off and follow him to the Jeep, where he would get me a fly. He picked up his stringer with three trout and I followed him.

When we got there, he opened the door. I pointed to the bag and said, "Are those the seven trout you caught down at the dam?"

He assured me they were. I then badged him and explained, "When coupled with the three on your stringer, you are two over the limit of eight and there will be a fine."

I gave him his ticket and thanked him for being so helpful. He just kept shaking his head, saying, "I should have known, I should have known."

DEER DANCERS

This job has taken me into many strange circumstances and places in the name of justice, but few were as unusual as one night right after I returned to Venango County. I was on a day off and had picked up a few home repair items in town and decided I could use a cold beer. I stopped at a tavern to have one and overheard two rough-looking men talking.

From the conversation, I determined that the guy doing the bragging claimed to have five deer hanging in his barn right then. It was months before any hunting season. He was trying to find buyers for them.

I sat across the bar, appearing to watch the 6 o'clock news on the TV, but always listening and tuned into the conversation of the big guy with the deer. He and his friend got up to leave without giving any indication of where his barn was or who he was. I followed and noted that the friend was driving, so the license plate wouldn't do any good. I had heard where they were heading, so I followed.

I paid the dollar cover at the door. A few minutes later I watched them enter. I found a seat within earshot, even though it didn't give me the best view of the girls dancing topless. I didn't want to be distracted. After seeing all the dancing beauties, the duo got up to leave. I still only knew the first name of the deer seller, so was forced to follow.

The trail took me through three towns and past nearly 15 semi-naked women, until around midnight I had enough information to turn over to the game officers for them to get a search warrant. This they did and staged a successful raid.

I never tried to recover the money I had spent on cover charges and tips at the various "joints" I had to visit while gathering evidence that night, but I always thought that it would have made for a lively exchange with the state comptroller. It was hard not to notice the beauty of some of the lithe, well-proportioned dancers while I was in search of the naked truth.

THE LITTLE WEE DOE

It was the first morning of doe season at Chapman Dam. My brother, Scott, and I had returned there for a hunt after ten years of my being out east. I was hunting with a walking stick and he had his .308. It promised to be a good time.

I hiked and trailed deer and kept trying to run one to him. I saw twenty-some deer that morning, but the only one that I pushed to Scott was a four-point buck. Darn our luck.

I was making a sweep away from the cars after a coffee break, when I noticed a man dragging a very small doe. I stopped and looked at it and noticed the lack of an ear tag.

"You forgot to tag it," I stated.

He looked at me and then at his car, not 100 yards away. Then with resignation in his voice he said, "Yeah, I guess I did. Would you get my tag out for me, please?" And he turned around.

I stood and talked while he tagged it, which he did with some reluctance after it became obvious I wasn't leaving until it was done. I wished him a good day and went on my way, knowing that had he been at the car with that untagged deer a few moments earlier when I was there, I would have cited him.

He probably is still wondering why I was so interested.

PLAYING BINGO WARRANT

By the time a citation goes to a warrant, it is usually evident that one of two things has occurred to the criminal. Either he feels he is too good to be arrested physically, due to his wealth or community status, or you will never find him. In over 90 percent of both cases, they are wrong.

It was a warm summer evening when I was called by a friendly local and told that there were four persons at the trailer park pond, fishing without fishing licenses, and they had told the caller that "no wardens will come in here."

Since I had a trapper friend who lived at the trailer park, whom I often visited, I couldn't imagine their feeling that way. I cited them. The two younger folks said there was no way they could pay the fines within the week. The older two, Earl and Pearl, assured me they would pay right away. Months later they had failed to make time payments and warrants were issued for their arrests. I'm not one for bashing in doors, even with a warrant, on a fish law violation, so I began biding my time. I only lived a mile away, so every time I went by, I would stop and knock.

The word quickly got out that the hunt was on, but Earl and Pearl were never home or at least never in the mood to answer their door. I loafed around the post office on public subsistence check day, and still they didn't show. I was starting to get itchy to catch them. Then I got the break I was waiting for.

I stopped and knocked on the door of their beaten-down trailer, and a neighbor came across the road. "They're up at the firehouse, calling bingo numbers tonight," she said, "What do you want to see them for?" She scurried back into the house when I told her, wishing she hadn't been so helpful for her new neighbors. She had just moved in.

As I walked through the door at the fire hall, Earl was on stage, calling numbers as they popped out of one of those little round cages with the balls in it. Pearl was working the floor, selling cards. Earl saw me right away, and I just pointed at him from behind the room full of people and held the warrant paper up at arm's length.

When "Bingo!" was called from the floor, Earl announced an intermission, and I met him coming off the stage. He was already reaching for his wallet. I collected the fines and costs right there and as inconspicuously as possible, and the fire hall never missed a game. I hope it was as good a fundraising night for them as it was for me.

CHAPTER 18:
Bad Habits

I never smoked. Sorry, that's my only defense.

VISITOR'S BOTTLE

One summer, the Game Commission had an intern program for warden "wannabes." Shawn was a young college kid that was involved in the program. One morning the phone rang and Lenny Hribar, the game warden, asked me if I could amuse Shawn for a day or so, while he was at a meeting. I was happy to oblige.

After getting all of my paperwork in line, I had Shawn meet me at my house. I had two young rookie deputies at that time, Erik and Mark. They would be riding with us, also. The three fish guys were all chronic tobacco chewers and Shawn also took a chew now and then.

As we rode the patrol that day, we were having a good time, checking fishermen and getting in and out of the car plenty to allow for necessary spitting. Along one particularly long stretch of road, things got quiet as I spit into my bottle and my guys held their juice. Shawn kind of garbled that he needed a jug. My guys knew the rules. Bob uses Bob's jug and only Bob uses it.

I told Shawn to reach over the back seat and get the "visitor's bottle." This had been one of my old bottles and was kept for emergencies only. It hadn't been washed before storage and had been capped in the sun all summer. As Shawn opened the cap, the resulting stench was akin to the dozen nightcrawlers that I once stored the same way in the trunk of my dad's car as a kid. It nauseated the three fish guys to gagging, but only gagging. But then we hadn't stuck our face over the bottle to spit, either.

WITH LEVI GARRETT IN NANTICOKE

Nanticoke is known within the state conservation agencies as having more than its fair share of "nay-sayers" when it comes to Fish and Game programs. This, I found after eight years with the town in the heart of my district, to be an unfair rap. I found salt-of-the-earth, hardworking, hard-hunting and hard-fishing men and women. Once you worked with them and got dirt on your uniform with them, they respected you as much or more than the people in any of my other assignment areas.

However, some of the Nanticokians did deserve the reputation.

Walleye fishing in the Susquehanna River gets to be its best just as the season closes in March. It was a warm, sunny Sunday, the week after the season closed, when I decided to run a river patrol in that direction. As evening set in, I was hidden on the West Nanticoke side of the river, observing with my 36-power spotting scope. Orange Hat, one of 15 fishermen, caught an 8-pound walleye and succumbed to temptation. He hid it under a log, rather than returning it immediately to the water as required by law.

Since all the fishermen were working jigs and obviously trying to catch walleye, I decided to make an example of the one "weak soul" and put an end to this violation. I also decided that since the eastside access to this large group of fishermen was remote and isolated, it would be easier to deal with one violator than a whole bunch. On top of all these negative forces was the fact that I was alone and it was quickly getting dark.

I made the trip up to the bridge, drove across it and down through Nanticoke and swung onto the railroad grade as the sun was setting in the west. I locked the state iron, my faithful Matador, and moseyed nonchalantly down to the creek bank. I directly approached Orange Hat and opened with, "How's the walleye fishing?"

"Oh, we're sucker fishing," was his reply.

This was my first notice that they all might be in cahoots. I asked to check his license and, having taken it off his hat, I slipped it into my pocket. Then I walked over to the log and lifted the hidden walleye by the gill plate.

"You caught this one a short while ago," I said.

"I don't know how it got there," he answered.

I conducted him to my state car and explained his options to settle on a field acknowledgement of guilt or to have a hearing. At this he became loud and began to bellow. The herd instinct took over, and I soon had the whole gang clustered around the car, bellowing.

My experience in the county had taught me that in dealing with these people, they were apt to get loud but seldom violent. However, 10 to 15 shouting men down a lonely railroad bed are distracting when you are writing a citation. Much of what they said was threatening, but none were taking aggressive postures, so I stood my ground. Yet writing was difficult and the night was fast coming on. I had to make a move.

An inspiration hit me, since all my rebuttal hadn't seemed to slacken the verbal abuse. I palmed the metal citation pad in my hand and suddenly "spiked" it on the hood of the aging Matador. At the sound they all startled and quieted. I reached deep into the pocket of my bulky winter patrol coat and slowly withdrew what I am sure they thought was some sort of crowd control weapon. It was a pack of Levi Garrett.

I unrolled the foil pack deliberately and loaded a large side-chew. They all stood stunned. I looked all around slowly, staring each man in the eye for a moment, then rerolled the wrapper and returned the pack to my pocket. I worked the chew for a few seconds, then spit like a true tobacco-chewing champion.

The advantage had become mine. The flock began to filter away up the railroad grade toward their homes, leaving Orange Hat alone to take his medicine.

SPILLING CHEW IN GAME GUY'S CAR

As luck would have it, one of the two game guys assigned to Venango County did not chew tobacco. In fact, he was appalled by it. He even was nasty about it when you chewed in his car. Probably, if you were not providing him free assistance, he would not have tolerated it. Despite this character flaw of officer Hribar's, I always enjoyed his company and, when time permitted, would ride a patrol with him.

It was a rainy bear season opener when I enlisted for a ride on the "wild side." Lenny's vehicle at the time was one of those blocky Scouts or such and, naturally, gruesome Game Commission green. As the day wore on, I clutched the plastic pollution sample bottle as we jostled through the logging roads and right-of-ways of the river hills. When we would stop to check a hunter, I religiously remembered to cap the bottle before setting it down on the floor between the seats.

Then, for some reason I no longer remember, we had to make a hasty exit of the car. I believe it was an ATV or two we were bailing out to check, but the bottle I had wedged between the seats, so it would not spill if forgotten, was forgotten. The check turned into an investigation and, since we were outside at the time, I had no reason to remember the bottle, spitting on the ground as I needed to.

After the paperwork was complete, we jumped back in the Scout. Lenny fired it up, as I loaded a fresh chew and reached for the bottle. I was too late. The vehicle lurched as it hit a pothole and the juice splashed. Then the jug upset as I fought to retain my balance and get hold of it before it totally drained its contents. My best efforts were unsuccessful.

Lenny didn't say much. Well, not much that I can type into this recollection of that incident, but I know he was not complimentary. I cleaned up what I could with some paper towels that were on the backseat floor, which Lenny had used earlier to wipe road-kill blood off his hands. I'm sure that in the spring, when the roads up here turn from mud to dust, that juice would have dried and you would never had noticed it on the rubber floor covering. Lenny was just too fussy about his vehicle.

SPITTING ON INSTRUCTOR'S BOAT

Paul Antolosky was a fine old fish warden when I came with the outfit. At the time he was the officer for Centre County. He had run the training facility for years and took great pride in his equipment and personal appearance. I found him to be a likeable chap, but had heard stories of his days as the training officer. Though I had never seen it, I was assured his ire could flare to flame with the right amount of fanning.

Now it was not my intention to fan the flames. I had no reason to even suspect they were smoldering this fine spring morning. A large group of deputies were gathered at Sayre Lake for boating and trailering skills training. I was on a day off and was granted an opportunity by my supervisor to attend the session, since my wife, Linda, was one of the deputies taking this advanced training course.

When I arrived, I figured my place would be to just stay out of the way. As I stood to the side, the day's events were outlined by Barry Mechling, the training officer at that time. There would be several officers and experienced deputies teaching each segment, and the trainees would rotate between stations.

Since it was such a nice sunny day, a pontoon boat had been rented and a video camera was set up on it to record, for later classes not blessed by such a fine day, the proper techniques demonstrated throughout the training. Should they get rained out, they would then at least be able to watch this valuable footage.

As the afternoon rolled around and proficiency had been demonstrated by all the trainees at operating the various boats and trailers in many different situations, it was decided to do some scenarios using an experienced deputy, a district officer and a trainee in a boat.

"We need a hooftie," Mechling announced.

A deputy strode forward to be a violator for the exercise. The routine check and subsequent warning were given or ticket was written and another scenario was set up. Later in the day, with the sun blazing, Mechling again announced the need for a "hooftie." When one volunteer stepped forward he was rejected for his military bearing and perfect uniform appearance.

"I mean a real hooftie," Mechling reiterated. "One that you would find in a canoe, fishing."

I pushed from the back of the crowd in my suspender-supported jeans and tee-shirt and spat at his feet. I got the job. I was to sit on the bow of a canoe with my feet dangling and be a fisherman without a license and no life preservers in the boat. Another young fellow was assigned to be the paddler of the canoe. We assumed our positions and the show was on.

Paul coached his deputy-operated patrol boat alongside our canoe, and the trainee did an excellent job of maneuvering. The experienced deputy started the routine questioning as the camera rolled on the pontoon boat nearby. "Sir, we need to see your fishing license," he politely requested.

I just stared at him.

"Sir," he repeated, "I need to check your fishing license."

Again he got only a stare.

"Do you have a fishing license, sir?" he tried.

But I was a player and knew the part.

Paul moved forward alongside the deputy and tried his luck.

"Let's go, we want to see a fishing license now."

I just kept on staring at him. I had their attention, and they had become personally involved. The patrol boat was drifting closer. Everyone was paying attention to the act and the camera was rolling. The relative position of the boats had been forgotten by all. I was going to have to do something to make them aware that they were about to ram the canoe, since the gap was narrowing.

Paul was caught up in the moment and knew he was supposed to be the hero, but knowing I was just an actor, I could play hardball. As he got frustrated, he looked me square in the eye and said, "Do you hear me, I want to see a fishing license?"

Without hesitation, I spit tobacco juice right on the side of his immaculate patrol boat and blurted out, "Yes sir, but I had to spit and didn't want to spit in the water with you watching, since it would be pollution, and I couldn't swallow, it makes me puke."

He never heard the explanation. He would have had me by the scruff of the neck had it not been for the audience and camera.

After the scenario was played out to the end, I took a handful of lake water and cleaned off the side of the boat. But I can tell you, there was no pretense of a warning in the scenario. I was issued the ticket.

CHEWING SCRAP

When the tobacco companies figured out everyone was onto their cigarette caper, they switched the official macho look. The new look was a cowboy rubbing snuff or a duck hunter loading a cheek full of side chew in a marsh, with a good friend and a dog. Somewhere, while watching all those ads for the next generation of cancer-causing filthy habits, I had an idea.

I'll bet that all those pretty girls that keep throwing themselves at the handsome man in a uniform, me, would let me alone so I could work if I had a chaw in. I went out and invested in my future. In no time at all I was able to do a side chew, eat my lunch and drink beer at the same time. Never once did I get sick.

For the next 20 years, I had a pack or two in a pocket at all times, except for a short break now and then to allow the sores inside my mouth to heal. It was, however, creating an image.

I never really evaluated that image much until one evening while sitting at a Federation of Sportsmen's Club meeting with then-Fish Commissioner Marilyn Black. Marilyn is a wonderful person and as good a commissioner as I ever worked with. She never said a word about my plastic spittoon that sat on the table in front of me all night, but the look of disgust she gave it made me rethink my logic. After that encounter, I increased my chewing to where I lost 20 pounds and spent four or five dollars a day on chew. But I became somewhat more discreet about where I set the bottle.

It was at this very same Federation of Sportsmen's Clubs meeting, as I sat spitting and chewing and listening and giving reports, that I realized that the image of the tobacco-chewing warden isn't offensive to all. I was there to be introduced by the commissioner. The county had been served for over five years by Jonesy as part of a district that included about half of Warren County. The sportsmen of Venango County had repeatedly requested that they once again have a "warden of their own."

When it came time for the agency reports, Mrs. Black rose and, with a smile, stated that she was proud to have assisted in granting their request and would like to introduce their "new warden," and that I would be serving Venango County only. She then asked me if I had a few words for the group.

I stood slowly, with the chew in, looked all around and opened with, "I appreciate that you folks have requested a warden to serve this county. I understand you have worked long and hard to this end. Well, here I am. I'm your prize."

At lunch break, I stepped to the door and emptied the jug around the back of the building and reloaded. An old timer came over and introduced himself to me. Then he smiled and said, "Any warden that chews scrap tobacco can't be all bad. Welcome to Venango County." I knew I had made a good move.

I am a strong believer in the necessity of an affiliation of sportsmen's clubs and the necessity for them to speak to their governmental agencies in a united voice. In this day and age of many national sportsmen's organizations, this united voice at a state level is missing. The Pennsylvania Federation of Sportsmen's Clubs has served the sportsmen of this state well for decades and continues to do so. I am proud of the personal and professional relationship I have had with these fine men and women.

MORE SPILLED CHEW

As a kid growing up, I was repeatedly told, "Don't cry over spilt milk." I kept telling mom I wouldn't if I could spill it without getting a lickin'. Once I grew out of the clumsy stage, I no longer had the problem. I had quit drinking milk.

The problem came back later when I was in my late 20s and I least expected it. I took up chewing tobacco to keep those bothersome pretty girls away. I would give them my shy look and let the chew juice dribble from my jowls, then smile. That did the trick. They were gone.

While on a late night patrol with Mike and Gary, two game deputies, we decided to take up a stationary position in a graveyard, near one of our prime suspect's shacks. He referred to it as his home. The poacher's mode of operation was to go out on foot with a flashlight behind the house, shoot a deer, gut it, and go back to the house to get one of his sons to help drag it in. Past tradition had it that when he returned to the deer, several game deputies or occasionally the real warden himself would be there to greet him.

After much small talk, they would all go in the house. At the kitchen table, paperwork would be completed and would change hands. Come springtime, the warden would go have coffee with the magistrate and pick up the warrant for failure-to-respond. Then he would go out and visit with the poacher again and give him a lift into town, where he would sit until his kids rounded up enough money to keep him out of jail. It was a friendly enough arrangement.

Mike, Gary and I decided to see if we couldn't get the process off and rolling one frosty November evening. Around midnight, I swung into the graveyard, went around the knoll and killed the lights. We sat until two or three in the morning, making small talk, listening for a shot and waiting to see a spotlight. Despite the cold, we had the windows cracked to keep them from fogging and to better hear any shots. Soon Gary, in the backseat, began to snore in the he-man tone of an honest 250-pounder. I switched from coffee to chew, since my bladder was full and I didn't want to open the door of the old

Jeep. To open the door meant the dome light would come on, and any poacher worth his salt would see that from miles away and bolt for cover.

I always had this theory that you could drain your body of liquids by chewing and spitting. You would have a full bladder, begin to chew and spit and dehydrate yourself and your body would reabsorb the contents of your bladder. The theory never worked.

As I sat in a trance, beginning to shiver, I realized that Mike was making the sounds of a little guy snoring. Kinda like a Chihuahua baying at the moon. I was, for all intents and purposes, alone in the night. The hours wore on. Around four-thirty in the morning, I was just letting the work-quit enter my mind, when I reached for the quart Styrofoam container on the dash in front of the steering wheel. It was now full with brown, slimy expectorate. I started it toward my mouth to spit, and the bottom caught the steering wheel. The contents hit me about chest high.

The door flew open, I cursed and gagged and carried on, and suddenly my sidekicks were back in action from a dead sleep. They jumped, cleared the car looking for cover, realized what was happening and began to laugh. We laughed until we were out of tears. I then cleaned up the Jeep with paper towels and we declared the shift over. After all, the dome light had been allowed to come on.

A bicycle was one of the unconventional ways I had of getting out and interacting with fishermen. If there were no fishermen around, I was still melting fat so the uniform fit.

CHAPTER 19:
The Clients

It takes all kinds. Without these folks and many others, I probably would have ended up working in a glass factory.

MURDER, ARSONIST'S SON

It was after the lake was stocked, but still a week before trout season when I got the call.

"There's a kid camping at Lake Irena and he's killing the trout."

I was with my deputy Gene that night when I walked into Lake Irena and spotted the small campfire at the upper end of the lake. One of us went around either side of the lake, a pincer movement.

Soon we had rounded up the 17-year-old. He had three or four violations. As the rains fell, we had him pack his backpack and tear down his tent. When all was loaded on the pack frame, he looked like a top-heavy ice cream cone, moving ahead of me in the glow of the mall lights.

Suddenly, as he tried to step across a small creek, he fell and floundered like a beached sea turtle. Gene, a powerful man at the time, just reached down and, with one hand, set him back on his feet. Soon we were on our way to the car.

"I'm going to take you over to the state police barracks until we can properly identify you," I offered.

"No problem, man. My dad works there, he'll get me out of this," he responded.

Now, most troopers I knew at the time would have consigned their kid into slavery for a violation of any laws. I couldn't wait to see who this character belonged to.

When we got to the barracks, I opened the doors for the "pack rat" and sat him on a bench with deputy Martin. I then went over to the desk.

"Sarge, this kid says his dad's a statey," I said. "I have four violations on him."

"Doesn't look like anybody's kid I know," came the reply.

I turned and went back to the kid and told him his story didn't wash. Eventually, with a little help from my friends at the barracks, I was able to get him identified. He was the son of an arsonist who was wanted in the murder of a deputy sheriff and his wife and three kids during a house-bombing. This fine father was still at large, as was his accomplice.

The kid found the money in the backpack to pay the fine.

A KICK IN THE HEAD

Club meetings are generally predictable. You go, listen to someone botch Robert's Rules of Order, and get the business of the club done, anyway. Then you are called on for your report. On special occasions, especially in the old days, you would tote a movie, screen and projector along, and the club would host the snacks and beer and all would sit and watch a conservation movie of some kind and have a good time.

It was just such a meeting in a little back-alley bar in Hazleton. The rod and gun club had a very efficient meeting, and we had moved beyond my report into setting up the movie. As one of the guys was bringing the pizza and beer into the backroom, I began to set up the screen and projector in front of one of the other doors, which opened into the hall across from the men's room. Suddenly there was a thump and the door bulged and shook the projector. I grabbed it and moved it and opened the door.

In the hall, one scruffy young guy was in the fetal position in the corner against the door, and two other ruffians were kicking him. He was screaming for help. I knew I wasn't big enough to break it up alone and was in our public relations suit, with no hardware to work with, so I turned to the room full of men and spotted two big ones.

"Ski! Stush!" I shouted. "Give me a hand breaking this up."

They came running and grabbed handfuls of scruffy characters. I shoved my badge in the rowdies' faces as they were being held and told them they were out of there. The big guys saw that they complied. The old owner came back and said the beer and pizza was on him for the job the fish warden did in throwing the ruffians out. He made it sound like I did it single-handedly. I liked him.

The pizza was exceptional that night and the beer was always cold there. I packed up the screen and stuff and headed home after the movie and talking with the club members a little. The next evening, less than a block away, a drug deal went sour and the kid on the floor was shot in the head at a very close range with a very big gun.

THE OLD MAN AND THE CANE

Lily Lake was a warden's enforcement nightmare. When I was there, a 60-horsepower limit was in effect, in a very small water-ski zone. Getting out to it was required to be "slow minimum height swell speed," and if you were doing anything else on the lake, it was electric motors only. The commission owned about 85 percent of the shoreline, but not all of it. Camping was not legal on our property, but the other landowners didn't mind. Swimming was prohibited except in the 10 or 15 acres of water that we did not own.

There was a camp set up down on the corner. A speedboat came out and was waterskiing in the ski zone. After a while, they just sat in the water with the skis floating and swam around. Sally, my deputy, was at the lake at the time and took the boat out. She warned them of the violation and told them to either ski or get off the pot.

An hour later, she came back to the lake and observed the same kid doing the same thing. This time she gave him a ticket. It turned out that he was the grandson of one of the lakeshore residents. Grandpa had sold his rights to the lakeshore, but still felt he could do what he wanted and so could his grandkid.

Grandpa was wrong and quite old. The kid was from up in the New England states.

Sally brought the ticket and check down to my house and I processed it, thinking the case over. Don't think. Never think.

Several weeks later, Sally and I were eating our lunches from paper sacks, sitting in the shade against a couple of big oak trees near the outhouses at Lily Lake. It was a delightful day, and the wind was just right to make this nicer than it sounds. Up the road from the area where the residents of the lake lived came an old man on a cane. I didn't realize that it was the same old geezer. Sally did, but didn't tip me off.

As we sat munching ham and cheese on rye and drinking our colas, he hobbled over to us, slow and steady. He stopped, glared at Sally, and then turned and unleashed his venom on me. I had worked there for several years and he thought he knew me. Sally had already proved she could take his abuse.

He spouted off about his "poor grandson" not knowing the rules, how we were taking advantage of nonresidents and on and on, hardly taking a breath. I just sat against the firm old oak, knees tucked up in front of me, chewing contentedly.

When he had run out of steam and paused, waiting for me to continue the argument, I didn't attack with reason or facts. I used psychology. I just swallowed my last mouthful of sandwich and looked at him. Then very deliberately, I said, "Old man, if you don't quit ruining my lunch break, I'm going to kick that cane right out from under you."

Sally had just taken a drink from her cola and it spurted from her nose, as she tried to suppress a laugh. He huffed and shuffled off down the road.

The check bounced. So I wrote the young lad a note and explained to him that we would have a warrant for his arrest. Should he ever decide to return, we would pick him up, unless he made it good.

He wrote explaining that it was his form of protest and then went on to say he felt for sure that the wardens in his home state would have only given him a warning and he wasn't going to pay.

I wrote back and told him that several of the wardens in his home state, near where he lived, were personal friends of mine, which they were, and I was forwarding a copy of the warrant to them.

He sent a good check.

TOO MANY HITS IN THE HEAD

Getting off on the right foot is an adage that I have always put a good bit of stock in. Generally, if someone likes you or what you are about in the beginning, it is hard for them to ever change that mindset, and vice versa.

I had been called by the office and was told that a man with a backhoe had phoned and said he was going to dig out the swamp behind his house. I was to investigate. When I arrived, it didn't take long to realize that the man was set on doing the dastardly deed to the point that the only means of stopping him might very easily have become physical.

I soon was on the radio and had a wetlands specialist from the then-Department of Environmental Resources heading in. He arrived and the irate landowner became even more enraged. He ranted and raved and could not be reasoned with. I finally decided the best course of action was to just assure him that if he felt he absolutely had to get into the wetlands before procuring the proper permits, he could expect a lot of bad legal things to happen to him, and we left.

When we arrived at the office, the Army Corps of Engineers wetlands man was on the phone, looking for an escort out to the site. Seems that Digger Dan was not satisfied with two professional evaluations of the situation, and he had summoned a federal agency to overrule the two state agencies. We figured, what the heck, the guy was not big enough to be physically threatening and had not indicated the presence of any weapon, so we returned after picking up the Army Corps man and the local county conservation agent.

After a site inspection, my third of the day, we all assured him once again that there would be dire legal consequences to pay should he continue on with his project. We left.

I thought the ordeal was beginning to become funny, since the area was only an acre or so and tens of generations had felt no need to disturb it and recognized its value as a sponge to protect the house from uphill rainwater. Now suddenly this old duffer, who had probably lived there himself 40 or 50 years, had bought a small backhoe and his Tonka Toy mentality was getting him into more trouble than he had ever been into, or so I thought.

With all the obvious hoopla over this investigation, I had forgotten that this was to be a day of a big event. Our new regional manager was reporting into the office. I was headed back to tell the longtime assistant manager, Cloyd, what was going on anyway, so I began thinking about the adage. That first impression one.

When I walked through the door, I heard Cloyd over the divider defending me to the new boss and explaining that the guy on the phone did not seem reasonable. In fact, Cloyd, who was reliably cool, calm and collected, had lost it with this guy.

In a heartbeat, before I could even get a coffee, the new boss whisked me out the door, got into my car, and we were off for my fourth visit to Digger Dan in a day. As we drove down, I was instructed to stay back, provide backup and the boss would smooth things over. Obviously I had mishandled this situation and was feeling like that best foot that you are supposed to put forward had stepped in a barnyard.

We arrived and were greeted at the door once again by a short, thick-shouldered old man with a large chip on his shoulder. I stood back and let the boss do the talking. Before the conversation could get going anywhere there was a flare and the boss was nose-to-nose with Digger Dan. Reason had been replaced on both sides by loud demands and accusations.

Then the most unusual thing happened. In the middle of a sentence Digger stopped, shook his head a few times and rubbed it with his hand. He looked at the boss and began to explain. "I was a prize fighter when I was young. Took too many hits in the head and now I'm a little punchy. Didn't mean to cause no trouble." He turned and went into the house.

We looked at each other and left in the car. I didn't know whether to be happy, sad or just relieved that the situation had quit escalating. When I drove by the next week, the backhoe had a "For Sale" sign on it. It sat like that without moving for over a year and then was gone.

LOST FOOTRACE, FOURTH OF JULY

Since high school I have been overweight. Despite the fact that I carry a "spare tire," I have been able to run. I prided myself on being able to sprint hard and pace well. I hadn't lost a foot race with a violator.

It was the Fourth of July, in the early 1990s. I was getting into my fortieth year and beginning to lose my edge. As I strolled around Justus Lake, a firecracker went off at the foot bridge on the upper end of the lake. I looked over and saw two young lads in their mid-teens. I began walking over, and they turned and began running out the path for the beach and pavilion area.

Looking off the bridge, I realized there were thousands of dead minnows. I took off at a jog to catch them. I kept them in sight and at times seemed to be closing on them over the half-mile distance to the beach. I had narrowed their lead to under a hundred yards, when we got to the beach area.

There had to be a thousand people using the pavilions and beach. The most I had ever seen. I visited each and every pavilion and checked the beach, but could not identify them.

They knew they were chased, but probably never realized they were the first to ever get away.

FRIEND OF A FRIEND'S KID

It was a warm evening during my rookie year. Linda and I were cruising up along Upper Two Mile Run in Venango County, when I spotted three teenagers fishing hand lines along the road. Fishing season was closed. There was a car, so when they ran away from the car into the wet bottomland and disappeared, I figured I was in business.

I had Linda drop me off just ahead and I circled back through the wooded hillside across the road. I didn't have long to wait, when the three of them came tripping out to the car. I took information and, since they were not yet 18, I told them I would see them with their parents the next evening.

Mr. Shearer, then the Fish Warden for Venango County, accompanied me to the first house. It was another old fellow who happened to be prominent in a local sportsmen's club. We talked with him and the kid. The kid insisted he hadn't been fishing. I knew I had seen them baiting and casting hand lines.

The father also insisted his kid would never do anything like that, he had raised him better. In the end it was Mr. Shearer's decision. He never doubted me. He just said he could tell the kid was lying, but since we didn't have any evidence we couldn't win the case.

I spent the next day with a rake trying to recover one of those hand-lines, but never did.

BEWARE THE COLD STARE

Warm, rainy weekends were always some of my favorites to work.

You weren't expected to be in the boat. Boaters are not hardy outdoor types and seldom are out in force in inclement weather. They watch baseball on TV at their cottage and find other things to do.

When it rains, you work fishermen. Illegal fishermen believe that fish wardens melt in the rain and won't be out on days like that, so you often write some good cases when it is raining.

This was just such a day. Don and I were patrolling in the Mountain Top area when we noticed a car with Minnesota plates parked along the road at Slocum Corners. We got into position and soon were observing two males fishing ardently.

We made our approach, knowing that we had an unusual situation. We were a long way from Minnesota. That indicated to us that these guys were not locals. The routine license check confirmed our suspicions that neither man had a license.

We took the pertinent information and found that they both had the name of McCurdy. I was somewhat doubtful, but when Don saw me begin to pressure for more identification, he called me aside. He told me that he recognized them from the Wilkes-Barre pool hall where he used to rack balls as a kid and that they had, in fact, good identification.

I then explained to them their options for settlement and impounded their fishing equipment. They would get their gear back the next day, when they had settled the cases via the Field Acknowledgement of Guilt that they had elected and had satisfied the fines.

We met them at the Mountain Top police station on a Sunday morning, in a drizzle, to complete the paperwork. The one officer on duty was on the road and the station was locked, so we conducted business in the parking lot. The shorter of the two men was very distant and never said anything that wasn't in direct response to a question. The whole time, both days, he just fixed a cold stare on me as I conducted business. It gave me the creeps. Don said he was always that way. I didn't like it.

Ten years passed and I moved across the state to the greener pastures I had long sought as a patrol district. I kept close with Don and we often exchanged visits and phone calls. One night the phone rang and it was Don. He worked a night beat as a photographer for the Wilkes-Barre newspaper.

"Guess who I just took a picture of?" he quizzed.

I didn't venture a guess, since his job often brought him in contact with everything from prominent sports figures to celebrities, politicians and the like.

"Michael McCurdy," he said.

The cold stare jumped from the distant recesses of my brain and flashed in front of my mind's eye.

"He just stabbed his brother to death in front of the pool hall," Don remarked. "They were leading him out of the jail for arraignment."

DEAF-MUTE PRAYING

To have been born with a disability or to have incurred one through the course of life is tragic. To suffer several, such as being deaf and mute, is devastating. But man is a survivor and persons with just such problems live normal lives. Some even commit crimes. Such was the case with the older deaf-mute man that I caught engaged in catching trout above and beyond the limit.

After talking with him the best I could, I spoke with his daughter. She insisted he had been getting away with "stuff like this for years and should be taught a lesson." I was looking for a reason to be lenient and was given reason to be the opposite. Life is strange that way when you're in this job.

The fellow had called and tried unsuccessfully to talk to my wife three times on the phone. Three times she had hung up. When I came through the door that night, she explained that we were having "prank calls" and gave some details.

I assured her I knew what it was and explained the situation. He was from New Jersey, and I had impounded all his equipment. I had given him the phone number and instructions on how to get to the state police barracks. If he came up with the fine money and wanted to pay and have his equipment returned before he left to go home, he was to call me.

Obviously he had rounded up the money. The phone rang again, and I understood that he wanted to meet me at the barracks in 30 minutes. I was talking to the daughter, who had relented and finally made the call for him, after making him suffer.

I arrived at the barracks, and since I was only meeting the one defendant to settle the case, I elected to just settle it in the foyer. There was one bench and a water fountain there in the entranceway, nothing more.

The fellow had come alone to settle the case. His daughter remained in the car. I waved to her as I entered. He sat on the bench. I sat down and began to fill out the paperwork. Once it was complete, I began explaining his options for hearings and such and he waved with his hands for me to stop. I then understood him to say, "I read lips." He knelt down on both knees directly in front of me, so he could see my lips as I slowly explained the charges.

As this was going on, two of my friends were completing their shift as troopers. They walked in and skirted around the defendant, looking at the situation, and on into the barracks. When all was settled and his equipment returned, I sent the defendant on his way.

As I entered the barracks for a moment of chit-chat and a brief thank-you, I was met by four laughing troopers. Between wiping tears from their eyes and hefty chuckles, one said, "We have heard we are tough and heard the game guys are tough, but you take the cake. Making them kneel in front of you and beg to be cited."

FIRE ON THE WATER

It was the second afternoon of trout season, Easter Sunday. It was sunny and Lake Irena was shoulder to shoulder. I worked around and listened to the complaints of "no fish." That was easy to understand. We had stocked 2,000 brookies, and if every other fisherman that fished the lake since starting time yesterday had caught only one fish, they should all be gone.

Easter Sunday fishermen are usually no problem, because they are the serious fishermen. A half-hearted fisherman would not ask the family's permission to go fishing on the holiday.

As I rounded the far corner of the lake, I saw a young guy ahead of me lay a pole down and go back into the woods. When I got there a few minutes later, still doing routine checks, he was leaning against a tree "just watching his friends."

"You weren't fishing?" I quizzed.

"Nope, never touched a pole."

Now I knew he was lying, so I got ID and he elected to settle on a field receipt. I told him I would meet him at the state police barracks across the road in an hour. He had to go get the money at home. He never showed. I filed the citation and it went to a warrant. When I took the warrant to the Hazleton Police Department, I was told that the best place to look for this guy was up in the "juvenile care" facility.

Sure enough he was there and probably going to stay a while. A juvenile hearing date was set. The woman that was the assigned judge was large and grandmotherly. She looked down from the bench with a scowl at me. The defendant was ushered into the room by a juvenile probation person, who sat next to him the whole time.

"Officer," she started, "he says he is guilty. He is in this facility for having committed 11 crimes, some of which are felonies, like arson. He has been here since he was 14. Now we send him home for a holiday with his family, and he commits the heinous crime of fishing without a license. While he obviously did wrong, it is the first wrong thing he ever did that didn't hurt anybody. I am going to extend his stay at this facility two days, if you will agree that is sufficient."

You can't argue with that kind of logic from a woman. Especially, when she is bigger than you and is the judge.

A-FRAME CAPER

Deputy Don and I had just launched a jet boat patrol on the Allegheny River at Parker and started downriver. We hadn't gone a mile when I spotted a jet ski parked against the bank with two fishing rods leaning against it with lines in the water. A family was camping just up the bank. I wanted to see a fishing license on somebody.

Don held the boat as I walked up.

"Who's fishing?" I asked.

"That's not ours," was the reply.

I looked around and could see no one else in sight.

"Any idea who belongs to the fishing gear?" I continued.

"One of the guys up at the next camp," came the reply.

I noted the direction pointed, told Don to stay with the boat, and headed up through the grass to the abandoned railroad grade for easier walking. I had gone about two hundred yards when I started smelling wood smoke. Then, much to my amazement, I walked into a cardboard refrigerator-box town. Everyone had a guard dog or two. It was squalor and filth and about fifty men, women and children.

With some of the citizens of the encampment I began to ask the same questions about the ownership of the fishing rods. After all, that was my business. I was feeling a little bit like the Lone Ranger would have if he had left Tonto holding the horses and then run into the Cavendish Gang.

Finally, one disheveled occupant replied, "See the guy in the A-frame," and pointed.

I followed his directions up over the old rail line where an A-frame shelter stood. It had sheets of plywood for the roof and floor. The ends were open. I noticed a plethora of bodies scattered about in sleeping bags. They all appeared to be sleeping.

Next to the A-frame was a large Cadillac with darkened windows. I silently approached police style, close along the driver's side of the car. I detected movement inside. I tapped on the window and a voice said, "Later!"

Pulling the door open, I loudly identified myself. "State Officer! Now."

There, sitting behind the steering wheel with a scale on the dash and what appeared to be a gallon baggie of marijuana on his lap sat a young bearded man. He looked dumfounded as I looked at him and his business product and tools.

I asked him if they were his fishing rods and he assured me they were.

I informed him we had a problem. He needed a fishing license which he readily admitted he did not have.

I then instructed him, "Dump all that oregano on the ground."

He stared a hole through me.

I repeated, "Dump all that oregano on the ground."

This time he slowly obliged me. I ground and scattered his product into the dust, dirt and grass.

I had him get out and explained how he could settle the fishing without a license case. He quickly decided he was guilty, paid, was given a receipt and I was gone back through the village to my nice safe boat.

We went back to Parker with the jet, borrowed the use of a phone, called the state police and I reported my incident.

The railroad grade is now a bicycle trail and tourists use it to bring money to our little municipalities. When this took place there were a lot of opponents to the bike trail idea. They certainly are better off now.

CHAPTER 20:
Barrels of Fun

Root beer barrels are fun. Beer barrels can be fun. Gun barrels made me nervous when I thought they were pointed at me.

SHOOT OUT, LEMON GATE

It was a warm May afternoon. I was stocking Nescopeck Creek in the game lands. I would load a float box at the Lemon Gate and my deputy Bob and his friend, Floyd, would float it downstream through a particularly picturesque piece of water. When they reached the end, they would carry the box out to their waiting truck and the day would be over. Meantime I would finish up the stocking of the creek, then return and patrol throughout the evening.

The float box was constructed with a rather large mesh wire of heavy gauge, to reduce the chance of tearing and dumping the whole load in one place. This particular day, when the trout came they were of less than average size, for whatever reason. As we loaded them into the box, many of the smaller ones went out the bottom through the mesh.

As the box pulled away, we were left with a riffle full of seven and eight-inch trout. While walking out, I passed two couples walking in carrying a cooler, which I assumed had minnows in it. I spoke to them and checked their licenses to save a walk-in later. One couple was in their early 20s and the other was nearing 50. All looked in order, so I moved on.

Hours later, as I was standing under the I-80 overpass, talking to fishermen, I saw a police car go by on the township road and head toward the game lands. It was flying with the lights flashing and siren blaring. I turned and looked and wondered, but because of the water level, I had no fear for the safety of my float box pullers. They had made the trip several times before and had never expressed any anxiety about in-stream dangers along the way.

Shortly, an ambulance came speeding up the same road. It also was wailing and flashing, but only aroused my curiosity, never alerted me. I continued to check fishermen and had a nice woods walks in the process. As darkness neared, I got into the Matador and went back upstream to where Bob and Floyd would be coming out with the box. They were gone, so I assumed that all went well.

I then drove up to the Lemon Gate to check fishermen's catches as they walked out the game lands road. When I checked the first fisherman, he told me a story that made me wonder, "What if?"

The two couples that I had checked earlier had walked back to the creek crossing where I had loaded the box and inadvertently stocked so many fish when they had slipped through the float box mesh. The couples had immediately seen the trout swarming in the riffle. They began to fish and the guys began to wade around among the fish, trying to get them to hit. Both men were drinking.

The younger of the two became loud and noisy and the other, his uncle, instructed him to "be quiet, you're scaring the fish." This led the younger fellow to rebel and, after some harsh words, he pushed the older man down into the water and was standing over him. Then the older fellow pulled a short revolver, loaded with snake-shot, and from his position lying in the creek, fired several shots into the face of the young man at point blank range. That's what all the sirens were about.

The younger man lost his sight, but lived. The older man did time in prison. I wondered, "What if I had arrived during the fight and the gunfire? Would I have been shot at? Or would I have drawn my own revolver and killed a man, thinking he was killing another and I was witnessing a murder?"

As the story was told to me, I couldn't help but think that a sport that is so much fun certainly has its downsides, like everything else. But you have to admit, people do go crazy over the Pennsylvania Fish and Boat Commission's trout stocking program.

THE REPEATING CANE

You train and train. You tell yourself always to be alert to the unexpected. You are always ready in the heated situations and the times you are outnumbered. You pay extra attention in the rain and in the dark. But you still get lackadaisical.

It was a hot July afternoon. I was responding to a "domestic"; just like they tell you in training, one of the worst situations you can get into. This was a "pissing match between two skunks." The complainant was a bum and lived in a shack. The accused was a well-to-do oil baron. Known to look rough, talk rough and be rich enough to get a good lawyer.

The complaint dealt with oil running on the ground near the first skunk's house, from the second skunk's well. I met with skunk number one and he pointed to the well beyond the "No Trespassing" posters that skunk number two had put up. It was a real Hatfield and McCoy situation.

I used my binoculars and could see no problem. I checked the ditch downstream and could see no problem. I told skunk one that there was no problem and he should not be dragging state agencies with limited time and budgets into the middle of pissing matches. Then I jumped in my car and left.

The weather was hot and miserable, sweltering. I drove back past the gate leading to the wells. It was now open. A gray van was pulling into the well site and stopping. Stupidity, my frequent copilot when I am alone, made me turn into the well road behind the van. I stopped 40 yards short of the van, on a raised access road with no turnaround. I stepped from the patrol vehicle and swung around my driver's side door to keep from getting my boots muddy. The emblem of the state agency that I am employed by was clearly visible to the old driver of the van, skunk two.

As I approached halfway to his van, I saw him reach around behind his seat. I saw a reflection from a long gun barrel and heard a click. My heart panicked and my mind and body froze. "That was a shotgun and I just heard the action close," said my mind. "There is no cover, start clearing leather. Get the gun out and be ready!" My body hesitated. I didn't clear. My heart and mind raced. I kept striding toward what I thought was my mortal enemy.

Skunk two swung from the van and grabbed the side behind the door to steady himself. He pointed his metal telescoping cane at me.

"What are you doing on my property?" he demanded.

I explained that I saw the gate open, had a complaint and was on my way up to his house to talk to him so he could show me the area, when I spotted him. All of which was a crock that my mind was spewing out as it exalted in having just lived through a life-and-death, shoot-or-don't-shoot situation, without having even looked panicky.

After getting the tour of the lease, I explained to skunk two that his was one of the neatest leases I had ever visited, and it was. He told me to ignore the signs if I ever wanted to check something, just go right ahead.

If skunk two had been of the wrong frame of mind and the cane had been a shotgun, I would have been gunned down. If I had cleared and been aiming at him when the cane came up alongside the van, skunk two would have most likely died. What in my mind kept me from reacting will always be a mystery.

Never in my life have I been more sure it was a gun being pointed at me and yet, somewhere in the recesses of the gray matter, commonsense was computing the available data and making a decision that I will always feel was one of my best.

HEY COP! BANG, YOU'RE DEAD!

I am a good conservation officer, but I am only a mediocre cop. I only eat doughnuts on the rare occasion. They make bad things happen to me. I get fatter, get heartburn, and they put me in touch with a part of the population that I don't normally have to deal with, the street people that don't fish and don't know anything about the outdoors.

Nonetheless, one fine spring morning I stopped in one of the many doughnut shops in Hazleton. The normal group was at the counter and a rough little street urchin was panhandling. He was about 12 and his life of crime was developing quite well. He was skinny, his clothes were dirty and he looked like he might have fleas.

"Hey cop, give me a dime," he insisted.

"Get a job," I responded, half kidding, half meaning it.

He panhandled on down the counter, until the owner of the establishment ushered him out. I sat a little longer than usual, working on educating the counter people on trout fishing, boating, hunting, wildflowers and anything else they don't normally experience in a town surrounded by strip-mines. Then I finished my second cream-filled éclair, slid to the floor of the shop with a thump and, hoisting up my gun belt, waddled for the door.

When I got into the parking lot the street urchin came wheeling around the corner of the building on a fenderless bicycle. It had a banana seat and a roll bar. He dismounted in a slide, drew a gun from the waist of his grungy black pants, assumed a really good combat stance and shouted, "Bang! You're dead!" He laughed, got on his bike and rode away.

It was only a toy gun, but the effect was real. I haven't eaten many doughnuts since.

GETTING A BANG OUT OF A CAMPFIRE

In the midst of a mall, a development and an airport is a little wooded sanctuary. It is the Hazle Township Community Park. It has a 20-acre impoundment called Lake Irena.

Lake Irena is heavily stocked with brook trout. They last only hours after stocking before they are supplying nourishment to the bodies of many a Hazletonian. I guess this is good. It keeps a lot of old-timers and kids off the streets. Some of these kids would be better off left on the streets, where they would at least get the supervision of a regular, full-time police force.

Lake Irena is not a wilderness. These kids thought it was. Beer parties ran rampant, as tent cities sprang up the Friday before trout season. Kids of all ages and of all sexes would frequent these blowouts, in honor of the gala annual piscatorial orgy. In that day and age, my job was strictly to keep the fish in the pond until the opening hour of the season and hold the annual trashing of the park to a minimum.

As much as I came to dislike these gatherings of the under-aged, I could not help but wonder if any of them even had parents. Nonetheless, it was tradition. My part was to walk around after dark and surprise as many of them as I could by appearing in the glow of their campfires, which were strictly forbidden yet numbered nearly a hundred, and convince them that in the shadows lurked a large contingent of uniformed, armed men prepared to shackle them and return them to their domicile if they got out of line.

I was on such a mission, working by myself at midnight, when I slithered in among a bunch of merrymakers. I was but a few feet behind the bulk of them, looking across the fire at 20 boys and girls, when I saw a young man stride toward them.

"State Fish Warden!" he shouted. Then, pulling a large .44 magnum handgun from under his coat, he aimed and discharged it into the fire, in my general direction. A shower of sparks jumped into the frosty night air.

"You know we don't allow fires here!" he yelled.

I knew him and had always identified him as one of the "better" kids that fished the lake. He was 18 and had a respectable job. He also had just made me mad.

I was on him verbally and in his face in a heartbeat. I took possession of the gun and led him from the group to my car. My intentions were to write him for impersonation of an officer, then have his parents meet me at the local state police barracks to recover his gun.

When we reached the car he was crying. He pleaded with me to take no action. He was to leave for the Marines on Monday morning, and this would certainly cost him his enlistment. I returned his gun, with instructions to put it in the trunk of his car and get it home. I promised him he would be cited if he was jerking me around.

A phone call Monday morning to the recruiter confirmed his story of enlistment. I told the recruiter what a good kid he was and that I had called just to put a good word in for him. I remained in that area for another five years and never saw his name in the paper for any trouble. Even good kids will be kids.

ONLY GUY THAT EVER SHOT AT ME

It had been a particularly disheartening union meeting. When I got back to Franklin, Leo Yahner, the game guy I was riding with, suggested we stop for a few beers. That sounded like a good idea.

We went into a tavern and sat and discussed the beating we had taken in negotiations. As we sat talking about the meeting and the different points of view that had come up and all the things you do to analyze a losing situation, Leo noticed a big guy sitting at the bar.

"That's the only guy that ever took a shot at me," Leo said, nodding toward the bar. "Sure you need another beer?"

"I'm not even sure I want to finish this one," I answered. I did but that was enough.

BARRELING SCHOOL BUS

It was one of my first stockings in my first district. I was full of enthusiasm and trying to get as much public relations out of the fish as I could. I would get on the truck and hand down the buckets, as the driver loaded them and chatted with the bucket carriers about how nice the fish were and "look at this big one." I was up and down on that truck a hundred times.

Then for a split second on a backcountry lane I didn't pay attention and began to swing down onto the roadbed. A school bus was squeezing between the lines of fish bucket carriers' cars, which were parked on both sides of the road. The bus was probably going a little too fast.

Someone screamed and I grabbed the mirror of the fish truck and the big, yellow fender just brushed my pant leg as I pulled myself up tight against the fish truck's door. Thank goodness someone else was paying attention or this would have been a very short book.

OIL DISSIDENTS

It had potential to be a real barn-burner of a pollution case. The neighbor to the old independent oil operator was the leader of an anti-regulatory group. They had stated on occasion during newspaper interviews that they would test the right of officers entering their property to enforce pollution laws. Naturally, right in the heat of the published discussion I found a pollution in the hub of their bailiwick. I met with Doug Neely from the Oil and Gas Division of DER and with a rookie officer, Jay Waskin, we headed out to the site. I had called ahead to let the well operator know we were coming. I told

Jay to stay on his toes, keep his eyes peeled and Doug and I would try to nonchalant them into a solution.

It went just about as expected. Upon arrival the old guy that operated the wells began leading us down to the site. I had been there the night before by walking up from the other road. In case things got ugly today, I wanted to already have my evidence, using the sure-to-be-disputed authority given me under the Fish Law.

Before we got very far, a group of five oil-producer desperados arrived and began trying to create a confrontation. I ignored them as did Doug and the nonchalanting went well. We got to the site, sat down on a log with the old guy and explained what we needed cleaned up and how we were going to deal with the fines. Our end was going smoothly.

Suddenly, Jay, a relatively short officer, was barking in one of the desperado's faces. He had backed him up against a tree. All the other players watched me. I stayed put and they didn't move. Soon all was calm again. Cleanup was agreed on, and I had made arrangements for collecting the necessary fine money. In the car I asked Jay what the excitement was all about.

"That guy's sweatshirt had ridden up above his jeans and he had a gun tucked in the front of his pants," Jay said. "I was just checking his carry permit."

I always felt good when using rookies for backups. They seemed so alert.

NOTHING AS DANGEROUS AS THE BOSS

After several complaints from a cooperative trout nursery about thievery from their holdover trout pond, I developed a plan. A group of 20-year-old certified vandals were camped downstream along a trout stream. They were making things ready for trout camp the following weekend and had no rods, or so they stated.

I had visited the camp at dark one evening earlier in the week. My suspicions were piqued. At 11 o'clock Friday evening, a week before the season, I once again saw the camp lights on and a fire going. Observation from across the creek showed a beer party in progress. I was on foot with a deputy. Another had taken my car and hidden it, staying with the vehicle. On the way there, I had radioed to the boss at the office, telling him of our mission. He said he would swing by in an hour or so, if he hadn't heard from us. A backup in this business is a luxury you don't often have. We would keep him posted.

Deputy Greg and I walked without lights past the camp, through the woods and secreted ourselves in the high grass along an access road to the pond. We would be able to watch the pond for activity. Before we could get properly hidden, a cruiser came by us. We thought it was a state police officer coming in to park and do reports and drink a coffee in this out-of-the way location. We ignored him, knowing he would leave soon and the action would probably pick up.

We oozed past the camp again. This time, some of the hoodlums were missing. Something was up. After 20 minutes of lying along the road, we saw the lights come on in the cruiser and it pulled out. It swung around the pond toward our position. Greg noted it was the boss in a marked car. We didn't want to give away our location, so we held fast. When the marked car neared where we lay in the grass, the driver swung wide to catch the pond in his lights. In so doing, he narrowly missed us lying there, then was gone.

He had no sooner left, when two voices began talking from the shadows across the pond. The hoodlums had been about ready to go into action when the car had pulled in, but instead they hid. They decided it was not a good time to be playing outlaw and to go back to the camp for awhile. We stopped them and asked lots of questions, but no violation had been committed. Greg and I decided the next time we worked that pond we would hide in a different place. The boss said he had never seen us lying there in the grass.

Float stocking trout to get them into off-the-road stream areas was popular with sportsmen, who volunteered for the often cold and wet duty, but called it "having fun." This picture is "getting ready to launch" on the Nescopeck Creek at the "Lemon Gate" on the State Game Lands. The "Nesky" was one of my favorite streams because of the challenge of getting trout into it. I used this ford in the creek as often as I could talk the drivers into it. Trucks got stuck, a fisherman got shot, violators cowered from my presence and one of the two pairs of waders seen here developed a major leak. This book would only be half the fun without this crossing.

CHAPTER 21:
Fun with Wildlife

Wild adventures with wildlife and domestic critters come with the job. Why? I'm not sure. I guess it was because our uniforms looked the same as the game guys and nobody took time to read the patches.

DEER CHOPPER RESCUE

One animal out of a population seldom makes a difference. A lone mouse eaten by a fox or a deer taken by a hunter is seldom noticed. But let the events of that lone animal's death, or two or three, be recorded by the media and it becomes the equivalent of a new endangered species. Such media coverage often causes a heroic effort, risking human life just to satisfy a public that doesn't understand.

It was the second week of buck season in Luzerne County, when two does and a buck, pushed by hunters, ventured onto the ice of Fenner's Ice Lake. The Ice Lake's ice wasn't ready for surface travel and they broke through in a cove, a hundred yards out. Nolfie, the Game Commission officer, and I were in his car and alerted by the radio to the media-perceived catastrophe. We headed over.

A crowd had formed before we arrived. There in the broken ice were three struggling deer. A TV crew arrived, having monitored the call on a scanner. We were between a rock and a hard place. We would have to make a move. Lassoing didn't work; not enough rope. Efforts to break the ice were a failure. A boat that arrived could neither break the ice nor help a crew to reach the deer.

Then, like magic, in the sky appeared the Pennsylvania State Police chopper. What they thought they could do was beyond my comprehension. The crowd "oohed" and "ahhed," as the chopper slipped lower and lower toward the lake. They were only feet off the water. The downdraft from the rotor was breaking the ice. The ice was blown out of the way the whole way to the shoreline. The deer struggled to the edge and lay panting.

We dried the exhausted animals with old blankets and dispersed the crowds. Soon it would be night. We stood guard until dark and then left. The next morning, I took a drive right after sunup to check on our deer. I had my doubts that they would make it. I felt that they would expire during the night. I was right. When I walked back from the road to where they were, I was shocked. I expected to find three dead deer. I found only three gut piles. Someone else had figured out the stress of the situation would take its toll.

GYPSY MOTH CATERPILLARS

Caterpillars make great bird feed and are not a part of our job. That is what I knew about these crawlies before the first great gypsy moth infestation of Luzerne and Carbon counties. I soon became aware that fuzzy caterpillars are not that good of a bird food and that they can attain populations that will completely eat a forest. That particular year, they were so bad they would have eaten green paint off of a car if they could get it to hold still.

I had a favorite lookout up on an old railroad abutment, probably one the Native Americans used when they were watching for enemies. From atop this cut-stone pillar, I could survey much of my domain on the Lehigh River. I would stand with field glasses and watch the canoes and kayaks. I could see life preservers and beer cans. When I saw what looked like a problem, I would head for the takeout and intercept them.

From the same point I could also look into several campsites that regularly hosted miscreants. This particular day, I was watching with my spotting scope as several fellows in their early 20s pistol-whipped some cans and bottles. I was analyzing the best approach for a "Lone Ranger," when I felt something nearing my groin inside my summer pants.

Needless to say, I panicked and dropped my pants high atop the pillar. I discovered a gypsy moth caterpillar crawling up my leg. I then began to notice that I had nearly 20 of the almost-grown insects on me. Man, is that creepy! I got them all off and went about my business, issuing paperwork without incident.

As I rode home in the car, an occasional caterpillar would appear on the car seat or dashboard, most likely still escaping from the folds of my uniform. I can't imagine sleeping in those tents that night where the defendants were camped.

BEAR TRAP BREAKING
Intrigued by wildlife all my life, I jumped at an opportunity to become friends with Gary Alt, the Game Commission's world-renowned bear biologist. Linda and I spent as many days as we could traveling, helping and photographing with him. When he started asking about our previous turkey hunting successes, it seemed only natural to invite him on a spring gobbler hunt.

He couldn't leave his project at that time of year, since the commission was hoping to capture a few bears for relocation, but he knew where there were a couple of turkeys. If we could come up bright and early, we could hunt together in the Pocono area and then check a few bear traps. Sounded like a plan.

We met Gary and soon had what sounded like a "slammer" gobbler yodeling to us, but for some reason we were unable to complete the equation. It was probably with hens. It would move and we would move. The morning took us nearly a half mile from where we started and, as it warmed up, Gary suggested we drop down over the hill and check a bear trap he had along a swamp, rather than go directly back to the car. Sounded like another good plan to me.

When we got there, we were met by a large female bear caught by one foot in a leg snare. She was not a happy camper. She had been held there for some time, since she had the dirt worn down around the anchor tree like a big dog on a leash. As we neared, Gary identified her and saw that we had her four cubs up a tree right next to her. For the most part she paced and then would lie down.

This was in a wooded housing development where Gary knew four sows, each with four cubs, lived. The people living there and watching the bears were convinced there were just two sows with four cubs each. They would never miss a sow and four cubs, while other areas in the state were just begging for bears. He could relocate five at one time, and everybody would be a winner.

Now we had to get a way to transport the bears, had to capture all of them, and we had to do it on the sly. Gary and I hiked for the cars with the shotguns and left Linda bear-sitting. Her job was to just relax and make sure the sow stayed tethered and the cubs stayed up the tree. An hour later we were back, and Gary's assistant was rolling in with a wheeled culvert trap for the transfer.

The first thing that needed to be done was to give the sow an injection to knock her out for processing. Linda would tease the "bear on a rope," while Gary did the darting. He would sneak across the expanse that the bear could reach, dart her in the butt, and lunge back to safety. The sow was easy to amuse. Linda only had to approach within a few feet, and she immediately got the bear's undivided attention. The sow was having so much fun that with one fell swoop she swatted a rock the size of a cantaloupe 30 feet into the air.

When Gary jabbed the bear and spun, I still believe her teeth missed the seat of his pants by less than an inch. Then the cable on the snare brought her up short. I often wondered how he had decided how long to make the cable and how he tested his conclusions. I figured he probably used summer help or guys like me.

Soon the sow was in lullaby land. We weighed and processed her and safely tucked her into the culvert trap, with hopes that she would have a nice sleep. Next, Linda, Gary's assistant and I stretched a fireman's rescue net. Then Gary shinnied 50 feet up into the tree to catch a cub by the scruff of the neck and throw it down to us. We would wrap it up in the net and the helper would process it and put it in the trap with its mom.

Two cubs weighed 11 pounds and two weighed 13. They were like buzz saws without a cord. Wrapping them up was a job for someone with little regard for life or limb, but then so was grabbing them by the scruff of the neck, especially 50 feet up. Since Gary had to improvise to bring this together so quickly, he had forgotten his climbing gear. He was only strapped to the tree with a piece of hemp rope. At the end of the exercise, he realized he had tied it to a belt loop of his dungarees and not to his leather belt. Oh well, we had the landing net.

After some time we had mama bear and her four kids loaded, and they were all up and playing in the culvert trap, if you call trying to get out of the air holes to eat the processors playing. They became content in short order, calming down after acquainting themselves with their new home, and we drove them out of there.

Now Gary had to decide where to take them.

"I would like to ship these guys to Somerset," he opined.

"Let me make a call," I offered.

I got on the phone and called my boss in Sweet Valley. I told him I wasn't busy that day. In fact it was a scheduled day off. I would haul the bear to Somerset with the state car and return the next day, since my parents lived near the Game Commission's southwest region office. In those days of no extra pay for extra work, they were glad to put me on the clock to justify the use of the state vehicle. There would be no overnight expenses.

Gary towed the bear to our home in Sugarloaf, and we attached the trap to the Fish Commission car. Then Linda and I were rolling for Somerset. We would meet several game guys there, and they would finish the bears' move, under cover of darkness, to the wilds of Will's Mountain. Then the next morning we would get the trap at Ligonier and return it to the northeast.

The trip down was relatively uneventful, except for being pulled over a few times by state troopers that just had to know if there was a bear in the trap. I assured them there was. They would look in and see the bears and ask the where-from and where-to questions, and then we were on our way. We delivered the bears and then visited with my folks for the evening.

The next morning was beautiful and spring-like. We hooked onto the empty trap at Ligonier and headed back to Luzerne County. As we were making the swing off Route 22 onto Route 220 at Hollidaysburg, the trap broke loose. The trailer tongue had broken right at the trap. The trap scampered forward toward oncoming traffic. I gassed the Matador and headed it off, before it could hit anybody else. It smacked three fenders of the state car and dented it slightly, leaving some paint marks.

Now I had a predicament. I couldn't leave the trap sit there and I couldn't move it. Traffic was reasonably heavy. Several motorists stopped and helped me get the trap pushed off the road. I then got out my Game Law Digest and called the local game warden, Larry Harshaw. He wasn't home, but I got his wife, Bonnie. "Good," I thought. "Somebody that can do something. No middleman." Usually you talk to a game or fish guy and they have to ask their wives how to solve the problem, anyway, so this time I had lucked out.

Bonnie asked where I was and I told her. She told me to look out the door toward Route 220 and I should see a small machine shop on the other side of the road. I said I had already left the trap in their parking lot.

"Great," she replied. "Go in and ask for so and so, he's a deputy."

I thanked her and hung up. I called the state police to report the accident, as we are required to do, and went and talked to the deputy. He assured me they would weld it where it sat, and they would get it back to the northeast somehow.

I met with the trooper who tried to issue me a citation, but was told not to by his superior in a phone conversation. I am not sure what I had done, but it dealt with faulty equipment. Then we were on our way home.

As I drove along, the thought occurred to me, "What if?" I could see the headlines now: "Five Bears Stocked in Hollidaysburg."

ATTACK RABBIT

Most days I could keep from laughing at funny things, until I got away from the situation to where the persons involved wouldn't know of my levity. But not always.

I had been riding with Nolfie for a little while one morning when he said, "Got to meet Officer Teddy Vesloski and see a lady about some bear damage. It broke into her rabbit cage. They sure do like rabbits."

Seemed routine enough. Go look around, make sure you find a few black bear hairs or tracks, make sure there was actually damage, get an estimate of the damages from the person and do one yourself. Fill out the paperwork and be on your way. We had done many over the years, bees, rabbits and various other items of interest to a bear's never-satiated stomach.

We met Teddy at the Mountain Top Police Department, loaded into one car and cruised the mile or two to the development where the damage had occurred. Nolfie and Teddy approached the door and I moseyed over and looked at the rabbit cage. It was flattened.

A middle-aged woman came to the door and only cracked it a little bit. Before Nolfie or Teddy could say anything, she pointed at me and blurted out, "You be careful, he's still on the loose."

I walked to the door to where I could listen.

"You watch behind you," she said, pointing to me.

"Yes ma'am," I said. "But the bear is probably long gone."

"I don't mean the bear!" she exclaimed. "I mean that rabbit of mine. He's an attack rabbit."

She was serious.

I had just seen the Monty Python film, "In Search of the Holy Grail," and could picture the attack rabbit tearing up the knight, one extremity at a time. I fought a chuckle. She looked gravely serious as she said, "You guys better step in before he bites one of you." As she ushered us through the door, I was starting to lose it.

"You don't believe me, do you? Well, he bit the neighbor kid and they had to take him to the hospital and get stitches," she said sternly.

It was not the time to laugh, but it was either laugh out loud or blow out my eyeballs from the pressure that was building, so I did. She looked at me indignantly. Nolfie gave me that hard fatherly look he used on me when I was being silly and he was trying to do serious business. Big Teddy was biting his lip. He looked at me and lost it, too.

I faced the lady and explained. "Ma'am, I know you are serious and just trying to keep us from getting hurt, but you are telling well over 18 feet and 700 pounds of game wardens armed with .357 magnum and .38 special handguns to be careful before your attack rabbit gets them. It just struck me as very funny."

Fortunately, she relaxed and saw the humor in the situation, too. I don't think Nolfie ever did, but then his name was on the incident report.

GARBAGE CAN SKUNK

The Game Commission vehicle fleet is like a bunch of wheeled arks. You never know what kind of critter you may be riding with when you get in.

This particular morning was no different. When I arrived at Nolfie's, he said, "We got to go pick up a garbage can and take it out to the game lands."

I wasn't busy, so it sounded like a good caper. We just went around the block to the doctor's house and the lady pointed to a garbage can. We lifted it onto the deer rack and tied it down with rubber bungees. We got in his state car and headed out I-80, got off on Rt. 309 and went down the Honey Hole Road. When we got up to the Pear Farm area of the game lands, I opened the gate and we drove up to the deer pit.

"You might want to stand back," Nolfie said. "Skunk."

So naturally I did. Nolfie carefully untied the can and set it on the ground, stood back, removed the lid and tilted it onto its side. The skunk crawled out a hole on the bottom of the can. The hole was so big that the skunk had to be riding the whole way spread-eagle, to keep from falling out. We chuckled at each possibility, as the skunk headed down into the woods.

"What if it would have dropped out when we were loading the can, between our feet?"

"Or better yet, what if it had fallen out of the can onto the Interstate and the car behind us had seen it happen and then hit it? They'd have thought the Game Commission was stocking skunks to hit on the road!"

RATTLER

Pleasant, sunny summer afternoons are meant for boat patrol, and when I was in the Luzerne County district the best place for a boat patrol was F.E. Walter Reservoir. The dam had a 100-plus-acre pool normally and provided 10- horsepower boating in an area that resembled the Canadian wilds. A few days each year, the fishing would be superb, but other than that it always seemed that the fish had lockjaw.

It was one of those lockjaw periods when I went on a routine boat patrol with deputy George. While deputies and district men were still working in blue jeans and flannel shirts most of the time, George was always in a finely tuned uniform. George looked sharp and was an excellent deputy. He took great pride in his affiliation with the organization and put a lot of effort into his appearance and training. George was an expert marksman with his service revolver. However, it was hard to convince George that our job was to protect snakes. He didn't especially care for them.

This particular afternoon, we were doing our "close the place up" patrol late in the evening. The sun was starting to cast long shadows and the hordes of tourists were heading "down the pike" for Philly and points south. It was time to just cruise around the lake and make sure no shoreline was missing and that the lake hadn't sprung any leaks.

We first did a cruise along the Bear Creek arm of the lake, and all was well. It was vacant and, as usual, we marveled at the scenery. We rounded the point and had made it all but a few hundred yards from the mouth of the

Lehigh River, when I noticed a snake swimming. Knowing how well George liked snakes, I slowly arced the boat's path to intercept it.

George was sitting in the bow of the 14-foot AlumaCraft boat and turned around in time to see why I was slowing down.

"George, get an oar and hoist him aboard. We'll give him a ride to the shore."

The order given was met with a stare of contempt and disbelief.

"George, I'm serious, I don't want to let it drown."

The face relaxed a little to mildly amused, but not responding. Finally, knowing I was getting the best of the situation, I told him, "Just slide the paddle under him and lift him on it and hold him out over the water. I'll run him into shore, so no one hits him with a prop."

George said nothing. Well, nothing I can put in this book, anyhow, and grabbed an oar and hoisted the snake to where we could see all of its 3-foot length. It was then that he noticed the rattles. I had suspected them all along. At that point, he dropped the oar and began to call me unkind names.

"George, don't shoot him," I cried. "He's only a little fellow and up here where he won't hurt anybody. Don't shoot, George. Put the gun away."

Finally one eye rolled my way, while the other continued to squint down the barrel and tracked the once-again-swimming snake. After a minute or so the snake made the safety of the shore and crawled behind a rock, as though he expected impending gunfire. Once George had reholstered, we recovered the dropped oar and continued our patrol, George occasionally looking at me as though he had discovered his best friend was the devil. Me, I just drove the boat and smirked.

REGAL WILD TURKEY

We were down near Catawissa in Columbia County, bowhunting with Linda's brother, Len. The hunt, as always, had been fun. After lunch, Linda lingered at the parking lot in the light drizzle, while Len and I headed back up on the mountain. While she was sitting there the Game Protector, Steve Smithonic, pulled in with a stocking truck and released some game-farm "wild" turkeys.

Steve talked to Linda and headed out. Then she noticed one of the birds had managed to get itself tangled in some green briars in the little creek that ran just off the edge of the parking lot. It was floundering in the flow and drowning. Linda waded in and extracted the turkey. She put it on the parking lot, and it just sat huddled as though it had accepted its fate. It didn't seem to be responding well to the rescue.

Since it was cold and raining and the turkey was getting no drier the longer it sat there, Linda lifted it into the van. She found a dry towel and wrapped it and held it by the heater for a half hour, until it had recuperated. Then she released it.

That is where she was, sitting in the van holding the turkey, when her brother returned for his tree stand. As avid turkey hunters, we had often espoused the virtues of the lordly wild turkey to him, as we told the stories of success and failures hunting this fine game bird.

All he said when he saw the wet, bedraggled, sad-looking critter in Linda's arms was, "Not the regal game bird I imagined."

BEAVER CHASE

The call came from game officer Lenny Hribar. There was a beaver stuck in the concrete basin at the outflow of Kahle Lake. Could I go with him to open the gate, so he could drive in?

"I wouldn't miss this for anything," I responded.

We met and drove down to the tailwater end of the lake and, sure enough, there was a 30 to 40-pound beaver swimming around and around in circles. It had climbed in the slope, but couldn't get out over the straight, slick walls.

Lenny had a plan and I couldn't wait. The area is about 20 yards square, with just enough water to come up to the running boards on a pair of hip boots on a tall man. Lenny donned his boots, took a noose stick, and lowered himself into the water.

I sat on the wall and cheered. Around and around they went, like a chess game, Lenny maneuvering for a checkmate. The beaver, ever so versatile in its moves, was diving under the now-muddy water. A half hour had passed and I was really enjoying it.

Every now and then a little of the April ice water would ease over the top of Lenny's boots when he tried to move too fast, or the beaver would make a dive and slap when he got too close. Occasional tail-slaps would send a spray of water high in the air over the arena, causing a rainbow in the morning sun and thoroughly splashing Lenny. It was quite a show.

Finally the beaver tired and was cornered, and Lenny got the noose around his neck. When the loop was tightened, the beaver became very indignant and the spray of water for a minute or two was terrific. In all the writhing to maintain balance on the slippery bottom, Lenny had swamped his boots quite well.

Eventually, between uproarious laughter and giggles that made my eyes water, I was handed a spitting-mad beaver on a stick. I eased him out over the dam and he was turned loose in the creek downstream. That's when I noticed them.

There were many large walleye stranded in scant inches of water just below the dam and downstream in stocked trout water. The very next morning would be the trout season opener and hordes of fishermen would descend on the area. I quickly devised a plan.

I returned to the Franklin office and rounded up some large, confiscated dip nets and Supervisor Hollen and I headed back down. I invited Lenny to join us, since I had helped him, but got an answer something like, "Fat chance, pal."

We spent several hours chasing and lifting splashing walleye up to 29 inches long with dip nets, until we were tired and soaked and muddy. They were all transported back into the lake.

I don't mind paybacks, but I hate it when they are so quick you can't enjoy the earning of them.

I GUESS I'LL HAVE TO KILL IT AGAIN

Deputies have real jobs and real families. Many of them work long and hard to earn a wage, then spend their evenings with the family and their weekends with the fish warden. These guys and gals are dedicated to making a difference for people that like to fish and boat. Keeping those recreations fun and safe is what motivates them.

Jimmy was just such a deputy. Any time I called, he was ready to go. He had four kids, two dogs, a house, a car and tuition payments to make. He had been laid off from his fulltime job due to cutbacks and was struggling to keep from losing his house.

I received a call just before midnight that a deer had been hit on the road at the Valmont Industrial Park. It was still flopping. The Pennsylvania State Police had called me, knowing that Bob Nolf, the local game officer, was on sick leave. They asked if I would take care of it.

Only a fool doesn't help out those guys and gals when they can. In the course of a year, the state police came to my assistance, one way or the other, ten times for every one time I got to return the favor. I was anxious to pay my debt.

I jumped in the truck and headed up. The deer, a small one, was still kicking when I arrived. I stopped at the barracks, told them not to let the shot bother them, and returned and put the issue snub-nose .38 to the deer's ear and touched off a round. It stiffened. I grabbed the four legs and swung it into the pickup and closed the tailgate and cap.

I was going to head out to one of the many deer pits that we had around the area at the time, and then I thought of Jimmy. I would give him the deer for venison if he wanted it, since it was along the way and would save about 20 miles of driving. I had a book of possession permits ready to go.

I knocked on Jimmy's door and he answered.

"Can you use a deer? I don't think she's too messed up," I said.

"Sure, just dump her out here," he responded, pointing. He was in a bathrobe and slippers.

I popped open the cap and the tailgate and out came a deer, somewhat running and staggering. It stopped alongside the house, between Jim's place and the neighbors, about 50 yards away.

"You better give her another one," Jim offered.

I did and, to my amazement, she actually did die this time.

After I got the neighbors calmed down and back to bed, I went and had coffee with the local cop that had arrived, blue lights flashing.

MINNOW AT SHERM'S

Minnows are just little fish. I have caught many fish and eaten them and many have not been any bigger than minnows. Some, such as smelt, I have eaten fins and all. I always figured there would be a time this reasoning and ability would come in handy. It certainly did one evening.

It was the night before trout season opened and my deputy Sherm had agreed to work with me. I was to pick him up at his sporting goods store. When I arrived, he had people waiting in line for licenses, so I set about amusing myself until he could empty the shop and lock up. As I roamed around in the store, I decided to have a look at his bait. I took the dip net and lifted a few minnows and a shiner about six inches long for a look.

As I was looking at them, Sherm spoke.

"You need a warrant to look in there," he said, kidding.

Sherm and I both knew that most of the people in the store didn't know he had become a deputy.

I looked at him defiantly, grabbed the big shiner and bit it in half. As I threw the severed tail section back into the tub, all were watching. They had followed my hand motion and not noticed that I had turned and spit the upper half into the other minnow trough.

Everyone was repulsed and convinced that I had bitten off and eaten the head of the minnow. Sherm went into a tirade about how I was going to have to pay for the fish I ate and he should charge me eating-fish rate and not bait-fish rate. Sherm never knew I had spit it into his tub, either. Unless he reads this he probably never will.

MINNOW AT HEMLOCK CREEK

In a business where image is everything, you must give thought to how you want to appear in the eyes of the group you are currently dealing with. I have always been image conscious and have tried to alter mine to meet the circumstances.

It was opening day of trout season on Hemlock Creek. We had word of some guys camped along the stream and thought we should go and check them. I was working with deputy Gene at the time. We had walked about half a mile when we came to the camp. We'd gotten there later than we hoped and missed any chance of getting preseason fishermen.

The three or four fishermen/campers were in their early twenties and hadn't had any luck. So they had come back to camp to have breakfast and let the sun warm the hollow before they tried again. On a slab of bark along the fire six emerald shiners were smoking, nailed to the wood. I looked at the group and ruled out satanic ritual. Since deputy Gene knew them all, I just stood and made small talk as there was no apparent violation.

Then the image thing hit me. They were probably cooking the minnows and somebody was going to have to eat them to keep his end of a macho bet. I walked over and picked one off the board and swallowed it after a quick chewing.

"Always liked them that way," I said and turned and walked off.

Gene ran into several of the guys at work the next week and they said they thought maybe I was crazy. My image-building had worked, just as planned.

THERE'S A BEAR

The eyes see what the mind tells them to see. This has been proven many times. Hunter education stresses this to help eliminate accidents. At the time, I was a hunter education instructor and had seen many demonstrations of the fact.

I was doing a slow boat patrol of the Francis E. Walter Reservoir one June evening, when I first noticed the "black bear" standing at the edge of the laurel, on the shore a hundred yards away. I watched and watched, but it did not move. Yet I knew in my mind it was a bear. I marveled at how still it was standing. Then the light faded and I couldn't make it out anymore.

A week or two later, my routine patrols again found me at the reservoir under the same light conditions, and there was the bear again. This time I had binoculars and, after tying the boat and getting a good solid rest for the binoculars, I could determine that what I was seeing was a burnt stump that had floated into its position along the laurel during the spring's high water.

"So," I thought, "if it fooled me ...." I began to get each deputy to ride with me when I knew the light would be right. I would tell them how we had been seeing a bear and they should bring their cameras along and say whatever it took to get them psyched.

As I rounded the bend in the river, I would point and exclaim, "Bear!" and they would get ballistic and take pictures. We would get back to the ramp and they would be telling people about the bear we saw. It made for a fun summer. But, as the summer faded and I again had each of them riding with me, I would point it out again and tell them what it actually was and let them see for themselves.

They were all disappointed when they realized it wasn't a real bear. I guess I would be, too, if I had a picture of a burnt stump in my wildlife photos scrapbook.

JUST GIVE HIM A ROOT

Del was a game deputy for Bob Nolf, the district game officer. We hit it off perfectly. I liked little, old, Santa-Claus-type guys, and Del had raised several smart-assed kids of his own. We worked perfectly together.

One sunny October afternoon, we were on a routine patrol, tuned to the Dallas Game Commission office on the portable radio, when we heard the call.

"Any 526 unit in the vicinity of Mountain Top, we have bears in a backyard. Woman said her kids are out there with them, and she is afraid to go out and get them. She sounds panicked."

They gave the name of the housing development.

"This is 526 F. We're right around the corner. E.T.A. about five minutes," I replied.

Well, this should break the monotony, I thought.

In the Pocono northeast part of Pennsylvania, man has made a dire mistake. He has taken some of the rarest and finest landforms found in the state, the acidic glacial bogs, and placed his homes in them by the thousands. Man didn't own them before building. The bears did and still do. Now man must tolerate the dual existence. The bears are generally not hunted in these overpopulated developments and as a result become quite brazen.

This sow and her two cubs were no different. When we arrived, the woman that had called in the complaint was standing with just her nose sticking out of the door. The sow was enjoying leftover people food from a garbage can, and the two cubs were just playing in the yard. The children that the woman had been hysterical about on the phone to Dallas had either made it back into the house or had been eaten. They were nowhere to be seen.

Del exited the car and swaggered past the sow and cubs and up on to the porch. I followed him, keeping an eye on the bear. She was belly-deep in a turned-over garbage can, only her butt sticking out.

"Ma'am, I'll show you how to do this. Not much to it," Del drawled, as we stood on the porch. He started down and I followed. He turned and whispered, "When I make my move, you run the cubs off in that direction," he said, pointing.

The old sow had a look around and went back into the can. Del just strolled right over to her and booted her in the butt as hard as he could, screaming, "Now get the hell out of here!" I attacked the cubs, screaming and clapping my hands.

The sow ran about 50 yards, banging into trees and stumps with the can over her head, and then stopped, backed out, "woofed," and ran off with the cubs in tow.

I guess the woman must have gotten good at it. I never knew the Game Commission to get another call from her while I worked there.

CHAPTER 22:
The Rest of the Job

When we were not stocking trout, running boats, walking streams or working pollutions, we were kept busy with other things. Here are a few that were amusing and a few that weren't.

THE DANCING COW

Being a "fish warden" is not all law enforcement. Many other projects that the agency gets involved in are yours to oversee. One such project was a joint effort. The local office of the Soil Conservation Service, the County Conservation District, our local chapter of Trout Unlimited and the Fish Commission became involved in fencing cattle out of creeks. The biggest project of the ones we became involved in required fencing two sides of nearly a half mile of stream on the Mitchell farm, just north of Cooperstown, in Venango County.

Streamside fencing is a method of controlling stream-bank erosion. Sugar Creek, being a fine trout stream with limited reproduction, was the chosen site. The representatives of the four agencies and the farmer worked diligently for a week or two digging holes and stringing electrical wire.

Eventually, all was ready to go. In erecting the stream-edge fence, we had left several crossings on the creek so the cattle could still get to the water and have access to the pasture across the creek from the barn. As a group of us stood by on a fine, high-sky summer day, the final electrical hookups were made, and Mr. Mitchell went across the creek and turned on the juice to the fence. Then he opened the barn and let the cows out. One large, old, "bell" cow came out first, stared at the fence for a few minutes and walked into the creek to have a drink. Her thirst quenched, her curiosity seemed heightened. Slowly she nosed toward the fence, still standing with her udder hanging in the water and all four feet planted on the stream bottom. Inch by inch she worked her way to the new upstream wire. Finally she was close enough to touch it. She was only inches from it with her nose. We waited with bated breath. Her pink tongue flashed out and wrapped around the wire.

If you have never seen a cow dance on water, you cannot appreciate the hilarity that rippled through the human ranks at this spectacle. With a little more juice she probably would have jumped over the moon.

SERVING WARRANTS

The case had been tough enough. The kid in the kayak on the private lake just didn't want to hear that he needed a life jacket. He ignored commands to stop and headed for shore. When he hit shore, he shouldered his boat and walked through a gate and onto a porch full of six or eight boisterous drunks that were just more trouble than the case was worth. Eventually, however, I got the paper issued and was back into my boat, without any major wrestling matches developing. But I knew better than to think it was over.

A check with the local police indicated the family was well to do and thought they were above the law. When I received a warrant of arrest in the mail for the actor a little time later, it certainly didn't surprise me. Off and on for the rest of the summer, I looked for the character but seldom actually knocked on his door. It had to do with a Great Dane that showed little or no desire to make friends with me. While I was sure the culprit was in the house some of these times at least, I couldn't seem to get past the gate.

Then early the next summer my luck changed. I was patrolling the lake again. As I launched the boat, I noticed what appeared to be the same kayak across the lake, paddling. My deputies, Bob and Don, and I headed over.

Sure enough, it was the young rebel that I had the warrant for. I followed him back into the lily pads, where he had headed when he saw it was the patrol boat, hoping, I guess, to go unnoticed. At my demand to stop, he once again just paddled along the shoreline as though he didn't hear me. Then, when in front of his summer home, he got out of the kayak, shouldered it and into the yard he went.

I was hot on his heels, as was Bob, while Don stayed with the patrol boat. Things were happening fast. Quickly a crowd came, pushing out the door as we were following him in. We were forced to retreat to the porch by the sheer numbers of drunks. While no one had physically threatened us or gave us a reason to thump them, collectively they had the upper hand. I made a command decision to send for help. We had no radio.

I barked to Bob to cover the back of the house, while I sent Don to go get the town cop; there was only one. I hoped the bluff would be sufficient. It didn't work.

As Bob left the porch, I heard the side door swing open out of sight and heard a voice holler, "Sic 'em!"

I had a vision of Bob having to shoot the Great Dane in self-defense or, if it got Bob, my having to, since we no longer had a boat to retreat to. What came charging out the door at Bob, with all the ferocity of an attack dog, was a miniature poodle, which Bob promptly kicked like a football against the fence. The dog was the first in the bunch to admit it was beaten. It came ki-yi-ing up on the porch. Then the threats of lawsuits for hurting the dog started randomly from the drunks.

I was starting to feel like I was going to win at this point, since I had depleted my reserves by a third and still hadn't lost any ground. As I kept the group of rowdies on the porch amused by hissing and snapping at them, Bob encountered the object of our chase, as he had tried to leave by the backdoor. Bob had stood ready, twirling his handcuffs, and caused the fleeing culprit to retreat to the house.

Then, just when hope was fading from my breast of any cavalry riding in, I heard the siren coming. There is no prettier sound to an officer's ears when things get sticky than a siren. At the very least, you are going to have someone to share the misery with.

Out jumped Tony the Cop, 5-feet, 6-inches of town cop. Spit-polished, but half my weight. The standoff was over. He went to the door, called the kid out and told him he was in big trouble. We loaded him in the car and off to the magistrate we went. There was no way this kid was going to pay a $10 fine and $11 cost, he said.

We waited with the kid in cuffs for about an hour, until the duty magistrate could get to his office. My batting average in front of this magistrate had been pretty dismal. If I had been playing baseball, I would have been stuck in the minor leagues. I didn't hold much hope, especially since the warrant had been issued in a different jurisdiction.

The magistrate listened to the testimony of my deputies, me and Tony the Cop, and then listened to the kid. I thought the kid was going to walk, having suffered enough by being in cuffs and delayed on a weekend afternoon. Things happen like that. But then the kid had to open his mouth one too many times.

"There is no way I am paying that fine. The costs should never exceed the fine," he ranted.

"You're right," the judge said. "I agree with you. You are not going to pay twenty-one dollars. You are going to pay forty-two dollars, or you are going to jail."

Reluctantly the kid dug out his wallet and paid. He decided not to appeal the case any more in front of this judge, on this day. We walked out of the court and stood talking around the locked patrol vehicles. We bid the judge good day and thanked him for coming out. The kid lingered nearby. After the judge had gone from sight, we got in our vehicles. As the kid went to get back into the cop car, Tony spoke.

"Sorry, this is not a taxi. You caused these guys a lot of trouble. You can walk the six miles over the mountain and think about what you should have done differently," and away he went.

I never saw the kayak or the kid again and, except for an occasional one-finger-wave from the porch as I patrolled along the shoreline, I never had any trouble at that summer home again.

MAKING A TRAINING VIDEO

The movie "Deliverance" had just swept the nation and the Lehigh River had been recently discovered for its fabulous whitewater boating opportunities. People were flocking in by the thousands to ride the standing waves with rafts, kayaks and canoes. Each Saturday, my deputies and I would be on the river with no other purpose than to try to keep everybody alive another day by checking them for life preservers and talking to the tourists about the threats the rapidly falling river contained.

I was checking several hundred boats a day, and the numbers soon caught the attention of the commission's Boating Division. They had just gotten one of the first video cameras and wanted to take some footage of me and my crew in action. A date was arranged.

We set up a check station at the Lehigh Tannery bridge. I was up on the bridge with the bullhorn and could look down into the boats going under the bridge, seeing if they had life preservers and how many. The boats without a sufficient number showing were ordered into the eddy, where my deputies would check them formally. Any in violation were sent up on the bridge, where I would write paperwork.

One canoe, traveling with a large group, had two young women in it. They had no life preservers and were ordered to shore. They came up on the bridge to receive their ticket, while the camera rolled at a very close range.

I could not help but notice that one girl, the stern paddler and thus the operator, was very well endowed. She had on a light-pink, gauzy top that was sheer, wet and clingy. As was the tradition in the early 1970s among city-type nature lovers, she was not wearing a bra. For all practical purposes she was bare-chested.

I stood several feet away from her and, straight-faced, looked her right in the eyes. I explained the citation procedure for the camera that I couldn't help but notice was not always focused on her face.

The citation was paid and I never saw the footage, but I doubt immensely it was because it didn't turn out. Somewhere, lost in the halls of great boating safety films, is some footage that shows the effects of cold water on young ladies without life preservers.

YELLOW BIKINI

Few things brighten an old warden's spring day more than detecting the first blossoms of the season. Sitting high atop F.E. Walter Dam with my spotting scope, I was running surveillance for illegal fishing or littering activity when I happened to focus on just such a sign of spring. There on the edge of the dam, near the parking lot, was a burst of bright yellow. As I focused closer, I could see a beautiful, nicely shaped young lady in a skimpy yellow bikini. I watched closely to detect whether or not she had a license, since she obviously was fishing. She stood casting and holding the rod.

The more I watched, the more I realized that this one was going to take some longer observing to solidify my case. Something was amiss. There were two very professional-looking cameras on tripods aimed at the object of my observation. However, no fishing license was apparent. Having cameras and friends to run them does not exclude a person from the licensing requirement, even dressed scantily in a string bikini. I made my move, driving down from the top of the dam to the scene of the action.

As I approached the young woman to ask for her license, for the first time my attention focused on the fishing rod. No line was on the reel. A Pocono group was making a promotional tourism film about recreation opportunities in the region, and they had figured that if their "angler" looked like that, nobody would notice if she caught a fish or not.

DIDN'T YOU HEAR

Some assignments are better than others. You can imagine how miserable I felt when I was told to report to Split Rock Lodge for a full week of hosting and guiding a large group of information-and-education specialists from all the state and provincial conservation departments. I resisted, arguing that my time could be better spent patrolling and checking for pollutions, but was finally overruled and agreed to have fun, instead, for a week.

The routine was typical for such gatherings. You would have seminars running during the day, with afternoons or mornings set aside for the participants to enjoy the area around them and get a look firsthand at how our state managed its resources. In the evening, after the participants returned, there was a hospitality room that lasted until the wee smalls, as you made new friends and related tales of the outdoors and actually used each other's expertise to assault mutual problems.

Many states sent entire entourages to this, so each information specialist could attend seminars that related to his field, while others were free to take advantage of the hospitality we were providing. My day was usually up at daylight, pick up someone at the airport or drop them off, and then come back and pick up a few fishermen and take them trout fishing. Since my district was nearby and I had some nice areas to take these folks to, I looked forward to showing off the local streams. We would fish for a few hours and then stop at a local pub for lunch.

Usually around three, when lunch was over, we would return to the stream and fish another hour or two, then return to the lodge for our evening meal. After the meal, I usually had another run to the airport to pick up or drop off a traveling dignitary. Then I would loaf around the hospitality room, being hospitable. To show your faith in the goodness of Pennsylvania-made products, it was imperative that you imbibe from the vast stores of the state's brews. And so it went for five or six days in a row.

Now, I will tell you that this was one of the last good old-fashioned-style conferences. It was before driving under the influence was recognized as the problem it is. It was also during a time when conferences were not only learning experiences, but also a reward to hardworking employees.

Thursday night, like so many other nights that week, the hospitality room remained open until the last wolf had howled. I forget what the arguments or problems we were solving were, but I remember the last four players that night. There was a Pennsylvania game warden, Clyde. Also present was the young man that was the chief and the entire education-and-information effort of the province of Saskatchewan. He dearly loved the little seven-ounce Rolling Rocks, "green grenades," in the tub of ice. A pretty girl representing Montana Big Sky Country and smoking a cigar was the third player. And lastly, me. We were holding court on some facet of environmental learning that long ago escaped me.

The next morning I was scheduled to take a VIP from one of the departments to the airport at 6 a.m. I didn't make the starting bell. It was 9 o'clock when officer Ohlsen, my roommate, shook me awake and warned that "Perry is looking for you, and he is steaming."

Bob Perry was my assistant supervisor and the prime organizer from the fish side of the event. He was a great guy to work for, but expected you to produce, on time. I quickly showered and got dressed and headed for the meeting hall. As I cleared the porch, I saw Bob round the bend, heading up toward our cabin. I could see the smoke flying from his ears, even before he spoke.

"Where have you been?" he demanded.

Without ever breaking stride, I kept heading for the meeting hall and called back over my shoulder, "Didn't you hear?"

I never heard another word about the incident. I often wondered what it was that Bob thought he hadn't heard.

NANTICOKE MEETINGS

Sportsmen's club meetings have been part of my life since I was just a little guy. My dad had belonged to several and when the situation permitted I would tag along.

When I reported to Luzerne County, there was no such thing as assigned hours or overtime. You would work ten or twelve hours a day, and then the boss would call and say that such-and-such club was having a meeting that evening and he wanted you to go. If you were lucky, you had time to eat dinner before you had to leave. One year I logged 70 evening meetings attended.

It was just such a call that sent me to the best meeting I ever attended. I had just arrived in the area when the boss called and said, "Nanticoke Conservation Club is having a meeting tonight at Jigger's Bar and asked if we would send somebody. The office staff and your neighboring officer have been to their meetings and they are rowdy, they drink and we can't get along with them."

"What makes you think I can?" I asked.

"Give it your best shot, but get there," the boss replied.

Now if that isn't a conversation that makes your dinner enjoyable, I don't know what is. I bolted down a quick meal and rolled 45 minutes north and was walking down the stairs to the meeting room in the downstairs of Jigger's as they finished the Pledge of Allegiance.

There were about 20 men at the meeting. The smallest man outsized me by about 5 inches and 50 pounds. They all had a chew of tobacco in and a pitcher of beer sat on each table. When I entered I was motioned to a chair. One old guy who acted like he had stopped right after work and began drinking to get ready for the meeting called out, "About time you got here. You better have a movie."

Well, I didn't. And now, for the first time, I was beginning to get a feeling that it wasn't the surly attitude of my neighboring officer or the stiffness of the office staff that had caused the problem. It might just be these guys didn't like the Fish Commission. I reasoned it couldn't be me that they disliked. Hell, I didn't know any of them yet.

I bided my time and the meeting went through the normal steps and a few low-level arguments about where the keys for the club's boats were going to be kept. A lot of clubs in "The Valley" own eight or ten boats that they leave chained up at the various lakes for members to use. I had never seen that and thought it was an excellent idea.

Finally, the president called on me and I gave my "dog and pony show" routine about fish stocking and boating safety.

"Sit down, boy, and show us a movie," came the cry from the same old guy.

I had listened to the names of those making motions and seconds during the meeting and realized that it might be an ethnic thing. I was the only one in the room whose last name didn't end in "ski, vich or czyk." I figured I had to make a move, so I rolled the dice.

"Fella, I don't know who you are and I don't care," I said, turning to his face and pointing across ten feet of tables with beer pitchers. "But I was sent here to work with this club and to establish a relationship and I'm going to do that if I have to get a name tag made with "S-K-I" on the end of it. And I don't have a damn movie."

Before I could say any more, the president pointed at the old guy and said, "Yeah, Stosh, sit down and shut up."

When the meeting was adjourned, I stayed and had a beer with the club officers. Soon we were working on a stream improvement project together.

NANTICOKE STREAM IMPROVEMENT

It was the next year on Harvey's Creek, the one depicted by Robert Kray in the Fish Commission's 1996 Trout and Salmon Stamp, that the true color of the Nanticoke Conservation Club showed through. The work was to start at eight o'clock in the morning. I arrived at 7:30.

When I got to the site and pulled in, the club was already there. They had several cases of Stegmaier beer iced down and were eating kielbasa and eggs with a cold one. It would have been impolite not to join them, so I did, as did the Fish Commission's Bellefonte stream improvement staff when they arrived. After we washed the grease and salt down with the last of the 16-ouncer, we dove into the work.

By the time the sun had reached the yardarm, we had finished two major devices and started a third, which we finished the following work session. The Bellefonte crew and I agreed that these guys were the hardest working, strongest group of men we had ever been involved with. We finished the kielbasa in sandwiches and washed them down, lazed in the sun and, just as we were to leave, a car pulled in.

It was a friend of mine, Joe Tweedle, who stopped to show us all a 28-inch brown trout he had taken up at the Delaware River on a fly at night. It made a great day. I worked for years with the crew from Nanticoke and attended their meetings and feel they were one of the best groups of guys I ever associated with. Joe went on to fame. He is the fisherman depicted on that 1996 trout stamp. He went to the stream and modeled for Kray.

RECOVERED TACKLE BOX RETURNED

Over the years I have recovered many lost items for persons. Usually gear that has fallen from the roof of their car or that they had set alongside it when loading for the trip home, but failed to remember as they drove off.

Just before dark one evening at F. E. Walter Dam, I noticed a nice, large tackle box sitting on the boat ramp. There was no one left in the parking lot, so I assumed that the person that had left it was gone and would possibly return looking for it. I picked it up and then left word at the dam headquarters that I had it and how to contact me.

The tackle box sat in my cellar for over a month and I didn't get a call. I decided no one was actively looking for it, so I would try to figure out who it belonged to. As I rooted around in it I could find nothing that was of any help. A regulation book for both New Jersey and Pennsylvania and a notebook that tallied the days' events were without name or address.

I did, however, notice among other things several Coleman lantern mantles in the tackle box, incidental to my search. Summer faded into fall and yet the tackle box sat in my cellar unclaimed. I really wanted the rightful owner to have it, rather than have it disappear into the great void of the Fish Commission's "items to be sold at an auction."

One evening in October, I hit a buck with an arrow just before quitting time and came home for a lantern to assist in my tracking the wounded animal. When I got my lantern out, I noticed a broken mantle and could not find any replacements where I usually kept them. I thought of those in the recovered tackle box. I figured I would use them and replace them when I forwarded the box to Harrisburg for sale. When I lifted the package of mantles, I saw a yellow piece of paper under it. It was a New Jersey fishing license with a name and address on it.

The next day, after taking the buck (with the help of the borrowed lantern mantles, I found it) to the butcher's, I located the owner of the tackle box through directory assistance. I mailed him his tackle box and a note apologizing for the missing mantles, saying I would replace them as soon as I got to a store. In short order the owner sent me a check for the postage, and a ten-dollar "reward." As I was on duty when I found the tackle box, I couldn't accept the "reward." So I signed him up for an Angler and Boater magazine subscription and mailed him one of our fish cookbooks.

He told me that after losing all his gear -- it was a well-stocked tackle box -- he had quit fishing. He was now looking forward to next summer with enthusiasm. It certainly felt good to reunite a man with his fishing tackle.

STOLEN LICENSE AND EQUIPMENT

It is amazing sometimes how crimes are solved. I was notified of a stolen fishing license by the guy that lost it. He said it had been on his ball cap and he felt it had been taken out of his boat, along with the cap, as he ate lunch in a diner. He was also missing a bunch of fishing gear. I took his name as a formality, with no hope of recovery. Stolen fishing gear is usually used and not sold, making it tough to recover.

I had taken the report on a Monday. On Friday I got a call from the Oil City Police Department, stating that they had done a routine traffic stop and, while citing the driver, the young male occupant had gotten mouthy. When they collected identification from him, it did not match with a fishing license he was wearing on a baseball cap. They asked, "Are there any charges you can file?"

I asked for the name on the ball cap and upon hearing it and recognizing it as the stolen one, told the police. Eventually they recovered the other fishing gear and the young fellow got to do some time in the county lockup. Like most crimes, it is eventually your mouth that gets you in trouble.

RIGHT WHERE I SAID

Every county has one or two. They are the guys that every sportsman thinks of when he hears the word "poacher." Most of them aren't very good at it because everybody, including the fish and game officers, knows their reputation.

Leroy was just such a character. To make it even more fun, he lived in my backyard, practically. Everywhere I went, I ran into him. He was a likable chap, except that he couldn't obey the law. He had taken many good game heads over the years, but then, since he didn't work, he certainly should have been able to know the animals' every move.

I don't think these poacher types know it, but what "endears" them to the honest sportsman isn't so much the fact that they get so many good heads of game. It is the fact that, for some reason, they want their picture plastered in the paper every time they shoot something, smiling from ear to ear.

One day as Leroy and I talked along Justus Lake, he said he had never caught a good muskie. Since the lake was making ice, I pointed to a spot where they always managed to catch or hook a few good muskies, in the 40 to 50-inch class.

Imagine my "delight" when I opened the paper a week later and there he was, holding a big Justus Lake muskie, smiling from ear to ear.

RAINY DAY DOE

It was the first day of doe season, 1975. The rain came in sheets as I hunted just outside of the park boundary at Chapman State Park. I had been invited to join the park crew hunting in the park, but didn't think it would be right. If the general public couldn't hunt there, then I shouldn't either, I reasoned.

I was getting soaked fast as the torrents continued down. I decided I might as well eat my tuna salad sandwich before the wax paper began to leak and made a mess of it. I had taken the first bite and leaned against a tree, when the shooting started down in the park. The park people and their friends had bounced some does, I figured. Maybe I should have taken them up on their offer. Suddenly there were two running does and I found one in the scope of Linda's .30-06, which I was hunting with, and down it went.

The drag was short and downhill and the wet leaves made the doe skid easily. I was soon at the parking lot, but still had a half mile to go to my pickup truck, parked along the road.

As I stood trying to decide whether to go for the truck and leave the deer or drag it to the truck, I got the chance to return a favor I owed.

A game deputy approached and gave the soggy tag the once-over and then checked my license. After some light-duty questioning, because the tag had almost melted in the rain, he bid me farewell.

"Are you satisfied I'm all legal?" I quizzed.

"Yes, I am," the deputy said, turning.

"Good," I said. "I'm Bob Steiner, the fish warden from over at Franklin."

I never believed in badge flashing and had appreciated this guy's boss, Dave Titus, handling my fishing check of him the same way the summer before.

GETTING EQUIPMENT

There are only two types of organizations that I would recommend you never work for. The first is the nonprofit organization. Few of them make enough money to pay you well. The other is an independently-funded agency of state government. As good an employer as the Fish and Boat Commission was, I never heard of management anywhere else "poor-mouthing" so much.

The commission never, in my career, seemed to have money to do anything except pay its bills. Innovative ideas that could have filled a warehouse went by the wayside for lack of funding. This is a shame for those that fish and recreate and expect the Fish and Boat Commission to protect the aquatic resource.

Without funding, a lot of good programs fizzle. When I first came on the job, union meetings were dominated by good soldiers arguing that we should barter for safety equipment and better boats, gun belts and such, not essentials for our families, like most unions. My first year in Luzerne County, I just went about my business, doing the job as best I could with the equipment I was issued. I had been taught as a kid, "You don't ask for stuff, you earn it."

One day late in July, I was at the office picking up paper supplies and dropping off reports, when the supervisor called me into his office.

"I have been checking your reports and noticed that you are not working after dark and have not run one boat patrol," I was told.

"I was never issued a boat or a flashlight," was my reply, "and I don't make enough money to buy them on my wages."

The equipment was issued within a few weeks, and my patrol capabilities expanded to reflect the new items. Early in my career, I had discovered how to deal with equipment needs. I felt contract negotiations should concentrate on caring for family needs, not work equipment.

MIND IF I FISH?

In the good old days, once you started working the Friday before the trout season opener, you worked until you couldn't see straight on Saturday.

It had rained a little during the night. Saturday morning, everything was muddy along the streams, and they were slightly discolored. I had stopped at a farmer's along the Big Wapwallopen Creek and had insured that his kids had a place to fish in the swimming hole. Once they were set up and ready to go, I had headed up toward the bridge.

Standing on the bridge in full uniform, I had decided to wait out the season starting bell. I only had about 20 minutes until it was time. I had just poured a cup of coffee from my Stanley, when a young fellow came running up to me, panting. "They're fishing up the creek around the bend," he got out.

I dumped the coffee, grabbed my fishing rod and pulled on hip boots and a raincoat. I headed up through the woods and watched from the bushes for a short while. One fellow was trailing his line in the water to straighten it. He should have changed line during the winter, but he had gotten lazy and now was paying the price.

Nothing illegal happened and the starting moment was only a few seconds away. I let my raincoat swing open, so my hardware showed, and approached on the high bank, six feet above the water. Nobody was on that side of the creek, and below me was a small lip of dry ground.

I spoke to the masses. "Mind if I jump down there (pointing to the dry spot) and make a few casts with you guys?"

Naturally they weren't enthused about having the fish warden show up to fish with them in their secret spot at the opening bell, but then only a fool would have said so. None spoke.

I jauntily jumped down to the dry spot and as I landed, my feet just kept right on sliding out from under me. The splash I sent up probably spooked every trout in the hole. I was mud from my boot heels to the little button on top of my baseball cap. It was wet mud, too. I got up cursing and splashing and sputtering. Nobody laughed, at least not on the outside.

I drove over the mountain, took a shower and got dry clothes on and worked the rest of the day. I wish I could have heard the after-fishing bar tales of the warden landing on his butt in the mud and the water. I'll bet I was responsible for many a good laugh in "The Valley" that night.

POLISH POLLYWOG

Even a game warden deserves a day off. Nolfie was one of the all-time great game wardens. He never seemed to take any time for himself. One day, however, on a sunny weekday, I convinced him to take a day off and go bass fishing with me. We had gotten passes to fish Fenner's Ice Lakes for panfish and bass.

Nolfie and I had a mutual friend, Sam, who was an inventor. He had sold the patent on a weedless, rubber floating frog to one of the major fishing tackle companies and now had invented a weedless, rubber pollywog. He had asked Nolfie to try them and let him know how they worked. Since Nolfie thought he was on a mission and not just having fun, he went fishing.

I situated him in the bow of my 17-foot Old Town wooden canoe and paddled into some likely looking bass cover. Nolfie caught a few nice bass and, as the day progressed, started bragging about this great weedless pollywog. It really was snag-proof. I was a devout Mr. Twister user at the time and would not switch and felt I was holding my own.

Eventually I eased Nolfie within casting distance of a beautiful flat full of lily pads and cajoled him into trying to hit a small opening, about halfway in, with that magic tadpole. His cast was only a little off to the long side. Perfect. If he gave a slight jerk, it would jump right into the opening where a huge bass had to be waiting.

He let the ripples settle and twitched the rod tip. The pollywog stayed put. He twitched a little harder. It stayed stuck. I began to giggle. The harder he jerked it, the harder I was laughing. Eventually we went in and unhooked the "Polish Pollywog" from its moorings on the lily stem.

Somewhere in my collection of mementos I have one of those pollywogs. I have used them with luck, but I have never bet on being able to cast into the thick of things without some consequences. I have never tied one on my line that I didn't think about that day with my now-deceased friend Bob Nolf.

LADY FRIEND'S MERCEDES

For an enforcement officer, losing your badge is likened to losing children if you are a nanny. Even when tolerated, it often draws severe consequences. That is why, I guess, that over these 20-some years I have only done it twice. Strangely enough, both incidents involved being with the same people, at different ends of the state, some ten years apart.

The second time it turned out that lost was lost. I had the shield in a leather badge case in my shirt pocket, while fishing on Lake Erie. The day was hot and windy and I decided to air my fat rolls. A gust of wind apparently sucked the shirt out of the boat unnoticed and the badge was gone.

The first time, though, it turned out that lost was not terminal.

It was way back in the days of polyester slacks and leisure suits. Shirts didn't have pockets then, so I slipped my badge case into a front pocket of my slacks. My wife and I were invited to dinner with this friend, a dentist, and his wife. We met and decided among ourselves that we would take his wife's silver Mercedes, rather than my cargo van with orange crates for back seats. Linda and I rode in the backseat of the car.

Not realizing for a day or two that the badge case was missing, I eventually figured out where I had lost it. A thorough search of the Mercedes' backseat, however, did not turn up the case. After a week or two, I figured I had better report it missing and take my medicine. After considerable correspondence with the main office, I was reissued a new badge and badge number. This necessitated a mountain of paperwork that resulted in everything being reissued to me with the new badge number affixed to it.

Months passed and, as another fall turkey season approached, I convinced my dentist buddy, a turkey hunting fanatic, that it just wasn't right hunting turkey in a silver Mercedes. He pondered having it painted in a camouflage pattern, but finally opted to sell it and get a real hunter's car. In short order he found a South American "diplomat" that was in dire need of a silver Mercedes and he had his son clean up the car for the transfer day. The son had a small car-cleaning business and had learned that under the seats of fancy cars you often find rewards over and above the price you charge.

While cleaning the Mercedes, he had torn out the back seat to vacuum and look for a little extra "loot," when he discovered my badge case. He pondered using it to impress his college buddies and women and decided against that, and was going to put it back under the seat. Then he realized that the "diplomat" might end up being mistaken for a D.E.A. agent if someone found it when they were installing the bullet-proof glass, and he scrapped that idea, too. There was nothing left to do but return it.

I was glad to have the badge back, but now my numbers didn't match. After some contemplation, I felt it best to notify the main office that the missing badge had resurfaced. It was critical that the memo be worded just right. After much thought, the memo was typed and sent. It read:

"Subject: Badge #77
To: Harrisburg, Law Enforcement Division
From: Robert Lynn Steiner, WCO, Luzerne Co.

I once again have badge #77 in my possession, reported lost this past spring. It was found under the backseat of a lady friend's silver Mercedes, where it must have slipped from my pants one evening while we were out."

We got trout into the Lehigh River backcountry with help from friends via helicopter in a fire-fighting water bucket and by rubber raft.

CHAPTER 23:
Rescues and Recoveries

Rescues are cool. Body recoveries, not so much. They both give you an adrenaline rush. They both can make you sick to the stomach.

RESCUE, LEHIGH RIVER

The truest form of river rescue is to talk people out of doing stupid things before they do them. This sounds simple enough, but it isn't often the case. Generally it takes a stupid person to think up some of the stupid, dangerous things people do, and then they are too stupid to understand what you are trying to tell them of the danger. These were just such people.

There was a scheduled release of water from F. E. Walter Reservoir. Since it had been announced far in advance, this meant I would have one of "those days." The water would be rising in the Lehigh River and the fishermen would be complaining to me that the boaters always got their way with the Army Corps of Engineers. While I don't believe they "always" got their way, they certainly held more sway than fishermen. Fishermen seemed to be ignored by the Corps.

There would be nearly a thousand accomplished boaters and rafters. People that were either expert at riding the high whitewater flows or under expert guidance on commercial trips. They would all wear wet suits and life jackets and would be instructed what to do in case of an upset. Guides were trained in dealing with hypothermia and carried emergency equipment. There was seldom a problem with this group of boaters.

There would also be a hundred or so who knew somebody that knew somebody that had a brother that had floated the brawling Lehigh River once last summer and said it was "a piece of cake." "River rats," the experienced folks, knew every rock that would be showing at every water level. These "float a day" people didn't know a thing about rafts, kayaks or canoes, they just had one. And it wasn't usually a very good one or anything near the right type for what they were about to experience. The dangers of foot trapping and hypothermia were never in their mind. They never had wet suits and seldom wore life jackets. My job was to keep them alive.

Diligently, I would show up at the most common launch sites and try to talk the "float a day" people out of it. I would recommend alternate tourist things to do or try to plead with the sensibilities of the woman that was in charge. Generally, I was successful. Occasionally, no matter how hard I tried I was unable to convince a group that they were risking their lives and going to inconvenience mine if they took the big deep-six. I would then look their equipment over with a fine-toothed comb for any problem. If I found a problem, I would then add, "And if you put that boat on the water with only that torn flotation device, I am also going to give you a ticket and then order you off the water." This usually worked. But not always.

It was a bright and sunny late April or early May day. The river was rising nicely and starting to get interesting. All the commercial trips were launched and on their way for a pleasant day of bouncing through splashing whitewater, careening off boulders and just adventuring in the great outdoors. Now was the time that the day trippers would usually be arriving. They didn't understand that the dam gates were only open for a couple of hours and you had to get on the flow and stay with it. It wouldn't be there all day. By evening the whole stream would be placid again. By noon, the upper-end launch sites would already be low.

The "float a day" folks were easy to spot. They would arrive in either a sports car or a mini-van. They would be redneck-looking, compared to the long-haired philosophers that had already left in their decked canoes and kayaks. The day-trippers would have either a hundred-dollar rubber raft more suited for swimming pools than river running or a 17-foot aluminum canoe with no decking. There would always be too many of them for the number of boats.

I arrived under the I-80 bridge on the east side of the river just in time to see such a trip getting ready to board their two open canoes. There were six persons and enough coolers, dogs and gear to sink a cruise ship. I went into my spiel. It appeared to me that they were dangerously unprepared. They assured me they were experienced river trippers, having day-tripped on the Delaware River many times and it was a bigger river. I explained the difference between flat water and whitewater and the skill levels necessary to accomplish the trip ahead of them. They were sure they could handle it. I was getting nowhere, so I went into my final tactic. I would have to check their safety equipment.

"May I see your life preservers, please?" I asked.

"We have them in bags to stay dry," came the reply.

"People with river sense wear them on this river folks. I'll have to see them," I countered.

"You're just hassling us now, man," came the reply.

They weren't as stupid as I had originally thought.

"I need you to unload the canoes and show me your flotation devices," I restated.

Fifteen minutes later they had everything unpacked but were without a flotation device.

"You must either buy flotation devices or pack up your gear. I can't permit you to make this trip without proper flotation gear," I ordered.

"Where can we buy some, man?" said the mouthpiece.

"Wilkes-Barre, twenty miles up that road," I said, beginning to give directions.

"I guess we'll just leave then," he finally conceded. "Let's get packing," he instructed his following of guys and girls.

My deputy Don and I got in the car and left, or so it appeared. As we headed up the road, Don looked at me and grinned.

"Now you know they're not going to leave, Stein," he said.

235

"I know, they know and you know that," I replied. "They aren't going to be talked out of it. They came for an experience. I guess I gotta let them have one," I continued. "We'll just go over to the west side of the river and go below that big chute. The canoes should fill up with water and sink without anyone getting hurt when they go through there. Then I'll order them in and cite them."

It only took a few minutes to get to the other side of the river and get downstream on the old railroad bed. We started down over the bank to stand on a big rock that hung out over the river. The way the water flowed, it would force all but the most experienced canoeists within six feet of shore at this point. I could jump in a canoe if I had to. As an afterthought, I told Don to grab a couple of rescue throw bags to take down with us.

The river was flowing a little better than I had thought, and the characters with the canoes were a little quicker than I thought, too, because as we reached the big rock I looked up to see the riffle full of floating gear and screaming people. A couple had made it to the far shore, as had one of the dogs. Swimming with the current, right for Don and me, were the others. As they got into range we threw the rescue rope bags out and they got hold of them and swung to shore. In a few minutes all was under control, except for the river being full of expensive camping gear and coolers.

On our bank of the river, we had four shivering, scared boaters. The canoes had eddied in, so Don and I dragged them up over the hill to where they could be retrieved. I left Don with the car and rounded up the whole group from both sides of the river and got them to their cars. Once they had warmed up, I got them to follow me back to the canoes.

As they began to load the canoes on their cars, I told them, "Don't be so anxious, those are my evidence." They stared incredulously.

"Remember on the other side I told you if you decided to go on the water after I left, you could all expect to get tickets? Well, you did and I'm goin' to give'm to you. So let's all get some identification out and let those canoes just lie there."

They weren't happy about it, I'm sure, but they survived and I'll bet they remember their life jackets now.

RUN, THEN JUMP

A kayak is not a proper patrol craft, but I was serving in a whitewater district and it seemed like a good idea at the time. The powers-to-be thought so, too, and issued me the first such patrol craft for the Commonwealth of Pennsylvania. Though they sent me to school for a few days to learn how to use the kayak, I didn't feel confident in it, so I decided some practice sessions were necessary.

Since one of the very first rules of all small-craft boating is to never go alone, and this is especially true with paddle craft, I set up some deputy training sessions. Since it was already summer and we were mostly young families at that time, we turned it into a kind of picnic. Steve and Patty lived in a development that had an access to a good run of water on the Lehigh River.

It had a sandy beach, so we went in swimming suits and took the kayak and a canoe.

I demonstrated some of the more basic stuff that you do in a kayak, and we took turns trying it. We all ended up wet and then went to Steve and Patty's for beer and pizza. We held several of these sessions, and I was starting to feel pretty confident with the boat. I had a plan.

There was a mild stretch of rocks and boulders that were canoe-eaters, between the two accesses above White Haven, where we were having these sessions. I would launch at the upper and, after we all had played, I would paddle down to the other beach and take out. If I got in trouble, there was an access road the whole way along where my deputies, Sherm, Earl and Steve, could shadow me and effect a rescue, if necessary.

I was paddling along and doing quite well, but I must have been looking too far ahead. Kayaking is like playing billiards. Each shot you take is only as good as the lie you have when the balls quit rolling. In kayaking, each rock you miss must leave you headed the correct way for the next rock. Somewhere along the line, my rhythm got funky and I was broadside on a boulder in a heartbeat. Tremendous water pressure was trying to bend the kayak in half backward, with me in it.

I had a lot of experience by now with the "wet exit," known as "abandon ship," in larger craft. I hurriedly got out of the cockpit and, in a desperate move, applied my weight to an extreme end of the boat. It popped free without any structural damage. Then it took off down the river. In my life preserver, I was no match for its sleek shape and it quickly was getting out of recovery distance.

The patrol car was on the access road, and I looked up to see Earl and Sherm thinking ever so slowly about rescuing me. I didn't need rescued. I was floating in complete control and working my way to the shoreline.

"Get the boat!" I screamed.

The race was on. As I bobbed down the river, edging ever toward the shore, I saw the boat way out ahead of me. It had miraculously chosen the near side to the access road, also. It was passing 20 yards off the edge, as it headed down through the rapidly flowing water.

I spotted the fisherman first and saw the boat heading right toward him. He was standing in front of a 6-foot-high boulder on the edge of a fairly deep pool. Since he had chest waders on, only his upper torso was showing and he was hugging tight to the boulder due to the depth of the water before him.

Suddenly in the air over his head, off the top of the boulder came Earl and Sherm. Both well over 6 feet tall and looking very gangly in flight. They had gotten a running jump off the boulder to intercept the boat, clothes and all. They had not seen the fisherman, and he hadn't seen them. The double splash threw water high into the air as they entered, and I am sure showered the guy fishing. They quickly had hold of the boat, and I came bobbing on down and got out at the next beach.

Before we could find the fisherman to apologize, he was gone. I guess you just have to know when it is not going to be a good evening for fishing.

MISSING BANKER

Game Commission officers are all too familiar with the smell of decaying animals along the road. As a close friend of several game officers, I had assisted in picking up hundreds of maggot-riddled deer carcasses in the first ten years of my career.

So when deputy Don and I were riding along the Bear Creek Road toward F.E. Walter Dam one spring afternoon and caught the aroma of decaying deer through our open car windows, we both gagged. I commented that we would leave that one for the Game boys. I further reasoned that it wouldn't hurt anything rotting there, the closest place to a wilderness we had in the county.

Several weeks later, Don and I were once again traveling the same route, when we noticed a profusion of emergency and police vehicles and people at the "dead deer" location. Among the group were two of my deputies assisting with loading a body bag.

We drove on by, not wanting to add to the confusion and feeling very stupid. It seems that a missing banker had been found, apparently assassinated. When we told the two deputies that helped with the bag about smelling it there long before, they thanked us for allowing the corpse to remain two weeks for ripening.

DEAD DOG DEAD

When you are around water in a professional capacity, sooner or later you will get involved with a "stiff." Badly decomposed bodies surface at the oddest places, when you least expect them.

It was a beautiful spring day and I was patrolling in the Dorrance area of Luzerne County, where there were five or six small ponds that periodically drew my attention. Spring days meant school picnics, littering and fishing without regard for license regulations or seasons, sizes and limits. I was assisted by several deputies and we had the route down pat.

We pulled into a little pond on a "blind attack" and saw five or six young people fishing and picnicking. One girl told me that she could not stand fishing and therefore wasn't. I checked the licenses of the anglers and left, not believing her for one minute. We moved the vehicle to a vantage point and set up an observation with a spotting scope. We watched for nearly an hour and the young woman did not fish. We moved on, but I still I wasn't satisfied.

Things were slow and several hours later we headed back to the pond. We used the blind arrival again, but she still wasn't fishing. I drove up, made some small talk with the group and prepared to leave, turning the car around. Just then, the girl that we had been watching, spoke.

"Did you guys see the dead body here?" she asked.

I looked at my deputy and rolled my eyes, then, parked and got out. She was right. There, bound tightly in a cardigan sweater with plastic shipping rope, was the chest bones of what looked like a smallish person. A young female was my first impression.

"My boyfriend just caught it," the girl offered.

I immediately secured the area, got identification from everyone present and sent my deputy to call the state police. He had to walk to a nearby house to borrow a phone to call back then. Sirens wailed in the distance almost immediately. Soon a host of uniforms and detectives were on scene, and the coroner was summoned. All present, including my deputy and me, gave statements. Finally, the remains were put in a body bag and loaded in an ambulance and taken to the morgue.

Because I like to know how cases end and I like to see my name in the paper, I watched the news closely for nearly two weeks. Nothing appeared. I couldn't take it any more, so I called the coroner. He said that after closer examination the body turned out to be that of a collie. I certainly was fooled, but then so were the other uniforms that put the dog parts in the body bag.

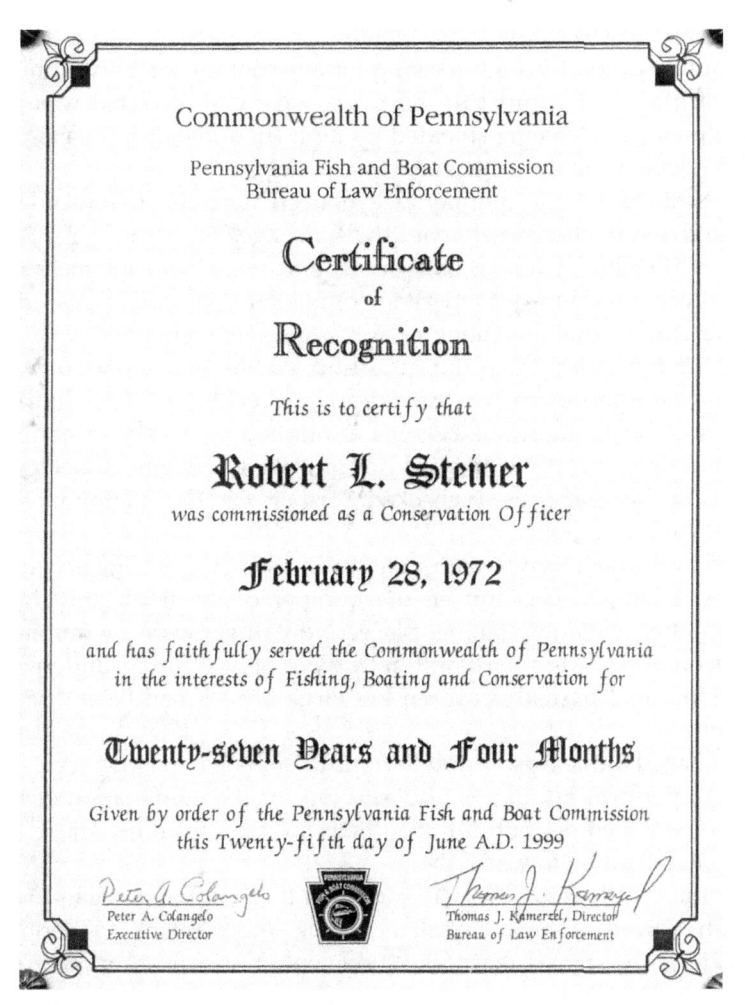

Commonwealth of Pennsylvania

Pennsylvania Fish and Boat Commission
Bureau of Law Enforcement

Certificate of Recognition

This is to certify that

Robert L. Steiner

was commissioned as a Conservation Officer

February 28, 1972

and has faithfully served the Commonwealth of Pennsylvania in the interests of Fishing, Boating and Conservation for

Twenty-seven Years and Four Months

Given by order of the Pennsylvania Fish and Boat Commission this Twenty-fifth day of June A.D. 1999

Peter A. Colangelo
Executive Director

Thomas J. Kamerzel, Director
Bureau of Law Enforcement

CHAPTER 24:
Sex in the Long Grass
(Rated R)

All the little animals frolic naked in the woods. Why would we be surprised when we stumble into folks enjoying the same delights? If you are remotely prudish or under the age of 18, skip this chapter. It is rated at least R.

GIGGLE AND GROAN
A friend of mine was riding with me on a fine, sunny spring day. He was on a week's vacation from his job, working at a foundry. He was considering being a deputy, so I took him to see what he would have to put up with.

We pulled up on the high parking lot overlooking Hickory Run Lake. By standing on the front bumper of the truck, we could see what was going on across the pond, while being shielded by high rhododendron bushes from the view of the persons on the other side.

As we stood on the bumper, we noticed a young fellow in his early twenties and a very chesty girl about the same age, sitting on a blanket on the other shore. They had fishing rods, a cooler and some bait containers sitting on the ground around them. This merited some attention, as it appeared that we were witnessing several violations, or at least possible ones.

I got the binoculars from the truck and watched for a period of 15 or 20 minutes as both parties cast, retrieved and baited hooks. She drank from a wine jug and he had several beers. I continued to watch in earnest now, because littering violations looked imminent. I left my friend with the binoculars in his hand as I checked farther up the shoreline for other fishermen, but found none.

When I returned, I saw a smirk on my friend's face as he watched through the glasses. I jumped back up on the bumper of the truck and right away noticed another violation taking place. Now they were swimming in an unauthorized zone in the park and both were only wearing underpants. The halter top that had partially covered her large breasts had been discarded on the shoreline.

I now faced a dilemma. I didn't want to appear to be a voyeur, yet I was obligated to perform my duties of observing for the culmination of the other violations. I watched on, but did take the binoculars from my friend, since he had no legal obligation to watch them.

Soon the couple returned, semi-nude, to the shore and began to dry each other with towels, which signaled to me their intent to soon depart. Unfortunately, the signals that this action sent them was of another sort, and soon they were totally nude, in a lovers' grasp on the ground.

The young man was as impressive in action as the lady was vocal, and soon the whole lakeside was privileged to her moans of ecstasy. As the young man was quite the performer, her vocalizations rang out for a full ten minutes.

My friend, having tired of the sounds of the show, looked at me and said, as though he were talking to the young stud, "Give her a break, already!"

As soon as the ecstasy ended and nude sunning progressed, a car with several fathers and their young boys pulled in. They got their gear from the car and the youngsters, rods in hand, ran for their favorite fishing spot. The spot was currently occupied by naked sunbathers. Had it not been for a lure snagging and the youngsters stopping to extricate it from a tree limb, they would have blundered, rather brashly, on the idyllic love scene.

However, enough noise was made that the nude "fishermen" were able to get dressed. As the couple packed up, they discarded a beer bottle and bait container into the weeds. I still had not seen a fishing license on either of them, but then most of the time they were wearing nothing to pin it on anyway.

I explained to my friend the various fish law violations and the park swimming and booze violations the couple had committed. He assured me he could keep a straight face as long as I did not mention the swimming. I made my intercepting approach as the couple reached their car and explained the fish law violations.

The young lady had a fishing license. Her friend from New York did not, and she wanted to pay his fine on a Field Acknowledgement of Guilt. She also wanted to pay her littering fine, as well. We did the paperwork and she paid and was given a receipt.

Knowing that my friend now felt the contact was over and had dropped his guard, I turned on my heel and, as we were walking away from the defendants' auto, stated, "Oh, and by the way, it's a state park violation to have alcohol in the park and swimming is allowed only at designated swimming areas."

My friend lost it, but contained his laughter internally until back in the patrol car. He then called me bad names.

YELLOW IS NOT A UNIFORM COLOR

It was a beautiful sunny afternoon in May. I had a new deputy. He had been with the Game Commission, then saw the light and made the switch. This was a coup for the Fish Commission. The young deputy, though married, had a reputation that matched his Corvette.

One day he showed up for patrol in a bright yellow shirt. Uniforms were not something that most deputies had at the time. We were working F. E. Walter Dam and things were slow, so we headed for Bear Creek, often a hot spot for unlawful activity in the form of littering, illegal fishing and such.

A car was parked along the berm a distance from the normal party area, and I decided to investigate. The deputy and I moved through the large pines and worked upstream, looking at the creek with binoculars. Soon I saw two persons lying on a blanket along the water, with their shirts off.

We were still a good ways away, so I observed with binoculars and discovered it was a boy and girl sunning themselves. I couldn't see a fishing rod, but they were near a good hole in the stream so I moved in, leaving the deputy sitting back a long ways so the pair wouldn't see his bright shirt.

Using all the stealth I possessed, I moved in to within about 20 yards. Just as I was determining that there was no fishing violation, the young fellow maneuvered the young lady onto her hands and knees and slipped her blue jeans down, and mounted her in a fashion named after man's best friend.

I could see nothing wrong with the way they were enjoying nature and I turned to leave. They were preoccupied and didn't see me, but my motion caught the attention of a Doberman they had tied to a nearby tree. The dog began quite a racket, but rather than focus his attention -- which already was focused -- on me, the young man just began shouting at the dog, without losing his concentration. I was able to slip out of the situation unnoticed.

The deputy remained with me until I transferred to another district, but always wore drab clothes on patrol after that, so he wouldn't be left sitting in the upper deck.

APPLE WHACKER

What you don't see through a spotting scope. Spotting scopes are a necessary part of long-range law enforcement surveillance and certainly assist you in knowing what is going on, so you don't have to guess. Sometimes, though, you are watching a scene for a fishing license or littering case and then what you see happening is beyond belief.

One of my favorite surveillance posts was high atop the F.E. Walter Dam. From there you could watch nearly two-thirds of the reservoir's shoreline and a half mile downriver. There was never a lack of activity, since the dam was but a few rural miles from the intersection of I-80 and the Northeast Extension of the Pennsylvania Turnpike.

One spring day, the lake water was up nearly 50 feet above normal pool and trout season had yet to open. Fishing on the dam was closed. On the east side above waterline, some very large boulders sat in the midday sun. As I worked the shore with the scope, I picked out a young man in his late teens fishing from one of these boulders. There was no easy way to get to him, so my deputy and I elected to watch a while and see if he caught any of the many stocked trout. Hopefully he would get bored of the sport and walk to his car, where we could apprehend him for the violation from the comfort of our patrol vehicle.

As we watched an osprey soar, we noted the illegal fisherman had retrieved, rebaited and cast again. Then from his coat pocket he pulled an apple. He polished it and began to eat it. While sitting on the end of the boulder, he worked his penis from his pants and sat polishing it as he ate the apple. We decided to take the long ride around to his car, feeling we had plenty of time with the violator preoccupied.

An hour later, when we cited him for the fishing violation, he assured us that despite being arrested he had had an enjoyable day in the woods. We were sure he had.

BIONIC EYE

It was a busy day in early June at the dam. Flowers were blooming, school was out, baseball season was in and outdoor enthusiasts were scampering all over the place like so many chipmunks. We went to the top of the dam to watch for a while and see what was going on. As we often did, we set out a paper and pencil and gave fishermen and persons with litter-possible containers identities.

"Green hat just cast again. Still can't see a license."

"So did red shirt, his buddy."

"The two with the Oriole ball caps have a cooler. He is drinking little beers in clear bottles and she is hitting on a jug of wine."

We would write down times and actions. After building a case for illegal fishing or littering, we would move to make the apprehension or call in another waiting deputy unit so we could continue with other surveillances.

The sun warmed and the birds sang and we were having a busy day and had no reason to leave.

"The couple with the Oriole hats are both fishing and I see no licenses," I remarked and logged as the afternoon wore on.

My deputy confirmed the action and initialed the log for later use in court. Several hours later, all but a few persons had left on their long journey home to the city. My interest had focused on the Oriole fans, who now had consumed much of their available booze and had bottles strewn everywhere. Additionally, I had only been able to locate his fishing license on his hat, but could not see hers. She had taken off her hat and thrown it on the blanket behind them, with their picnic stuff.

As I next swept the scope to that side of the dam to log the action, I was greeted by their absence, but their gear remained. Where they were, the water plunged straight away to the deepest part of the reservoir, and I immediately feared the worst. Had they slipped from the cliff-like boulders and ended up in 60 feet of cold water? Booze causes balance issues.

I searched with the scope for any sign of an answer. Between two large rocks, writhing in the moss and wildflowers were two naked torsos. I logged this as well and resumed my checks of other happenings.

After completing whatever it was they were doing, they must have decided they had enough sun for one day and began to pack up. They put all their bottles and garbage in the cooler and the Oriole hats in a tote bag. Then they walked the half mile to the parking area.

Still not having seen the young fisherwoman's license, but most of the rest of her, I felt it my job to stop them and check for the missing item. The conversation went something like this:

"State Conservation Officers. Good evening, folks. I would like to thank you for so thoroughly picking up your bottles and other garbage. Miss, I noticed you fishing off and on this afternoon and didn't see your license. I believe it must be on your Oriole ball cap like your friend's. I believe you put them in that tote bag. May I see it please?"

She rummaged through her tote bag and produced a valid license. I checked it, turned and began to walk away. The sequence of her personal afternoon "events" began to sink in, so she spoke.

"Excuse me officer, but how did you know all of that?"

"I have a bionic eye," I replied and walked into the sunset, my snickering deputy following.

NAKED HIKING DIVER

F.E. Walter Reservoir is the first wilderness north of the Philadelphia area. It's a little over an hour on the Northeast Extension of the turnpike and you have arrived. Shed all your worldly woes and play in the woods. Thousands of visitors do just that each and every year.

Although camping is not permitted at the lake, there are some large tracts of land above the dam that attract the rough-and-ready types. With a backpack, a five-pound can of ravioli and a clean pair of socks, they would embark on a weekend in the wilds with real bears and snakes and deer and fish wardens.

After a day of heavy hiking, the trail would near water and camp would be made. Before slipping into their sleeping bags, the hikers would take a refreshing dip in any available water. Now, as a backpacker you cannot possibly bath in your underwear, since you only have one pair with you, so you leave them on a rock to air in the last rays of sun. You get refreshed, reclothed and then go back to camp. Occasionally we would chance on these situations as we patrolled the perimeter of the lake with our boat, which was amazingly quiet for its vintage.

One sunny day I was patrolling with Earl, a delight of a deputy. For all the hours he put in on patrol with me in the five years or so that he served, he never seemed to be there when we would encounter "nature's children" at play in their altogether as often happened.

As we boated up the Bear Creek arm of the lake, we noticed a pretty, blonde, weekend wood sprite hiking along the shoreline. She was tall, slender, twenty-ish and beautifully earthy. After all, it was the early 1970s. She appeared to be enjoying the lovely, sunny afternoon in the wilderness. We remarked on the fact that she was hiking alone on the wildest portion of the terrain and continued up the lake.

Seeing few fishermen, we began the trip back down the lake at a faster rate. As we rounded the bend where we had last seen her, Earl bent down and away, trying to light a cigarette. The wind from the moving boat was giving him fits. I looked toward the shore just in time to see the wood sprite in a high, arcing dive from a huge lakeside boulder, without a stitch on. The sight remains etched in my brain like a fine engraving on a good shotgun. Earl didn't see her.

Earl wanted to return to warn her against the illegality of swimming in the lake. I kept heading the patrol back to the launch, leaving him only with the memory of a backpack covered by lace underwear drying in the sun, next to a pair of hiking boots.

THE NEARLY ABANDONED CANOE

The Bear Creek arm of F.E. Walter Reservoir looks like a scene out of the far north of Canada. It's no wonder it attracts so many outdoor enthusiasts. Hunters and fishermen found the land challenging. Others found it inspiring. Young couples found it remote and romantic. I found it to be a place to work where what happened next during a day could not be guessed at by the wildest imagination.

One hot August evening, Don and I ran a routine patrol. The sun was fast fading, but the air had yet to begin to cool. As we reached the incoming creek, where our prop depth dictated we turn around, Don noted a canoe without any occupants along the shoreline. It appeared to have drifted in. We approached the canoe, fearing the worst. Kids swimming from the canoe could have drowned. An old timer could have hooked a large fish and lost his balance. The thought of an all-night search was rambling in my head.

As we pulled slowly to within a few feet of the canoe, two heads, a teenage boy and girl, popped up on the far side. The water was about ten feet deep there and they were clinging to the side of the boat. I was still thinking "rescue," when Don broke the silence.

"State Waterways Officers. May we see two life preservers, please?" he said.

With one hand on the edge of the canoe, each of the teens began flinging blue jeans and underwear aside in the bottom of the canoe, digging for the personal flotation devices. Soon, still shielded from our view by the canoe and absolutely nothing else, they held up the PFDs. I turned the boat and pulled away.

Once we got out of hearing distance, I turned to Don and remarked, "I honestly thought they were in trouble."

He replied, "They would have been if their parents had been in the boat with us."

HE'S RUBBING HER FRONT

Stocking fish has a flavor all its own. Every day is routine. Wait on the truck, carry buckets until your arms hurt, laugh with your help, but always get the fish in alive. The more remote the section is to stock, the bigger the challenge and the more ingenious you get. Sometimes you scare yourself.

When I came up with a helicopter with a firefighting bucket attached to use for stocking the Lehigh River above the F.E. Walter reservoir, I was a local hero. This opened three or four miles of trout fishing to anyone willing to work for them. Real sportsmen praised the effort.

One sunny May afternoon, we were loading the stocking chopper at the parking lot of the dam. A young couple in their early twenties was standing around, watching. Obviously they were on holiday from the city. They marveled at the operation. The chopper pilot, a southerner with Viet Nam experience, would hover while loading the bucket with water from the dam. Then he would land on the parking lot, so we could load the fish. He'd take off and disappear into the wild blue yonder to dump the trout. He would be gone for ten minutes, then return and the scenario would be repeated.

After watching five or six trips, the young couple disappeared. The rest of us sat on the hood of our vehicles, chatting between loads. Soon we could hear the chopper returning and the radio crackled to the support truck on the ground.

"You know that couple that was down there? Well, they're up here on a rock and she has her shirt off and he's rubbing her back."

The pilot dropped down to get water, we loaded him with more fish and he was off again. Minutes ticked by and the drone of the machine could be heard coming back down the valley. Again the radio crackled.

"Now he's rubbing her front."

All those within hearing chuckled, as only a bunch of dirty old fishermen can.

Once more the pilot picked up water, we reloaded him and he left. More time passed and the hot afternoon sun beat down. The chopper again came down the valley. He loaded water and to our surprise headed up over the rocks, where the young couple had become romantically engaged. As he topped the ridge he sent 300 gallons of cold water spraying down through the tree tops.

Then the radio crackled: "That sure put that fire out!"

NO LADY, YOUR LICENSE (FOXBURG FLASHER)

Every day has its highlight. Even if you have a brilliant light flash early in the day, you don't stop hoping for a larger, whiter light. That is the beauty of this job. Any minute can bring a story or a tale that will be told and retold when you sit with other old retired wardens and close friends.

Don and I were patrolling the Allegheny River between Kennerdell and East Brady in the jet boat. The 30 miles of river make for a long day and the scheduled 12 hours had its usual share of hardcore fishermen, canoes, wildlife, nice bikinis and violations.

As we returned up the river, we tried to check only those boats we hadn't checked during our downstream journey. We were appreciating a day on the river when everybody cooperates, nobody gets hurt, and the weather is perfect. The kind of day you sign on for.

At Foxburg we saw a small, green fishing boat with a man and woman fishing. She was quite heavy and he was not much lighter. As we observed through binoculars, they both cast and retrieved and eventually we were able to identify a license on his hat. However, despite another five to ten minutes, we couldn't see a license on her. We putted the jet-boat in and slid it alongside their boat.

"Good evening," Don said. "State officers. Having any luck?"

After the usual small talk, he then asked to see fishing licenses. The gentleman handed his hat to Don, as I held the boat in position. As I observed the woman, I noticed she was beginning to panic. She couldn't locate her license. Then like a flash it happened. She must have realized that as the evening had cooled, she had pulled a red sweatshirt on over her red tee-shirt. She quickly but firmly grasped the bottom edge of the shirts, thinking she had only the sweatshirt, and jerked her arm high overhead. We had a point blank view of one large, flabby breast chilled well by the evening air.

Don was speechless, but being a veteran of these situations, I never lost my composure. Without hesitation or any noticeable reaction, I said, "No ma'am, your license."

She began to flush the color of her shirts. She carefully parted them and exposed a license. We didn't check it closely; I only nodded and we pulled away, thanking them. I know that sound carries forever over calm water, so it was well over a mile up the river until I throttled back the motor and looked at Don. I am sure anybody listening from the remote shore wondered what on earth those two wardens were belly laughing about.

SAND SPRINGS SLAYING

It was late July or early August, hot and sunny. I had one crew of deputies patrolling, besides myself and a deputy. We had worked the water release on the Lehigh River, making sure all the whitewater enthusiasts recreated safely. After a six-hour morning shift, we piled into one car and went for lunch. As we returned from lunch to the afternoon patrol, we noticed a Jeep with out-of-state plates. There were several small bluegill ponds farther back the road, so we decided to check them for fishermen. We unlocked the gate and headed in.

Suddenly, in the high, uncut grass on the Game Lands access road, I spotted an item of clothing. It was a pink halter top. Since dead bodies and victims of all kinds tended to show up along the interstate highway in areas like this, we went on with caution. The jovial crew became sober.

Then I spotted a body lying face down in the high grass, just beyond a pair of blue jeans thrown to the side of the road. About the same time, I saw a young man step behind a tree along the road. A scramble ensued as uniformed officers began bailing out, taking cover and shouting orders to the perceived murderer/rapist. The young man froze and I began to move in a circuitous route to gain a full view of him.

Only then did the panty-clad "body" giggle and speak. She assured us she was just fine and that they were young romantics and not perpetrator and victim. The young lady sat up, covering herself as well as she could and we retreated to the car.

I returned with the halter top that had piqued our curiosity in the beginning and gave it to her. I told her she probably should get dressed, since we were only going in to turn the car around and would certainly return that way. As we passed them on the way out, they were holding hands and laughing. The rest of us didn't hold hands, but we certainly laughed, too.

FAT GIRL'S OFFER

Rich people do not like to be arrested. In fact, they dislike it so much they are willing to pay extra not to be. I always figured sooner or later, someone would try to bribe me. It was sooner.

I was working with my deputy, "Bear," along the Nescopeck Creek in the area of Drums, when I noticed two young women fishing. One was as skinny as a rail. The other made up for it. She had to weigh four times what her friend weighed.

After parking the car, Bear and I worked through the trees and bushes and maneuvered between the two women and their camp. We watched a little longer and determined that without a doubt they were both fishing.

"Good afternoon, ladies," I spoke as I strode toward them in a nonchalant manner. "How's fishing? Need to see your licenses."

"We can't show you licenses, but we can show you two guys a good time," the obese lady offered. Her string-bean friend just smiled. "That's our cabin right there," she continued, pointing at a small, log creekside cabin.

Being somewhat naive at the time, the situation hadn't quite sunk in. The ladies started for the cabin and I followed.

Bear grabbed my arm and whispered, "They want you and me to have sex instead of giving them a fine."

Now that made the situation pretty clear. A bribe.

"Let's just see a license or an ID," I said as I approached the cabin door.

"You sure, honey?" the big one cooed as a last effort.

"I'm sure," I insisted.

Papers were signed outside on a picnic table in front of God and everybody and the fines were paid in cash. We returned to the car and had ridden several miles, when Bear started to giggle. This was somewhat out of character for him.

"Just visualized you making love to that big girl back there," he said.

I laughed even harder. When the tears quit on both of us, he said, "That wasn't that funny."

"Yes, it was," I retorted. "If we were going to accept the bribe that was your girl. Mine was the skinny one."

The chuckling started all over.

SKIN BOOKS

It was late on a night patrol one weekend when I swung into the development where my deputy Earl lived. Earl was the all-American pretty boy.

In those days gays and such were not understood or accepted. Civilization's tolerance of the gay lifestyle was low. There was a lot of overt contempt displayed at its mention.

As we rounded the corner, Earl noticed two discarded magazines littered along the road. I immediately backed up, thinking that they were either evidence or possibly girlie magazines. Either would have been worth stopping for. Earl got out and retrieved them.

Earl reached from his door and scooped them up and pulled them into the car. He threw them behind the seat without looking, until we got to the nightlight near his driveway. When he grabbed them from the backseat, they were boy-and-boy pornography. Earl opened his door to throw them back out.

"That's littering," I cautioned.

"I can't take them in the house," he argued.

"I didn't pick them up," I reminded him. "Throw them in your garbage can."

"What if the garbage man sees them? He knows me," Earl worried.

"Guess you should have thought of that," I said.

He jumped out of the car, leaving them in front of the front seat. I put them in a dumpster behind a grocery store on the way home and worried him for years where they would show up next.

NAKED BOATER

I feel that being selected to train cadets is quite an honor. I tried to approach this opportunity to mold new officers from a professional stance. I believe the Fish Commission selects the finest raw materials available and, once they have been cut and formed, they are sent into the field to be finished by the old artisans. Being selected to put the finishing touches on one of these guys or gals certainly is an honor.

When I picked Tom Tarkowski up at the Inn at Franklin, I formed a first opinion. One that I had to overcome during the next week. He reminded me of a guy that sucker-punched me at a high school football game, who I had always wanted to get even with. I had to keep this from becoming my chance. It is amazing how those things stick in the macho side of your brain.

Tom, I am happy to report, did an excellent job during his week with me, and my reports indicated that. But there was this one incident.

We had been on the river on the Oil City pool and then headed north in the jet boat, checking fishermen. We had written a few cases and, overall, the day had been good. We had a deputy traveling with us as we headed into the barn to park the boat and call it a day.

But you always feel like you owe the people that pay the freight that one last check. There was a camp at the mouth of Lower Two Mile Run, and I sent the deputy and Tom down to do the check, while I stayed in an advantageous position to watch and evaluate. Everything went smoothly and they came back up to my position.

"What did she ask you guys?" I queried, having heard some but not all of the conversation with the middle-aged woman they had checked.

"She wanted to know if we were here trying to catch the naked guy driving the boat," Tom replied.

"That would be a sight," I stated and laughed.

"I think she was serious," Tom reiterated.

I just looked at the deputy. He smiled and shook his head, yes.

We headed for the city of Franklin and noticed a large crowd of official vehicles on the boat ramp at Third Street. I looked back at my deputy, grimaced, and told Tom, now driving, to head down to the ramp. When we arrived, I saw the chief of the city police department and approached him. He explained what had happened.

Seems a local businessman had had too much to drink after some marital problems and took his boat out on the water to work on his all-over tan. He had temporarily lost control of reality. It was a shame, since he had never had any previous legal problems. I asked the chief if he felt the guy was a boating-under-the-influence case, and he just raised his eyebrows at me to signify, "No doubt."

"What is he being charged with?" I asked.

"Public indecency and drunk and disorderly," was the reply from the chief.

"Think he needs a B.U.I.?" I queried.

"Not unless you have to," said the chief.

"Guess you won't be needing us, then."

We loaded up and rode on out to limit the congestion in the area.

Tom had learned the two most important lessons I could teach him. That cooperation with other agencies is of the utmost importance was the first. An officer's discretion is his strongest ally was the second. After five years, I have not seen the defendant's name again in relation to any crimes. It would have been a shame to overreact to his one moment of failed judgment. Piling charges on a down-and-out suspect can totally ruin their life and it is "only another case" to the officer. The suspect is as much a part of the citizenry you serve as the rest of the other folks.

KAYAK CLASS SHOWER

The Lehigh River is a brawling whitewater stream. To patrol it required special skills. I was sent to Allentown to acquire these skills. A kayaking and canoeing course was my assignment. I was the only representative of our agency at this civilian-run and operated course, or so I thought. It happened that a new employee, later to become chief of one of the boating functions, was also in attendance.

We were assigned tents in the Girl Scout camp for quarters. Not exactly the Holiday Inn. I was a camper, but I took one look at the accommodations, crawling with mice and spiders, and I decided my sleeping would be done in the backseat of the Matador. I am convinced that the average Girl Scout is a lot tougher than I am.

We spent all day practicing Eskimo rolls, wet exits and other get-soaked-in-the-polluted-river maneuvers. I participated and became somewhat proficient in the many required skills. I spent the whole day in a pair of coveralls with shoulder patches. This was a co-ed, as in college girls, class. I was the only uniform.

Being one of the first to successfully master all the required skills, on Saturday I jumped in my car and headed from the river back to the camp. I needed a shower to clean off the mud and grime of the day's activities. I had noticed showers in the camp. I had also noticed they were all labeled, "Girls."

I quickly headed into one of the many shower rooms and undressed, placing my coveralls, patches up, smack in the middle of the doorway. Anybody entering would have to step across them. I felt this was necessary, because the shower stalls were arranged in a group of four, all facing each other and without doors. Privacy in the Girl Scouts, like in the army, must not have been a consideration at that time. I was about to find out just how little of a consideration it was.

I soaped up from head to toe and was fighting the age-old problem of soap in the eyes, when I heard a young lady's voice.

"Mind if we shower with you?" she nonchalantly asked.

How can a chubby, naked man respond to a question like that, knowing full well that when he gets the soap out of his eyes he is going to be the only naked male in sight? The location of the voice told me that my privacy had already been violated. The coveralls and patches had not elicited the respect I expected.

The three girls who occupied the three vacant, open-front stalls began to shower. I tried to keep from going blind, as I hurriedly dried and clothed myself and exited amid schoolgirl giggles. I thought that at least I was the only Fish Commission employee at the place, so word of this would never get out. Nobody really knew me except by my name on the registration form. I thought I was safe.

I reported to the chow hall when the bell rang. I took a heaping plate of spaghetti and sat down. A young fellow wearing suspenders and a Mickey Mouse tee-shirt sat next to me at the table. He introduced himself and told me that he had noticed my shoulder patches. He said he had just taken a job with the commission. At least he didn't know about the compromising situation I had just endured. Not yet.

The door opened and three attractive young ladies made their way to the chow line. I recognized them, even with their clothes on. They got plates of the hearty fare and proceeded to walk toward me. This was not a good sign. As they approached the picnic table with just the new guy and me sitting at it, I feared the worse. I wasn't disappointed. The same melodious voice rang out clear throughout the mess hall, "Since we showered with you, do you mind if we eat with you, too?"

People all around stopped eating and stared, then whispered among themselves. I'm sure in the minds of some that weekend I was a scoundrel. In others I was a hero. One thing for sure, the secret was out.

MAYDAY

It was a hot, sunny day at the end of July or early August. I was working with a deputy and things were slow. The area around Mountain Top has a bunch of little, unnamed ponds. Summer fishermen often fished these, and they were always worth a check.

I remembered the location of a pond that I had seen when on game patrol the year before. When we pulled in, we saw a boat on the water. Since I had been there last, a very large, beautiful home had been built on one end of the pond.

Through binoculars, we observed the fisherman in the boat and determined that he was operating an electric motor without the required registration numbering on the side. With a handheld loudspeaker, I hailed him to shore. He came in as ordered, but then the whole deal took on a new light.

The fisherman was a skinny old man and certainly not an unarmed threat. However, he refused to comply with our demand of identification. I explained the violation, but it fell on deaf ears. He only cursed and walked for his truck.

He got into the truck and I blocked his exit with the patrol vehicle. I then stepped to his driver's door and stood dumbfounded as he picked up his CB radio and called on the emergency network, "Mayday, Mayday. I am being arrested by a fish warden. I need immediate help. Call Mr. Jones at (phone number)."

In a minute the response came back over the CB that "help is on the way." I didn't want to get physical over a $25 fine, but I was sure things were going to get interesting in a moment or two. We did not have radios of our own at the time.

In a few minutes another man, Mr. Jones, the owner of the property, arrived and we headed him off and explained the violation to him. The old violator was his caretaker. It all ended on a calm note, with Mr. Jones telling "Skinny" that he would pay the fine, and the citation was issued.

But it wasn't over yet. I opened my big mouth and commented on the beauty of the new home. Before I could find a way out, I was on a tour of the building. It was plush. If it was mine I would have taken my shoes off. As we entered an upstairs hallway lined with bedrooms, a string of shots rang out. I looked for cover, and then realized that it was only firecrackers leftover from the Fourth of July. There must be other persons present that we had not seen, since the four of us were all right there.

Mr. Jones continued to open doors to show us one plush bedroom after the other. I was just getting the idea that this place looked more like a brothel than a home, when he swung a door open and just as quickly closed it. A young man and a girl with her blouse and bra lying on the bed were entangled in a lover's embrace that seemed to have a lot of momentum. Mr. Jones just looked at us and said, "My son."

The tour ended on that note.

About the Author

Robert Lynn "Bob" Steiner graduated in 1967 from Jeannette, Pennsylvania, High School with an "A" in English and not much else. He found himself in the U.S. Coast Guard thirteen days later, where he learned to paint buoys in New York Harbor, clean toilets at Air Station Annette Island, Alaska, and run typewriters in Gloucester and Atlantic City, New Jersey.

Bob was hired by the Pennsylvania Fish Commission in February of 1972. They called on his USCG Alaskan experience to clean fish-rearing tanks at their Walnut Creek and Union City stations. He moved into Law Enforcement in September of 1974 and worked in the Southwest, Northeast and Northcentral Regions, teaching fishing, boating safety and working undercover based out of the Northwest Region Office.

Offered a choice of three county districts, none of which he wanted, Bob was assigned to Southern Luzerne County, anyhow. He spent nearly nine years there, making many lifelong friends, working hard with both fish and game officers and laughing lots.

In 1984 Bob was reassigned to Venango County, where he worked diligently stocking fish, running a jet boat and fighting pollution in the gas and oil fields. He was named Pennsylvania Fish and Boat Commission Officer of the Year in 1993, despite always having fun.

Bob spent several summers acting in a temporary supervisor capacity as needed and eventually was promoted to assistant supervisor for the Northwest Region for the last few years of his career.

Bob and his wife, Linda, live in a log home on 30-some acres in northwestern Pennsylvania. Retired since 1999, Bob writes, plays guitar, hikes, bikes, hunts, fishes, canoes and is still having fun.

Made in the USA
Middletown, DE
10 November 2022